STATE-BUILDING AND DEMOCRATIZATION IN BOSNIA AND HERZEGOVINA

Southeast European Studies

Series Editor: Florian Bieber, Centre for Southeast European Studies,
University of Graz, Austria

The Balkans are a region of Europe widely associated over the past decades with violence and war. Beyond this violence, the region has experienced rapid change in recent times, including democratization and economic and social transformation. New scholarship is emerging which seeks to move away from the focus on violence alone to an understanding of the region in a broader context drawing on new empirical research.

The Southeast European Studies Series seeks to provide a forum for this new scholarship. Publishing cutting-edge, original research and contributing to a more profound understanding of Southeastern Europe while focusing on contemporary perspectives the series aims to explain the past and seeks to examine how it shapes the present. Focusing on original empirical research and innovative theoretical perspectives on the region, the series includes original monographs and edited collections. It is interdisciplinary in scope, publishing high-level research in political science, history, anthropology, sociology, law and economics and accessible to readers interested in Southeast Europe and beyond.

Other titles in the series

A Discourse Analysis of Corruption
Instituting Neoliberalism Against Corruption in Albania, 1998–2005
Blendi Kajsiu

The Politics of Social Ties
Immigrants in an Ethnic Homeland
Mila Dragojević

After Ethnic Conflict
Policy-making in Post-conflict Bosnia and Macedonia
Cvete Koneska

Croatia in the European Union
Changes, Development and Perspectives
Edited by Pero Maldini and Davor Pauković

Sense, a news agency specializing in covering trials at the International Criminal Tribunal for the former Yugoslavia. Before moving to the Netherlands, Iva worked in Sarajevo, as an analyst at the Special War Crimes Department of the State Prosecutor's office. Previous writings include a chapter in *Prosecuting War Crimes: Lessons and Legacies of the ICTY* (Routledge, 2013) and an article about ICTY archives in the UK journal *History* (Wiley-Blackwell, 2013).

Acknowledgments

Many people deserve recognition and thanks for their support to us throughout this book project, and there are too many to mention them all. However, there are some we would like to highlight.

First of all, we would like to thank Brenda Sharp and Rob Sorsby at Ashgate for supporting this project. We are also indebted to Florian Bieber for his support in publishing the volume in this Ashgate series.

We would furthermore like to thank the Association for the Study of Nationalities (ASN) and its conference director Dominique Arel. The original idea for this edition came out of two panels that were presented at the Annual Conference of the ASN at Columbia University, New York City in 2011. We would like to thank the panelists and all commentators in the audience who have helped to shape the individual papers in this volume.

In addition, we would like to thank Canterbury Christ Church University for providing financial means for the completion of this volume. This money was provided via the RIEF 2013 fund, and we are particularly grateful to David Bates for providing this support. We are also really thankful to Julia Grimm, who brought a fresh set of eyes to the project, ensuring the final editing and review of this volume, as well as indexing. Liza-Franziska Kummrow provided some last minute editorial support, which helped to increase the quality of this volume.

We also wish to thank a number of family members, friends and colleagues for their support. In particular Zeynep Arkan, Michael Burgess, Jasmina Colić, Jelena Džankić, Sarah Lieberman, Armina Mujanović, Claire Parker, Malindi Parker, Bernhard Stahl and Jens Woelk.

Finally, we would like to thank our parents, Peter and Regina Keil and Diana and George Perry for their continued encouragement and their moral support throughout our academic and practical endeavors. This book is dedicated to them.

Introduction: State-Building and Democratization in Bosnia and Herzegovina

Soeren Keil and Valery Perry

In the aftermath of the enormous efforts in Afghanistan and Iraq, which have demonstrated the significant financial and human costs involved in international political–military interventions, there is increasing wariness among decision-makers and citizens alike on the wisdom of engaging in state-building and democratization initiatives abroad. Perhaps of even more concern, the unfolding of the Arab Spring has demonstrated that political reform is not necessarily linear or based on progressive liberal constitutional principles; the uncertainty of outcomes and the economic and security chaos that can fill a social vacuum may make some uncomfortably wistful for the certainty of dictatorship. After the relative ease of political transition in Central and East Europe in the wake of the Cold War, the uneven developments in other regions around the world seem to suggest that resources poured into rule of law consolidation, military stabilization, police training, human rights advocacy and democracy promotion may very well yield few tangible results, particularly in the short- to medium-term.

Much has been written on whether or not certain preconditions are needed to ensure the success of a democratization and state-consolidation effort.[1] In addition, the timing of an intervention—in terms of initial engagement, scope, length and exit—may affect the short- and long-term success. While one can argue that every case is *sui generis*, there are reasonable lessons to be learned from a variety of past or ongoing cases. For example, the early intervention in Macedonia offers an example of a case that reflects lessons learned from previously failed prevention in Bosnia and Kosovo, where full-scale war erupted before any effective intervention was implemented. The limited intervention in Libya has left behind a country that is devastated and divided, and in which new conflicts continue to erupt. As demonstrated by Mateja Peter in this volume, the ongoing discussions about the closure of the Office of the High Representative (OHR) in Bosnia shows what can happen if a mission suffers from mission creep. Getting it right is extremely important for the prospects of democracy promotion and state-building, but getting it right is always context- and actor-specific.

---

1 For example, work by Almond and Verba (1963) focuses on the role of political culture and its influence on democratization. A similar argument in relation to democratization and effective statehood has been made by Putnam (1994).

When considering the fits and starts of such political transitions, the case of Bosnia and Herzegovina (BiH)[2] offers a useful case study of international state-building and democratization efforts. International engagement in BiH now spans more than two decades, if engagement prior to and during the wars of Yugoslav succession is counted, and the civilian and military investment has been significant. BiH provides a useful lens into the forest and trees of these intervention efforts, and can potentially offer lessons to be learned, and practices to be avoided. Most critically, if state-building and democratization efforts are unsuccessful in a continental European country that is a one-hour flight from Vienna, an eight-hour drive from Venice, and which before the war boasted a good, modern lifestyle (if one built on a shaky economic foundation), then what are the prospects for other fragile states that lack such beneficial conditions?

This volume aims to explore these issues, within a timeframe that allows sufficient time for reflection while still being current enough to have policy relevance. The authors selected have a combination of academic and on-the-ground policy implementation experience, ensuring a combination of theory-based comparative practice, and real-world diplomatic and development reality. This short introduction provides a basic summary of the political background and context in BiH, a short overview of the main theoretical framework used, and outlines the key arguments of the contributing experts. Taken together, it is difficult to be optimistic, not only because of the stagnant reform environment in BiH, but because of the missed opportunities, the massive investments in time, money and resources and the continued inability of the international actors involved to understand the real dynamics underlying BiH politics, and the risks of placing all hopes in a handful of politicians who have very little interest in reform.

Background

As editing of this volume was completed in June 2014, the country was recovering from a year of increasing social unrest and a natural disaster that revealed the extent to which the government (at all levels) is unable to fulfill its basic functions. Summer 2013 saw the rise of the "Babylution" in Sarajevo, as thousands demonstrated to show their dissatisfaction with the government's inability to agree on legislation that would allow for the issuance of identification numbers for newborn babies. In February 2014 protestors took to the streets again, first in the industrial, labor-stronghold of Tuzla, and then in cities throughout the Federation. What began as protests based on months of unpaid wages turned into a broader movement reflecting widespread dissatisfaction with basic socio-economic concerns and the inability of the government to improve the situation. These protests took on a more urgent tone, as government and political party buildings were set on fire in

---

2   The terms Bosnia or BiH will be used as a short form throughout this volume, and refer to the whole country.

several cities, including the burning of the Presidency building in Sarajevo. In the aftermath of these protests, several cantonal governments fell, and a new form of civic engagement emerged in the form of the so-called "plenums," an exercise in direct democracy through which participants issued demands and called for changes. While the civic actions primarily took place in the Federation, there were signs of increased dissatisfaction in the Republika Srpska (RS) as well, though the more centralized and oppressive civic atmosphere in that entity limited the scope for such visible public protest.

The plenums and protests continued throughout the spring, though they lost momentum, as politics (and society) returned to business as usual. The plenum participants from the beginning rejected a political role, noting that they did not seek political involvement but wanted to serve as a "corrective" aimed at guiding governments forward. The nature of their engagement changed significantly when BiH experienced its worst flooding in over a century in May 2014. Central and north-east BiH were hit with three months of rain in just three days, devastating the region as rivers flooded towns, leading to landslides and unearthing landmines and even some unmarked wartime graves. Some of the plenum organizers shifted their work to humanitarian relief; however as of this writing (June 2014), there is little sign of sustained civic involvement—let along political engagement—by this civic phenomenon, in general or related to the October 2014 general elections.

Most commentators agree that some sort of change is long overdue (Bieber 2014, Keil 2014a, Perry 2014). As the contributions in this volume will demonstrate, the current public unrest in Bosnia is due largely to a failure in establishing an effective and functioning state, and ensuring that Bosnia's democratization would lead to a system based on representation and accountable politics.

Bosnia and Herzegovina was established in the aftermath of the wars that ensued as Yugoslavia at first slowly, and then quickly, dissolved. Following declarations of independence by the Yugoslav republics of Slovenia and Croatia in June 1991, violence first came to Slovenia in 1991 in a 10-day crisis that was rather easily resolved. A longer war erupted in Croatia, including a long stalemate in which nearly one third of Croatian territory was held by Serbian separatists until a military offensive in the summer of 1995 led to Zagreb reclaiming all of its territory. The war in BiH was the longest, the most intense and the bloodiest, reflecting the historical heterogeneity that required untangling by force to enable the ethno-territorial visions of the warring parties (Silber and Little 1996; Burg and Shoup 1999). Fighting raged for three and a half years, taking the lives of approximately 100,000 people and displacing nearly half the population of 4 million. The war was fought among the Bosniaks (Muslims), the Bosnian Croats (Catholics) and Bosnian Serbs (Orthodox Christians), though many persons of mixed or undeclared background were also affected by the war as political officials and various armies and paramilitaries used force to fight either for an independent BiH, the creation of "ethnically pure" mini-states or for annexation to neighboring Croatia or rump-Yugoslavia (Serbia and Montenegro). The first year of the war in particular was marked by massive population transfers, transforming a highly heterogeneous and diverse population mosaic into a country marked by more substantial ethnically "clean" swathes of territory (Toal and Dahlman 2011). Serb forces, benefitting from arms and other means of support from the former Yugoslav military (the JNA) and a range of Serbian paramilitaries, moved rapidly in 1992 to establish a new ethnic map and front lines that would more or less remain until the end of the war. Rural and urban populations shifted with significant consequence for the cultural and demographic life of the country's cities (Stefansson 2008).

Figure I.1 Map of Bosnia and Herzegovina[3]

After years of failed attempts at securing a peace deal, a United States-led initiative in summer 1995, supported by military force used both in Croatia's Operation Storm and in NATO bombing of Serb positions in BiH, finally led the warring parties (including the then Presidents of neighboring Croatia and Serbia) to agree to and then sign a peace deal—the General Framework Agreement for

---

3   Map taken from the website of the US State Department. Available at: http://www.state.gov/p/eur/ci/bk/ (last accessed March 2, 2014).

Peace, or Dayton Accords (Holbrooke 1999, Burg and Shoup 1999). The resulting post-Dayton BiH was (and remains) a fragmented, complicated, ethnically-gerrymandered construction whose map reflects both the front lines of the war and the actual minefields left in its wake.[4] BiH's constitutional, governing structure and internal boundaries were legitimized through the Dayton Agreement, and reflect the dominant political preferences and results of ethnic cleansing rather than historical continuity or administrative logic. The small country consists of a convoluted patchwork of state, entity, cantonal, and municipal levels of government crafted to appease the varying formerly warring factions by ensuring everyone got a piece of the post-war pie. As explained in more detail in Valery Perry's chapter, the state created at Dayton was intentionally weak. BiH consists of two highly autonomous entities which enjoy the bulk of powers and competencies. The Federation of Bosnia and Herzegovina (FBiH), often referred to as the "Muslim-Croat Federation," was created as a part of the 1994 Washington Agreement to end that war, and comprises 51 percent of the territory of BiH. The Republika Srpska (RS), makes up 49 percent of the territory of BiH, and while illegally declared independent in January 1992 as BiH's problems began to unravel, was legitimized at Dayton. The entities are structured differently, with the RS highly centralized and the FBiH highly decentralized, with powers devolved to 10 cantons. (Five of these cantons have Bosniak majorities,[5] three have Croat majorities,[6] and two are mixed.[7]) The result is a lop-sided, asymmetric federation which could technically work if there were political will, but in fact cannot function (Keil 2014b). The long-recognized obstacles and weaknesses of the system have become increasingly clear since a degradation of the reform environment began in 2006—a phenomenon discussed by several authors in this volume.

The strict power-sharing system and the continued dominance of ethnically exclusive parties have resulted in a situation that has been described as a permanent crisis (Džihić 2011). Indeed, it is possible to look at this permanent crisis from different angles and analyze it in different periods. From 1995 until 1997, the crisis focused on the reestablishment of any form of statehood and governance structures in the country. While the Office of the High Representative was included in the General Framework Agreement for Peace (GFAP) in Annex 10 to provide a civilian implementation capability, in this period of time the primary intervention mechanism was military, with nearly 60,000 NATO troops deployed throughout the country, and an over-riding focus on the implementation of the military components of Dayton. Military intervention and peace-building through robust (military) means was therefore at the heart of the Dayton Peace Agreement, and the civilian aspects were in many ways afterthoughts. The elections in

---

4   On the governing structures in Bosnia see Keil, 2013, Bieber 2006 and Bose 2002.

5   Una Sana (Bihać), Tuzla, Zenica-Doboj, Bosanski- Podrinje (Goražde) and Sarajevo.

6   Posavina, West Herzegovina, and Canton 10 (Livno).

7   Central Bosnia (Travnik) and Herzegovina-Neretva (Mostar).

September 1996 brought to power the same parties that were responsible for the war in Bosnia. They had no intention of working together and establishing a functional state; in fact Croat and Serb nationalists fought against the very idea of Bosnian statehood and independence during the war, and continued their attacks on the Bosnian state after the end of violence through political means. The situation quickly developed into a state of paralysis, to which the international community reacted with heavier *civilian* intervention. In December 1997, at a meeting of those countries overseeing the peace agreement for Bosnia,[8] it was decided that the High Representative would hold extended powers to impose laws and dismiss officials (PIC 1997).[9] As a consequence major decisions, including, for example, issues concerning state symbols, entity constitutions and military reform, could be decided by unaccountable international actors, with subsequent local governmental adoption or legitimization a secondary concern.

Bosnia's crisis evolved from a predominantly military intervention focused on separating the formerly warring parties to a more explicit civilian intervention, pressuring and even imposing a step-by-step state-building and democratization approach. BiH parties —either out of strategic choice or default—became more and more reliant on the intervention of the High Representative, and BiH citizens became part of not only a consolidated post-war chimera of a state, but of an international state-building operation as well. From 1997–2006 the civilian push for peace implementation and democratic consolidation remained heavy, first by High Representative Wolfgang Petritsch, and then by Paddy Ashdown. Entity constitutions were reformed, the defense apparatus restructured, a state-wide value added tax put in place, new justice sector bodies introduced, and more.

Yet, when heavy international intervention stopped after 2006, when the new High Representative Christian Schwartz-Schilling, along with some increasingly fatigued and distracted (by Iraq and Afghanistan) international actors believed—or wanted to believe, or wanted to test—that Bosnia could now function efficiently, a new form of crisis emerged. Local political elites showed an impressive lack of interest in finding compromises in any sector, including on fundamental decisions concerning a new constitutional framework. As Mateja Peter demonstrates in her chapter, this is where the country remains today, stuck between a rock and a hard place. On the one hand, significant international intervention is not viewed as a viable option in the face of domestic political opposition and reluctance (Germany, some other EU states) or outright opposition (Russia and some other members of the international community). On the other hand, the period since 2006 has demonstrated that Bosnia is still far from being a self-sustaining functional

---

8   The Peace Implementation Council (PIC) oversees the implementation of the Dayton Peace Agreement. It consists of representatives from several countries that have an interest in Bosnia, and have been involved in the military and civilian mission. Members include the USA, Russia, Turkey, the EU, Germany, France and the UK, among others.

9   The High Representative is appointed by the PIC and has so far always been from an EU Member State.

democracy; it is more of an electoral oligarchy. Political rivalries, continued threats of secession from the RS, calls for a Croat entity and permanent criticism of the existing constitutional and institutional framework have become normal in Bosnia's political discourse. This is in line with consistent and effective political attacks on some of the institutions of the state, as pointed out by Meagan Smith-Hrle in her review of the judicial system. Some argue that this symbolizes a failure of state-building in Bosnia (Cohen 2013). Others have been more outspoken about the need for functional power-sharing institutions in Bosnia (McCrudden and O'Leary 2013). Some, such as Valery Perry in this volume, have argued that a stronger focus on constitutional and electoral structures that empower citizens rather than political interests could help to overcome this crisis.

There is general consensus that change is required to overcome what has become a perpetual crisis in Bosnian politics. The authors in this volume look at different policy areas, and at this crisis and the need for change from different perspectives. They have all been working on issues related to state-building and democratization in Bosnia for many years and have spent significant time in the country. All contributors hope to add to the discussion about the future of Bosnia by providing first-hand analysis of state-building and democratization in different areas, and from different perspectives.

Key Definitions

The two key concepts used throughout this volume are state-building and democratization. These concepts have found considerable recognition in the academic literature in recent years. State-building has been defined as the (re)-establishment of statehood, including state institutions, economic reconstruction and the physical rebuilding of a polity torn apart by violent conflict (Paris 2004, Sisk and Paris 2007, Chandler 2009, 2010, Ghani and Lockhart 2009). Democratization, in short, refers to the process of regime change from an authoritarian (or semi-authoritarian) regime towards democratic governance. This process can occur either slowly and over a period of time or through a revolution and violent regime change. There is general consensus that the building of deep-rooted democracy consists of more than just establishing free and fair elections and includes elements such as the establishment of the rule of law, democratic accountability, civil society participation and the protection of fundamental rights (Linz and Stepan 1996, Diamond 1999, 2008, Grugel 2002). In the case of Bosnia and Herzegovina, both processes have been strongly connected, in particular through the Dayton Peace Agreement, the aim of which was to stop the violence and to establish a functional state and democratic governance via power-sharing arrangements (Bieber 2006, Belloni 2008).

Different actors have left their footprint in Bosnia's state-building and democratization process. While the initial spasms of democratization occurred internally with elections in 1991 as a result of which three nationalist parties shared power for a short period of time,[10] later attempts to democratize the country in the post-war period were driven by external actors including the Council of Europe, the OSCE, the Office of the High Representative and the EU. However, the initial process of democratization and Bosnia's move towards independent statehood in 1991 and 1992 are also connected to the end of Cold War empires, subsequent socio-political vacuums, and the outbreak of violence and full-scale war, a connection that can be observed in other countries as well (Snyder 2000, Zakosek 2008). Likewise, while the process leading to Bosnia's declaration of independence has been initiated by local actors, the process of establishing and manifesting Bosnia's statehood after 1995 was heavily influenced by international actors. From NATO's Implementation and Stabilization Forces (IFOR, SFOR) to the International Criminal Tribunal for the former Yugoslavia (ICTY), external actors have had a profound impact on the environment for state-building and democratization in post-war Bosnia. Because of this, many commentators have argued that Bosnia has become a prime example of post-Cold War international state-building, some even claiming that international actors have established a new neo-colonial protectorate (Chandler 2000, Knaus and Martin 2003). Others have pointed out that international actors only intervened when local actors failed to take important policy decisions. Victor Bojkov (2003) for example describes Bosnia as a "controlled democracy" instead of an outright protectorate.

The discussion on how much external influence there has been on policy change and long-term state-building and democratization in Bosnia and Herzegovina is also reflected in this volume. In some areas, such as party politics, constitutional and judicial reform, external actors have provided important frameworks and guidelines, though ultimately key decisions rest with local actors. In other areas, such as dealing with war criminals and security sector reform, there has been a much heavier exogenous footprint. While the distinction is often difficult to discern, the authors in this volume have aimed to look at change within different policy areas through the complex interplay of the internal and international actors involved. Bosnia and Herzegovina remains a highly complex case of international state-building and democratization, and the contributions in this book demonstrate that in some areas important progress has been made (such as the establishment of a Ministry of Defense at the state level), while in others progress is absent (such as constitutional reform). The assessment of the authors is therefore mixed. While some progress has been made, and the likelihood of large-scale violence is relatively low in Bosnia today, the country is still far from being a consolidated democratic state on an irreversible road toward political and economic stability. The unrest in early 2014 might lead to more long-term changes, but the authors in this volume remain skeptical about the future of Bosnia unless more deep-rooted changes take place within the elite culture and the political structure of the country. Furthermore, a readjustment of international policy towards Bosnia is

---

10   For more on the developments in Bosnia in the early 1990s and especially the reasons that led to the war see Anđelić 2003.

required to enable and facilitate these deep-rooted reforms, which should provide a framework in which Bosnia's statehood consolidation and democratization are embedded in Euro-Atlantic integration processes.

Contributions

The contributing authors in this volume each tell a different but inter-related part of the story of post-war BiH and its uncertain, shaky future. Valery Perry's chapter reviews the country's constitutional framework and efforts to change it –all of which to date have failed. Perry's combination of 15 years of work in BiH, including issues related to constitutional reform and democratization strategies, together with an academic foundation, provide space for practical and theoretical reflection. Her explanation of the constitutional and political status quo provides background information on the country's political dynamics and dominant internal and external incentives that could either promote or inhibit reform. Perry's chapter in addition reviews efforts to promote an independent civil society in the country to counter the often anti-reform political forces and institutions that have been blocking implementation of the peace agreement, and reform in general.

John Hulsey's contribution explores Bosnia's electoral system and the resulting party system, identifying the underlying structural explanations behind the lack of significant political change, while at the same time reviewing the proliferation of a very large number of party options that continue to suggest more political plurality than in fact exists. Hulsey's academic research on the impact of electoral systems on political outcomes provides an understanding of the electoral engineering tactics that can affect broader political party strategies. This electoral system—like the country's constitutional structure in general—was sculpted to maintain the status quo and the interests of the main formally warring parties that seek to ensure that the state remains divided along three ethnic pillars.

Meagan Smith-Hrle contributes a thorough overview of reform and continuing challenges in the country's justice sector. Hrle has over a decade of experience in BiH, ranging from work with the Human Rights Chamber to the rule of law programs at the OSCE Mission to BiH, and can provide a first-hand insight into the objectives, processes and continuing weaknesses of reform. The story she tells echoes themes in the other chapters—namely the weak roots of even "successful" reforms; the continuing and escalating challenges from the RS against any state-strengthening reforms; and the puzzling role and reaction of international actors who continue to support such programs in spite of the relative lack of lasting improvements.

Kurt Bassuener provides a review of the Bosnian security situation, looking at the on-the-ground situation and the limits of reforms implemented or attempted in the military, defense and internal security (police) spheres. Bassuener has nearly two decades of policy experience in the Balkans, including tenure at the Office of the High Representative and several years of experience on the ground in BiH with the Democratization Policy Council. Based on extensive field research, his analysis points out a broad number of concerns. While some reforms—for example in the defense sector—have been lauded as significant, upon scratching the surface one sees that reforms are often skin-deep, cosmetic, and still linked to overriding political forces and factors that could easily render such reforms irrelevant. Together with his assessment of some of the internal and external reasons for this limited substantive reform, his outlook is bleak.

Adnan Efendić and Azra Hadžiahmetović provide an overview of the Bosnian economic situation nearly two decades after the war. They bring an economist's eye to the topic, focusing on the numbers and statistics that form the backbone of "the dismal science" to paint a picture of the real impact of the post-war political environment on the bread and butter everyday concerns of the country's citizens. This chapter reviews the dominant economic trends since the peace agreement, breaking the peace into three different timeframes for analysis. The impact of the grey economy and BiH's reliance on external remittances receive special attention. Their prognosis is bleak, as they tie the lack of real economic reform and progress to the country's convoluted political structure.

Mateja Peter introduces the reader to the people and dynamics acting within two of the main international organizations presently working in BiH—the Office of the High Representative (OHR) and the EU Delegation to BiH, including the EU Special Representative (EUSR). Based on extensive fieldwork, her analysis explores the different worldviews and mindsets that decision-makers and staff in each of these bodies have, particularly on the question whether the OHR should close, and the EU should take over. She focuses on the premise that OHR employees tend to view the BiH situation through a "post-war" lens, while EU counterparts cling to a prism of "pre-EU enlargement" to drive both their activities and their analysis of the political situation.

Iva Vukušić provides an overview of a critical and perhaps unintended outgrowth of the wars in BiH and in Yugoslavia in general, as she assesses the impact of the International Criminal Tribunal for the former Yugoslavia (ICTY) on international transitional justice, human rights jurisprudence and reconciliation in Bosnia. Vukušić has a lot of experience with the court through her work as a journalist, and has been in close contact with stakeholders and participants in The Hague, BiH and other countries in the region. Her review starts from the early days of the Court, when there were no precedents or easy-to-reference guideposts for procedure or success. She continues by looking at key elements of good practice in the ICTY that affect both the current caseload as well as other international courts (such as the International Criminal Court), and also the challenges and limitations of this aspect of retributive justice. She concludes that the expectations for the court in terms of its impact on reconciliation were overstated and inflated at the beginning of the process, and that while the ICTY has contributed to a process of coming to terms with the past, it will only be one part of a much bigger puzzle.

The final part of this book examines some of the issues that have affected state-building and democratization in Bosnia and Herzegovina in a comparative perspective. Tina Mavrikos-Adamou and Soeren Keil focus particularly on similarities in other Balkan countries, and argue that Bosnia has become an example for institutional learning for other political elites in post-Yugoslav countries as well as for international actors.

Tina Mavrikos-Adamou introduces a study of the country's dysfunctional political dynamic and the resulting impact on the party system. Mavrikos-Adamou has a research interest in democratization efforts and civic movements in Southeastern Europe, and integrates past work in conflict resolution into this chapter to consider potential lessons that might be learned in light of the international experiences in the Balkans over the past two decades. She explains that the country's constitutional and electoral structure, together with the impact of the war and a weak democratic tradition, conspire to create a political party system dominated by elites—a leader-driven, rather than platform or results driven system. She also briefly explores similar trends in Kosovo, to provide a backdrop for comparison.

Soeren Keil's chapter focuses on Bosnia's power-sharing system in comparative perspective. Looking at the use of consociationalism and multinational federalism, he demonstrates how lessons have been learnt in other post-war countries in the former Yugoslavia, particularly in Macedonia and Kosovo. His overall analysis demonstrates that while power-sharing might be necessary in a divided society like Bosnia, a general consensus on the state must exist before institutions based on consensus and cooperation can function properly. He also explores similar institutions in Macedonia and Kosovo and argues that more flexible provisions in these two countries have allowed for the power-sharing arrangements to function better and contribute to more efficient governance. However, his conclusion points out that all three states remain contested and that there seems to be a direct link between different ethnic groups agreeing on the nature of a state and the functioning of power-sharing institutions.

Florian Bieber's conclusion summarizes the main arguments presented in the individual chapters and provides a larger picture, and first assessment of the internal and external state-building and democratization efforts in Bosnia. Labelling Bosnia as a failed success, he argues that some aspects of the Dayton Agreement have improved the situation in the country, such as the absence of violence and growing inter-ethnic trust. However, overall, the situation remains fragile and Dayton failed to provide state structures and a political framework which would allow for effective democratic decision-making.

While the contributions in this book are strong and illuminating, the picture that they paint is dim and gloomy. Extensive efforts have failed to produce a lasting consensus for democratic peace and power-sharing in BiH, as the leading political parties cling to significant differences in interpreting the Dayton constitution. Further, the political aims of the parties remain the same as in 1991, with various factions more or less successful in achieving such aims, contributing to an increasing sense of grievance and injustice among some parties. These internal political dynamics are playing out in the full view of a still large international presence, meaning that not only can the international community not admit that they have witnessed the unfolding of events, but that hundreds of millions of international dollars and Euros have in fact funded either the unsatisfactory status quo, or the even more concerning rollback of reform. Whatever the ultimate outcome of BiH's political stalemate may be in the medium- to long-term future, both internal and external actors will have played a full hand in the deal.

Bibliography

Almond, G and Verba, S. (1963) *The Civic Culture (Political Attitudes and Democracy in Five Nations)*. Princeton: Princeton University Press.

Anđelić, N. (2003) *Bosnia-Hercegovina: The End of a Legacy*. Portland: Frank Cass.

Belloni, R. (2008) Statebuilding and International Intervention in Bosnia. London: Routledge.

Bieber, F. (2014) Is Change Coming (finally)? Thoughts on the Bosnian Protests. Available from: http://fbieber.wordpress.com/2014/02/09/is-change-coming-finally-thoughts-on-the-bosnian-protests/ [Accessed March 2, 2014].

——. (2006) *Post-War Bosnia (Ethnicity, Inequality and Public Sector Governance)*. Basingstoke: Palgrave-Macmillan.

Bojkov, V. (2003) Democracy in Bosnia and Herzegovina: Post-1995 Political System and its Functioning. *Southeast European Politics,* Vol. 6, pp. 41–67.

Bose, S. (2002) *Bosnia after Dayton. Nationalist Partition and International Intervention*. London: Hurst & Company.

Burg, S. and Shoup, P. (1999) *The War in Bosnia-Herzegovina (Ethnic Conflict and International Intervention*. Armonk, London: M.E. Sharpe.

Chandler, D. (2002) *Bosnia – Faking Democracy after Dayton*. 2nd edition, London: Pluto Press.

——. (2009) Introduction. In *Statebuilding and Intervention. Policies, Practices and Paradigms*, David Chandler (ed). London: Routledge, pp. 1–14.

——. (2010) *International Statebuilding: The Rise of Post-Liberal Governance*. London: Routledge.

Cohen, R. (2013) Enough of the Daytonians, *The New York Times*, July 18. Available from: http://www.nytimes.com/2013/07/19/opinion/global/roger-cohen-enough-of-the-daytonians.html?_r=0 [Accessed March 2, 2014].

Diamond, L. (2008) *The Spirit of Democracy: The Struggle to Build Free Societies Throughout the World*. New York: Times Books.

——. (1999) *Developing Democracy: Toward Consolidation*. Baltimore: John Hopkins University Press.

Džihić, V. (2011) Bosnien und Herzegowina in der Sackgasse? Struktur und Dynamik der Krise fünfzehn Jahre nach Dayton, *Südosteuropa*, Vol. 59(1), pp. 50–76.

Ghani, A. and Lockhart, C. (2009) *Fixing Failed States*. Oxford and New York: Oxford University Press.

Grugel, J. (2002) *Democratization: A Critical Introduction.* Basingstoke and New York: Palgrave Macmillan.

Holbrooke, R. (1999) *To End a War.* New York: The Modern Library.

Keil, S. (2013) Multinational Federalism in Bosnia and Herzegovina. Farnham, Burlington: Ashgate.

——. (2014a) Bosnia's Only Starting on Road to Democracy. *Balkan Insight,* Available from: http://www.balkaninsight.com/en/article/bosnia-s-only-starting-on-road-to-democracy [Accessed March 2, 2014].

——. (2014b) Building a Federation within a Federation—The Curious Case of the Federation of Bosnia and Herzegovina. *L'Europe en Formation,* 369, pp. 114–125.

Knaus, G. and Martin, F. (2003) Travails of the European Raj – Lessons from Bosnia and Herzegovina. *Journal of Democracy,* Vol. 14, pp. 60–74.

Linz, J. and Stepan, A. (1996) *Problems of Democratic Transition and Consolidation. Southern Europe, Southern America and Post- Communist Europe.* Baltimore and London: The John Hopkins University Press. McCrudden, C. and O'Leary, B. (2013) *Courts and Consociations. Human Rights versus Power-Sharing.* Oxford, New York: Oxford University Press.

Paris, R. (2004) *At War's End: Building Peace after Civil Conflict.* Cambridge: Cambridge University Press.

Peace Implementation Council (PIC) (1997) Summary of Conclusions. Available from: http://www.ohr.int/pic/default.asp?content_id=5183 [Accessed March 2, 2014].

Perry, V. (2014) Elite-Driven Reform Will Not Save Bosnia. *Balkan Insight,* Available from: http://www.balkaninsight.com/en/article/elite-driven-reform-will-not-save-bosnia [Accessed March 12, 2014].

Putnam, R. (1994) *Making Democracy Work (Civic Traditions in Modern Italy).* Princeton and Chichester: Princeton University Press.

Silber, L. and Little, A. (1996) *The Death of Yugoslavia.* London: Penguin Books and BBC Books.

Sisk, T. and Paris, R. (2007) Managing Contradictions: The Inherent Dilemmas of Postwar Statebuilding. *International Peace Academy/Research Partnership on Postwar Statebuilding,* November 2007. Available from: http://www.ipinst. org/media/pdf/publications/iparpps.pdf [Accessed March 2, 2014].

Snyder, J. (2000) *From Voting to Violence: Democratization and Nationalist Conflict.* New York and London: W.W. Norton & Company.

Stefansson, A. (2008) Urban Exile: Locals, Newcomers and the Cultural Transformation of Sarajevo. In *The New Bosnian Mosaic: Identifies, Memories and Moral Claims in a Post-War Society,* X. Bougarel, E. Helms, and G. Duijzings (eds). Farnham: Ashgate. Pp. 59–77.

Toal, G. and Dahlman, C. (2011) *Bosnia Remade: Ethnic Cleansing and Its Reversal.* Oxford, New York: Oxford University Press.

Zakosek, N. (2008) Democratization, State-building and War: The Cases of Serbia and Croatia. *Democratization,* Vol. 15, pp. 588–610.

Chapter 1

Constitutional Reform Processes in Bosnia and Herzegovina: Top-down Failure, Bottom-up Potential, Continued Stalemate

Valery Perry

Introduction

While the need for constitutional reform in Bosnia and Herzegovina (BiH) has been acknowledged by many internal and external actors for well over a decade, since the failure of the 2006 "April Package" and the subsequent Prud and Butmir processes, expectations for comprehensive reform have receded to the point where it is rarely even discussed publically. Instead there has been a steady domestic—and primarily Republika Srpska (RS)-driven—resistance to integrative political reforms of *any* kind. The constitutional stagnation is facilitated by an apparent American willingness to cede policymaking on BiH's political future to the European Union (EU), and an EU aversion to demanding integrative reforms as a part of the enlargement process; in essence allowing domestic minimalist agendas regarding reform to prevail. Past efforts to compel (impose) or financially persuade (pay for) state integration through externally-driven institution-building have been replaced by a seeming acceptance of disintegrative realities. Cohesion and stability in BiH hinges on the hope that the magnetic power of Europe will somehow bind the post-Dayton construct together in some minimally functional way.

In such an environment, is constitutional reform still on the agenda? The need for "Sejdić-Finci" reform to ensure minimal compliance with the European Court of Human Rights (ECtHR) has changed from a chance to broadly remove discriminatory provisions in the constitution to a narrow exercise driven by leading party interests in maintaining the status quo—or even in accelerating the decline of functioning state institutions. Beyond Sejdić-Finci, there is almost no political discourse on constitutional reform.[1] Rather than seeking "big bang" packages, there

---

1 Briefly, the Sejdić-Finci case refers to a judgement from the European Court of Human Rights that found that the BiH Constitution's limitation of participation in the institution of the three-person presidency to a Serb (from the RS), and a Bosniak and Croat (from the Federation) is discriminatory to persons who do not identify as one of these three groups. This is explained in more detail below, and in the Hulsey chapter.

is a sense that any reform will be incremental and piecemeal, starting (perhaps) with reform of the Federation's constitution. While the US played a key role in the April Package and subsequent spin-offs, the notion of an externally-brokered deal is being replaced by a belief (or hope) that the EU accession process in itself will be sufficient to—if not resolve BiH's structural problems—at least ensure minimal ability to function as a candidate country and eventual EU member state.

One is increasingly likely to hear the words "constitutional reform" not from external actors but from BiH civil society activists. There are increasing numbers of NGOs either talking about the issue in a broad academic sense or offering their own recommendations. While from 2005–2009 the processes were nearly exclusively elite-driven, top-down and closed-door by nature, since 2009 there has been an increasing interest among international actors as well in promoting grassroots, bottom-up involvement in a long-term process of constitutional reform. Is a civil society approach to constitutional reform in BiH a practical way to move forward, a sign that external actors have given up on reform through the elites, or a side-show to avoid forcing difficult questions to the political center stage?

This paper will review the status of constitutional reform, with a focus on the shift from a top-down and comprehensive approach with a visible if not revolutionary goal at the end, to an incremental, bottom-up approach that is less definable for its imagined end goal than for its contribution to a process. Following a review of the arguments for reform, a summary of top-down efforts to date provides background on initiatives since 2006. This is followed by a review of general civil society development issues in BiH, and a review of bottom-up civic efforts to support constitutional reform. The chapter concludes that while civic efforts for reform are necessary, they will not gain traction in an environment in which nearly all of the domestic and international incentives for political behavior are focused on elite level actors who have no rational incentive to change the status quo.

BiH Constitutional Reform—Top-Down

The need for constitutional reform had been broadly recognized by international organizations and BiH observers alike for years, as efforts at reform and rationalization continuously met with the implications of the unwieldy and asymmetric Dayton constitution based on institutional overlap and inefficiencies that burden an already poor and feeble country. Institutional weaknesses were seen early on as having an impact on both functionality as well as the basic enjoyment of human rights and equality. As early as 1998, the Bosniak member of the BiH Presidency Alija Izetbegović filed a case with the BiH Constitutional Court challenging the legality of several provisions of the entity constitutions, and in particular the entity definitions of constituent peoples. At that point, the RS constitution recognized only Serbs as its constituent people, and the Federation (FBiH) constitution recognized only Bosniaks and Croats, grounding

Izetbegović's contention that the exclusion of some constituent peoples from the entity constitutions violated BiH's constitution, which itself acknowledges BiH's *three* constituent peoples (Case U 5/98). The Court found that all three peoples must be guaranteed equal status and rights throughout BiH, a decision made by international and Bosniak judges, with the Croat and Serb judges expressing critical reservations (ICG April 2002). Implementation of this court decision was ignored, as it challenged the ethnic preferences that some parties wanted to maintain, and it was only implemented after the Office of the High Representative (OHR)-driven negotiations and a final imposed decision (CoE SG 2002). This early example of attempted reform highlighted the resistance to changes that would reduce the ethnic preferences some BiH politicians sought to maintain.

Following some years of OHR-driven integrative state-reform efforts, the European Commission for Democracy through Law (the Venice Commission) issued a report in March 2005 on outstanding constitutional issues in BiH entitled *The Opinion on the Constitutional Situation in Bosnia and Herzegovina and the Powers of the High Representative.* This assessment of the BiH constitution's compliance with the European Convention for the Protection of Human Rights and Fundamental Freedoms and the European Charter of Local Self-Government provided an opportunity to comment on the constitution's practicality, efficiency, rationality and non-democratic provenance (Venice Commission 2005). The Commission highlighted numerous issues of concern inherent in BiH's constitutional arrangements, including the impact of an extraordinarily weak state, incapable of "effectively ensur[ing] compliance with the commitments of the country with respect to the Council of Europe and the international community in general." Furthermore, the lack of precise conditions for the use of the vital national interest veto, the entity veto, and the House of Peoples was criticized, all of which can effectively delay or halt the legislative process at multiple stages (Bahtić-Kunrath 2011). Finally, the duplication of effort and competencies between the collective Presidency and the Council of Ministers was also highlighted as an area that needed improvement (Venice Commission 2005, 26–38). In addition, the Commission noted that BiH's "Constitution was drafted and adopted without involving the citizens of BiH and without applying procedures which could have provided democratic legitimacy" (Ibid., point 6). It further concluded that BiH's constitution would have to be changed to make the country fit for EU integration.

Similar observations have been made by independent BiH analysts. For example, the Foreign Policy Initiative (FPI), a Sarajevo-based policy organization, released a report entitled *Governance Structures in BiH: Capacity, Ownership, EU Integration, Functioning State* in 2007. The report identified governance challenges presented by the current state structure, including the implementation gap between state framework legislation and entity level implementation, and the phenomenon of institutional layering that accompanied the construction of state-level framework laws and competencies without an accompanying dismantling of lower level powers (FPI, 2007, 14). FPI recommended streamlined parliamentary processes in the spirit of the April package, clarification of state and entity competencies, the establishment of enforcement mechanisms to ensure lower-level compliance with state or joint policies, and a constitutional supremacy clause specifying that state law would prevail over all inconsistent entity legislation (Ibid., 20–21).

Moving beyond words and prescription, the most substantive policy effort to achieve meaningful and sweeping constitutional reform was unfolding in 2005 and 2006 (Sebastian 2007). What became known as the April Package began as a process of consultation among American diplomats and advisors with the leadership of eight ruling parties. After months of talks, a package of constitutional amendments was agreed upon, including an indirectly elected Presidency with one president and two vice-presidents, a stronger Council of Ministers with more clearly defined competencies and led by a Prime Minister, a larger Parliament including an enhanced House of Representatives and a reformed House of Peoples (limited to issues of vital national interest), two new state-level ministries (Agriculture, and Science and Technology) and a more streamlined and articulated agreement on the competencies held by the state and the entities (April Package 2006, Amendment I).

At the time of discussions many observers felt the reforms were too modest, though in hindsight and in light of the disintegrating political atmosphere since 2006 they are now appreciated as having been rather sweeping and significant. In spite of the agreement among the participating parties, the package ultimately failed by a narrow two-vote margin in the Parliamentary Assembly. While the process was accompanied by a minimal amount of broader consultation, there was limited effort to build a broader civic constituency for the proposed reforms (Hays and Crosby 2006). Ultimately, 16 parliamentarians voted against it, including six from SBiH (Party for Bosnia and Herzegovina), and five from the then newly-formed HDZ 1990 (Croat Democratic Union 1990).[2]

Following the failure of the April Package, there were two progressively less ambitious efforts at constitutional reform. The "Prud Process" from November 2008—January 2009, failed to generate concrete proposals other than some fundamental political principles for reform, and, with heavy US pressure, the first (and only) amendment to the BiH constitution—the incorporation of the Brčko District under the jurisdiction of BiH state institutions and the Constitutional Court (CoE PA 2010). The "Butmir Process" followed, as the US and the EU sought to resurrect some of the amendments included in the April Package, including increasing the powers of the House of Representatives and the Council of Ministers, decreasing the powers of the presidency, limiting the role of the House

---

2 The SBiH members of parliament who voted against were Beriz Belkić, Nijaz Duraković, Mehmed Suljkanović, Adem Huskić, Azra Hadžiahmehtović, and Senija Kapetanović; the HDZ 1990 MPs who voted against were Vinko Zorić, Martin Raguž, Ruža Sopta, Filip Andrić and Ivo Lozančić; the remaining five no-votes were from Sead Avdić (Independent), Mladen Potočnik (Republican), Mirko Blagojević (SRS), Muhamed Moranjkić (BOSS), and Mehmed Žilić (SDA).

of Peoples, and creating a stronger executive with a prime minister capable of assuming most of the functions of the presidency (ICG 2009). The Butmir Process also failed to garner support among the parties, and it ended without agreement.

Why did these efforts all fail? There are many inter-connected explanations. BiH's electoral calendar is generally thought to have affected the potential of all of these initiatives, making politicians less willing to compromise in order to ensure electoral support (ICG 2009, Sebastian 2011). The escalating zero-sum feud between Milorad Dodik and Haris Silajdžić that took off in 2006 poisoned the atmosphere for reform and compromise of any kind (Bilefsky 2009; Azinović, Bassuener and Weber 2011). The end result has been a period of time since 2006 characterized by political stalemate punctuated by regression.

A long saga that came to dominate debates on the need for constitutional reform is the so-called Sejdić-Finci reform issue. In December 2009, the ECtHR delivered its judgment in the *Case of Sejdić and Finci vs. Bosnia and Herzegovina*. The case challenged the inability of representatives of the Jewish and Roma communities (or any other non-constituent peoples) seeking election to BiH's Presidency and House of Peoples—each of which is constitutionally limited to BiH's three constituent peoples (Case of Sejdić and Finci 2009). The Court found that limiting participation in these bodies to just BiH's constituent peoples constituted unjustified discrimination. In 2010, a commission was formed in parliament to seek to address this issue; however it was hobbled by procedural and quorum problems and had no results. A second Commission was formed in the autumn of 2011, including 13 Commission members representing BiH's various political parties.

In 2011 the Commission agreed to very narrowly define its task to just addressing the reforms required for the House of Peoples (HoP) and the Presidency, to the chagrin of some parties (SDP, HDZ, SDA) who had hoped to use the forum to address some broader interests in constitutional reform. However even this circumscribed approach was hamstrung. A very minimalist, and some would say cosmetic reform to the HoP that would provide for two representatives of the others to be appointed to the Federation and one from the RS, failed to move forward as concerns about the Presidency reform remained deadlocked. A critical point of contention regarding the Presidency is the RS interest in continuing to have a directly elected presidency, while the Croat parties in the Federation broadly seek either an indirect election to avoid being "Komšić'd" again in the future, or their own electoral unit that would to some extent fulfill their interests in a third (Croat) entity.[3] Some parties have also raised the issue of the lack of opportunity for cross-entity representation, or have noted the so-called Pilav case still pending decision

---

3   When voting for the Bosniak and Croat members of the three-person Presidency, all Federation voters can elect to cast their vote for either the Bosniak or Croat candidate. Some claim that the election of Željko Komšić, a Croat from SDP, was not reflective of the Croat vote, but of the votes of Bosniaks (Arslanagić Oct. 2010).

at the ECtHR in Strasbourg.[4] The Commission met in late 2011 and into 2012, and ultimately announced their inability to find a solution, handing the responsibility from the institutions to the parties. As of the end of 2014, there was no remedy.

Another issue that deserves mention is the international community's increasing call for reform of the Federation. Since the signing of the Washington Agreement in 1994, this 51 percent of the country has been an unwieldy amalgam of 10 cantons that are either majority Bosniak, majority Croat or mixed. Each canton is further organized into municipalities, so the structure of the Federation government results in a three-tiered system (ICG 2010). The cumbersome Federation structure results in high costs for public administration, under-served citizens at the mercy of municipal and cantonal officials playing competency ping-pong, and a structure that invites ethno-nationally focused patronage which has a built-in interest in maintaining the status quo.

For these reasons, in 2013 the US and EU called for reform of that entity in and of itself, and outside the context of state-level reform. This served a number of practical and political interests. Practically, as noted it is clear that the Federation *is* inefficient, ineffective and costly (Keil 2014). In comparison the more centralized RS is a model of order and efficiency (though at the cost of almost all political pluralism within the entity (ICG 2011)). Politically, this option allows the international community to support reform without alarming or provoking the most powerful politician in BiH—RS President Milorad Dodik. Dodik has made it clear that he is fine with a push for Federation reform—as long as it has absolutely no impact on his entity, in any way. Dodik has been equally insistent on ensuring that the words "constitutional reform" are eliminated from the debate. A Federation "expert group" heavily supported by the US Embassy delivered a set of 181 recommendations in spring 2013, and drafted these into a new constitution in autumn 2013.[5] There was little expectation for adoption, and little confidence that BiH's broader problems could be fixed in this manner, particularly as parties already at the start of 2014 began to position themselves for the upcoming autumn general elections.

Constitutional reform has been so difficult precisely because there is no political will for change by several parties satisfied with the status quo, and addressing this issue head on is a reminder that the country remains in a state of frozen conflict (Biščević 2010). If there were an iota of political will for a more effective, streamlined and human rights-based government structure and function (the presumed goals of reform), then the current Dayton constitution would in many ways be flexible enough to provide that framework. (The need

---

4   The Appeal of Ilijas Pilav is a case concerning the denial of a political party's request to list a Bosniak from the Republika Srpska (RS) as a candidate for the RS seat of the Presidency of BiH. After exhausting BiH remedies, the case was appealed to the ECtHR, where it is currently pending (Appeal 2006; Mustajbegović 2007). On this issue see also John Hulsey's chapter in this volume.

5   Available at http://ustavnareformafbih.blogspot.com/

to remedy the exposed discrimination inherent in the Sejdić-Finci case is a very important exception.)

As a result of the lack of any shared vision for the country, every aspect of constitutional reform has been turned into an existential struggle among the representatives of the three constituent peoples vying for their own ends. Perceptions of constitutional reform in the RS are heavily influenced by past efforts, political rhetoric, and the media. RS political leaders have consistently reinforced the sense that *any* reform would require the RS to give up political power and resources without gaining anything in return, and should therefore be thwarted. Croat interests in reform revolve around ensuring equal representation in BiH state structures, if not through a *de jure* third entity, then through processes and protections that provide them with *de facto* third entity status. Positions among Bosniaks vary widely as well—from Haris Silajdžić's "Bosnia without entities" (CSCE 2007), to Bakir Izetbegović's call for constitutional reform to promote the potential of EU membership (Arslanagić 2010; Mulabegović 2010; Quinn 2010). In general, Bosniak politicians (as well as politicians who would consider themselves to be "Bosnian" in spite of the lack of such a legal category) are most comfortable with the idea of more substantial constitutional reform and a stronger state government.[6] Some argue that this is because of a commitment to diversity, while others argue that this is a mathematical calculation based on the fact that they would form a plurality within a more unified BiH (Bieber 2006).

In such an environment, a number of bottom-up approaches to reform have been initiated. Some have been expert-driven, lengthy processes, while others have been single, stand-alone activities. Following a brief review on the state of civil society in BiH, several of these efforts are described below.

The State of Civil Society in BiH

The notion that constitutional reform—perhaps the Holy Grail of post-Dayton reform—might be addressed and influenced by civil society begs the question of whether or not civil society is up to the task. In fact, it is fair to consider the impact of civil society in this process in *any* country, as constitutional reform is a tall order.[7] This section will briefly review the state of civil society in BiH.

---

6   An August 2010 NDI public opinion poll indicated that 78 percent of Bosniaks favored abolishing the entities as a level of government (NDI 2010).

7   In 2011 Iceland worked through a state-initiated, bottom-up driven process to draft a new constitution for a country seeking to rebuild social and political trust after the financial crisis. This very innovative process worked through a series of events, including an initial assembly of almost 1000 randomly-selected citizens, and a Council comprised of citizens and experts, who worked to draft the text over the course of several months (Fillmore-Patrick 2013; Olafsson 2011)

Discussions about civil society by external actors or observers in BiH tend to be focused on structured organizations with a potential interest in and ability to influence public policy—non-governmental organizations (NGOs) or civil society organizations (CSOs).[8] External actors tend not to focus on book clubs, volunteers or other informal social networks, let alone civic actors that do not possess a progressive reform agenda. Any broad definition of civil society must also include sports groups and veterans associations, both of which in fact receive a large percentage of BiH civil society funding,[9] as well as religious groups and trade unions (both of which have been highly politicized). However, in BiH's post-war experience, civil society has broadly been viewed by outsiders as a non-partisan (i.e., NGOs not affiliated *formally* with any one political party) potential tool that may help in peace implementation and long-term democratic consolidation (USAID 2004). Therefore, for the purposes of this paper, the term civil society will be used to refer to formal organizations working in the policy advocacy realm.

A great deal has been written on post-war civil society development efforts in BiH, and this brief summary only reviews some broadly recognized trends. As a result of the large number of donors that flooded the country after the war, BiH NGOs have been developed, groomed, trained, briefed, advised, tested, funded, evaluated, propped-up, de-funded, and cajoled. The sheer amount of attention and money spent in efforts to build or strengthen a civil society capable of serving as a counter-weight to the ruling parties means that the environment has been distorted by the influx of aid and (often) good intentions (Carothers 1999, Ottaway and Carothers 2000). The notion of civil society being shaped and debilitated by a dependency trap has been thoroughly discussed, as have other criticisms of the outsized influence of external actors on the emergence of civil society in BiH including the fostering of a project-based mentality; the impact of aid distortion; the focus on civil society as service delivery; a tendency to focus on short-term international "trends" in targeting funding rather than long-term local needs (for example, heightening interest in anti-trafficking projects even if that is not a stated local need); the competition among NGOs that is created by the scramble for funding; a focus on the urban-elites; the pros and cons of the professionalization of NGOs (and unbalanced relationships between the two); and weak donor coordination (Belloni 2001, Bieber 2002, USAID 2004, Reich 2006, World Bank 2006, Belloni and Hemmer 2010, BCSDN 2012, Sebastian 2012, Verkoren and

---

8 While various organizations use these terms in various specific ways, these terms are used interchangeably in this paper.

9 A report from the Center for the Promotion of Civil Society (CPCS) looked at data for 2010, finding that 34.3 percent of grants were made to sports associations, 16 percent to disabled veterans, 21.6 percent to groups providing social services and 28.2 percent to other types of CSOs (CPCS 2010). The OSCE Mission to Bosnia and Herzegovina did independent research on municipal level support to CSOs in 2009–2010, finding that, "Out of approximately 60,000,000 KM reserved for CSOs, 70 percent is allocated to war related associations, sports clubs, cultural and religious organizations" (OSCE unpublished).

van Leeuwen 2012, Puljek-Shank and Memišević 2013). It is not just critics making these observations; for example USAID is itself aware of the continuing challenges in this development sector (Barnes 2004, USAID 2009).

Anecdotally, NGOs also suffer from a credibility gap with citizens, as a skeptical citizenry often lumps civil society actors in the same lot as politicians, viewing them all as in it "just for the money," biased and at times even nefariously motivated. Whether these views are based on their direct and real experience with various segments of civil society—the professional or the volunteer; the policy advocates or activists; the independent or pseudo-independent—does not matter, as the monolithic notion of "civil society" means they are all painted with the same brush. As noted above, studies by the Center for the Promotion of Civil Society (CPCS) and OSCE shows that a significant amount of money invested in the NGO sector by the BiH government is given to social care, sports groups, and war veterans associations (CPCS 2010; OSCE unpublished). As the latter two groups often have close ties to political parties, it is reasonable to expect that this practice has an impact on the average person's thoughts on civil society, as advocacy organizations and think tanks tend to be limited to larger urban areas.

These criticisms should not suggest that there are no positive aspects of BiH civil society, though this angle has not received as much attention as the more critical research. Whether in terms of service delivery, offering cultural and educational opportunities in communities that would otherwise be unserved, or seeking to change the interaction between civil society and government at all levels, NGOs have been able to make an impact at this level (Barnes 2004, Belloni 2007, Sejfija 2006, CPCS 2010). Anecdotally speaking, externally funded activities—often not at all political—offer small communities in particular opportunities for entertainment of engagement that would otherwise not exist. However, in terms of consolidation or success at the macro or systemic level, successes have often been out of reach. On the policy side, NGOs cannot point to a major legislative "win" that might serve as the basis for some momentum, or help them to demonstrate their capacity and potential.[10] In June 2013 a series of civic protests related to the issuances of citizen ID numbers inspired many people to begin to think that perhaps citizens had had enough; however, after several weeks even these demonstrations lost steam, and a law with provisions contrary to the wishes of protestors was ultimately adopted (Zuvela 2013). Protests in 2014 also failed to maintain momentum.

---

10   When asking BiH observers whether they can identify substantial policy "wins," one suggestion often raised is related to the campaign by the Center for Civic Initiatives (CCI) for the direct election of mayors. The campaign did succeed in changing the law to allow for direct election of mayors; a step seen as having the potential to increase accountability at the local level. CCI receives funding from USAID. However, some critics will point out that CCI had much more support from the US government and other international actors in this endeavor, which greatly increased the chances for success (USAID 2004; OSCE/ODIHR 2004).

Why have NGOs advocating for political reform been unable to make more of an impact? While some of this is related to organizational weaknesses, the broader environment in which they operate cannot be ignored. The country formalized and structured by Dayton and the state constitution therein were not drafted to ensure maximal engagement by diverse citizen constituencies; the Dayton structure was developed by and for the wartime elites, and has never enjoyed confirmed public legitimacy. While written in 2001, a description of this environment is still applicable in 2013: "The lack of transparency and accountability and the dearth of the rule of law and good governance make public scrutiny a chimera. Bosnian civil society has neither the leverage nor the potential resources to perform the task handed over by the international community" (Belloni 2001, 172). Further, Belloni's description of the way in which elites maintain the status quo remains accurate a decade later: "By fostering community isolation, mobilization and a general feeling of insecurity, ethnic elites legitimize each other and maintain a tight grip on their constituencies. At the same time, internal dissent, as expressed by those who question the existing social order by promoting and defending the possibility of a multi-ethnic polity, is often repressed and marginalized" (Belloni 2001, 173.) It is not theoretically *impossible* to think that civil society might play a meaningful role in constitutional reform efforts. However, it is fair to consider that this would be one of civil society's biggest challenges.

Is international support for civil society driven by a real interest in civil society or is it a more cynical reaction to the failures of working with BiH's Dayton structures and elites (Belloni 2001)? This is an intriguing question in general, but in particular as it relates to efforts to engage civil society in constitutional reform. Further, there is a risk that viewing "civil society" as a panacea can ignore broader factors related to the lack of democratic consolidation or the inability of a society to reach a lasting peace. A World Bank report looking at the role of civil society in peace-building notes that "Conflict is generally driven by macro-level factors" (World Bank 2006, 23), and "The assumption that many local peace initiatives will automatically influence peace building at the macro level has been proved wrong" (Ibid., 25). It is reasonable to think that while civil society should not be purposely excluded from elite level reform efforts, neither should it be expected to successfully shoulder the burden alone in the existing non-conducive socio-political environment.

Rethinking Constitutional Reform – Bottom Up Efforts

While the failure of the April Package put the issue of constitutional reform on the public radar screen, there had been some limited prior bottom-up efforts. The Center for Security Studies (CSS) implemented a project entitled "Dialogue on the People's Constitution of BiH" in 2003 and 2004 with funding from Norway, engaging experts and intellectuals on the topic of the functionality (or non-functionality) of BiH institutions (CSS). A mixed group of youth convened by the

Children's Movement for Creative Education developed a Youth Constitution for BiH as a part of their youth outreach and engagement activities.[11]

However, the bulk of civic efforts began after the failure of the April Package, as donors began to work with (or through) existing NGOs to seek ideas and proposals for how to move forward. This engagement often shared many characteristics in common. Donors sought to work with established NGOs, to benefit from existing capacity rather than create new bodies that might exist just for the length of the project. They tended to support organizations with past experience and current capacity to produce policy analysis and recommendations; or in the case of engaging with activist organizations, with NGOs with experience in street actions and outreach. None of the NGOs noted below have any *formal* affiliation with political parties (though members may have been active in one or more parties as individuals), and their organizational means ranged from the voluntary and negligibly funded to the larger NGOs with operational and/or project funding. In terms of ideology, all of the NGOs supported share a basic commitment to progressive reform grounded in human rights. The NGOs and members were often (but not solely) based in Sarajevo but with projects and membership throughout the country.

In 2007–2008 the Helsinki Committee for Human Rights in BiH (HCHR) in Sarajevo implemented a constitutional reform project with support from the Heinrich Boell Stiftung, organizing roundtables in Bugojno, Livno/Drvar, Foča/Goražde and Sarajevo, working with returnees, NGOs and municipalities to identify participants and involve officials as well as citizens. The resulting recommendations were rather broad, calling for an inclusive reform process that protected the rights of individual citizens and national minorities and met international human rights standards. Recommendations were shared through a conference and publicized through the media, but in the absence of sustained follow-up gained no traction.[12]

The Swiss Development Cooperation Office in BiH (SDC 2010) has supported a multi-year phased project entitled, "Contribution to Constitutional Reform" (CCR), with the most recent phase wrapping up in late 2013. The CCR project defined its vision as follows: "Constitutional changes are [the] result of wide compromise, representing the interest of the entire citizenry of BiH, achieved through democratic process led by authorities in conjunction with civil; society organizations, the media and the broader public. Strong emphasis is given to the state and nation building in BiH" (SDC 2010 3). Initial phases included media

---

11 For more information on this organization see the web site at http://www. childrensmovement.org/index.php?option=com_content&view=article&id=46&Item id=69.

12 Helsinki Committee for Human Rights in BiH, www.bh-hchr.org . While there are 3 other local organizations with the word "Helsinki" in them in BiH (Helsinki Odbor in the RS, (Bijeljina) Helsinki Parliament (Banja Luka); Helsinki Parliament for Youth (Tuzla)), the four have little cooperation.

monitoring, academic research, public debates, public opinion research, advocacy, women's engagement, study trips to Zurich and presentation of ideas to the Parliament. A number of local NGOs have been engaged by the Swiss in the project, including the Human Rights Center of the University of Sarajevo (HRC), the Alumni Association of the Centre for Interdisciplinary Postgraduate Studies (ACIPS), the Institute for Social Science Research at the University of Sarajevo Faculty of Political Science, Zašto ne? (*Why Not?*), the Association of Democratic Initiatives (ADI), and the entity associations of cities and municipalities.

Two packages of reform proposals largely in line with the Venice Commission recommendations were drafted. One was developed by ACIPS through the project, "Our Position on the Constitution" (*Naš stav za Ustav*), in partnership with the Institute for Social Science Research of the Faculty for Political Science of Sarajevo University.[13] In developing the amendments, ACIPS considered two approaches: one "radical," calling for significant structural change to the constitution, and one "acceptable," providing for minimal change to the constitution in recognition of the perceived political realities, ultimately settling on the "acceptable" option as the more possible of the two options.[14]

The ACIPS proposal consisted of five constitutional amendments, including the protection of collective rights; reforms to the House of Peoples to both include the representation of the Others[15] as well as to enable both entity parliaments and the Assembly of Brčko District to select its representatives; and a reformed BiH Presidency, with a single, indirectly elected President, voted for by the HoP, and with fewer competencies than the current Presidency. The amendments were presented at roundtable discussions in Mostar, Banja Luka, Brčko and Bihać, and civic petition events held in Doboj, Bijeljina, Trebinje, Drvar, Višegrad, Foča and Sarajevo (SDC 2010). The initiative secured media space in *Oslobođenje*, *DANI* and *Dnevni Avaz*, as well as on Federal Television (FTV). (Although Radio Televizija Republike Srpske (RTRS) came to take a statement at one of the petition signings, the footage was never aired.) Activists presented the Amendments to the main political parties, gaining support from the SDP platform parties (SDP, SDA, People's Party Working for Progress, Croatian Party of Rights BiH), PDP and HDZ 1990. SNSD opposed it publicly but noted some interest behind closed doors, while SBiH and HDZ BiH, were opposed to the proposals.[16]

---

13   Alumni Association of the Centre for Interdisciplinary Postgraduate Studies (ACIPS), http://www.acips.ba/eng/. ACIPS is often associated with the Social Democratic Party, due to the profile of some of its members (alumni of the CIPS Master's program.) However, ACIPS is not affiliated with SDP.

14   Interview with ACIPS (April 2011).

15   The "Others" is a term used to demote those citizens in the country who do not self-identify as one of the three constituent peoples.

16   Interview with ACIPS (April 2011). ACIPS has prepared other papers on the topic of the constitution as well. For example, "European Movement for a European

The second set of amendments was by the Young Lawyers Association, subsequently renamed the Law Institute (LI).[17] The LI brought together a group of legal experts and drafted proposals including reforms related to local self-government, expanded human rights protections and state competencies, and a State Supreme Court (the group could not agree on whether to eliminate the entity supreme courts and compromised on recommending establishment of a state supreme court, while maintaining the entity supreme courts) and reforms to address the Sejdić-Finci decision. This initiative also included consultations, a public debate, and presentations in the Parliament, including with the Clubs of Delegates.

The US supported civic efforts as well.[18] A third comprehensive set of civil society driven amendments was drafted by *Forum Građana Tuzle* (FGT, or Forum of Citizens of Tuzla), with support from the National Endowment for Democracy (NED) and USAID (via the Center for Civic Initiatives).[19] FGT developed proposals including a Presidency comprised of one President and three Deputy Presidents elected indirectly by the House of Representatives; a 31-member House of Peoples representing constituent peoples and national minorities from both Entities; and a 10-member Constitutional Court comprised of three Bosniaks, three Serbs, three Croats, and one national minority judge nominated by the Parliamentary Assembly from a list produced by the High Judicial and Prosecutorial Council.[20] The proposals were presented in the newspapers *Nezavisne Novine* (Banja Luka), *Dnevni List* (Mostar), and *Oslobođenje* (Sarajevo), discussed in roundtable discussions and discussed with all main political parties.

While these efforts represent the main comprehensive non-elite initiatives since the failure of the April Package, there have been other relevant efforts as well, each of which vary in scope. In 2009, the FPI prepared a report on civil society and constitutional reform to provide insight and recommendations for more effectively engaging civil society in the process (FPI 2009). In 2011 the think-tank Analitika prepared an analysis on the ECtHR decision and options for *Sejdić-Finci*

Constitution," by Sead S. Fetahagić and Saida Mustajbegović, available at http://www.acips.ba/bos/uploads/publikacije/europski%20pokret%20za%20evropski%20ustav.pdf

17   Law Institute of Bosnia and Herzegovina, http://www.lawinstitute.ba/. The Law Institute was founded in 2009. It is not affiliated with any political party.

18   NED provided ACIPS with funding to refine their drafted package of amendments to ensure better protection of the "others," resulting in a publication entitled, "Democracy Without Citizens? Looking for a Model of Political Participation of All Constitutional Categories in Bosnia and Herzegovina," in 2012. Available at http://www.acips.ba/bos/uploads/istrazivanja/Democracy%20Without%20Citizens.pdf

19   Forum Građana Tuzle (FGT), www.forumtz.com. FGT had received funds from the National Endowment for Democracy and others, on a variety of issues. FGT is not affiliated with any political party.

20   Forum of Tuzla Citizens, Constitutional Reforms in Bosnia and Herzegovina—Civil Initiative Project, Proposal of amendments and addenda to the Constitution of Bosnia and Herzegovina (2010).

implementation, offering particularly unique food for thought on remedies for the Presidency.[21] The proposals were shared with BiH officials and parties, and debates held to discuss the issues from a variety of perspectives, but beyond disseminating the proposal Analitika has not engaged in more aggressive advocacy.

In 2011 a civil society effort called Koalicija-143 was established, bringing together 16 NGOs from throughout BiH to press for constitutional reforms that would strengthen local self-governance at the municipal level.[22] As of late 2013 it was re-formed around three core NGOs, and publicly launched its model for reform. In winter 2012, 13 women's NGOs were brought together through a Swedish women's initiative (*Kvinna till Kvinna*) to seek ways to involve women in any future constitutional reform processes, in an attempt to provide an alternative to the all-male, elite-driven efforts to date. In 2013 this initiative began working with another women's initiative for constitutional reform being funded by the Swiss and organized by the TPO Foundation[23]; the two networks jointly launched a platform and set of amendments for "gender sensitive" reform which also addressed broader political reform needs.[24] The European Research Center organized a winter 2012 event to discuss the role of civil society in constitutional reform, including learning from the experience of Serbia and its constitutional reforms as it prepares for future EU membership. The Public International Law and Policy Group (PILPG) implemented a project with support from USAID from 2011–14 to strengthen civil society capacities to influence constitutional reform efforts. This effort includes support to NGOs and coalitions (focused on youth and women) interested in reform, legal research, and liaison capacities with the international community in the interest of more harmonized policy approaches.[25] The Swiss have continued additional phases of their support, again involving law faculties and law students working with Swiss legal scholars, debates, and the involvement of NGOs.

Ideas and Activities, but Still No Traction

While all of these efforts show an increased interest among BiH and international actors alike in promoting a more inclusive, bottom-up approach to constitutional reform, there has been nothing close to an April Package-like initiative in terms

---

21   The full text of the book, *New/Old Constitutional Engineering?*, is available at http://www.analitika.ba/en/node/149.

22   Interview, Sarajevo, May 2011.

23   Transkulturna Psihosocijalna Obrazovna Fondacija.

24   The reform proposal is available at http://tpo.ba/inicijativa/dokumenti/P%20 Ust%20proCol%20Final%20Web%20.pdf. A previous gender sensitive reform effort, limited to gender issues, was prepared in 2008 with the support of UNIFEM.

25   PILPG was involved in encouraging the two separate noted women's initiatives to merge, as well as a number of targeted NGO efforts on topics such as ensuring an EU Supremacy Clause, and establishing agricultural competencies at the state level.

of scope or possibility. Despite these efforts, however, there not only has been no constitutional reform, but no noticeable change in the terms of debate; no consistent aggressive advocacy reform by *any* actors; and no wellspring of public support for reform, as average citizens still do not see the link between the constitutional structure and their day to day lives. In fact the environment to even *discuss* reform has worsened. Two sets of explanations (often inter-related) can help to explain the lack of civic traction: technical/project weaknesses and political/policy weaknesses.

Technical/Project Weaknesses

First, many of the various civic efforts ended before achieving "civic traction." For each of the more sustained efforts (ACIPS, LI, FGT), funding ended during various phases of the projects, often leading to gaps in implementation and momentum. This shows the practical constraints of time-limited funding on dedicated work; however, it also shows the impact of "projectization," the lack of member-supported policy NGOs, and the lack of ability of volunteers to engage. This problem was compounded by the impact of the election cycle, which often (some would say mistakenly) leads NGOs to wait out the storm until they can resume their work. Those efforts that have lacked dedicated funding have worked on a shoestring, organizing stand-alone events, but limiting their engagement to what was possible in light of other responsibilities and priorities. However, the support by the Swiss—who have funded numerous multi-year cycles—suggests that lack of traction is not simply an issue of money.

Second, these efforts were all limited in terms of their exposure to the population as a whole. The number of grassroots debates was limited, and the vast majority of communities in BiH did not have the opportunity to hear directly about the various proposals. Those NGOs that used the media were unable to sustain a long-term and consistent campaign; summaries were published, but there was no steady, daily drip of outreach, advocacy and explanation that might counter the standard daily litany of politics. When one considers the space that politicians have in the media to sell their message, every day, civic outreach possibilities can seem extremely limited. One individual interviewed in the course of the PILPG effort noted that it is impossible to fight the 24-hour propaganda machine with leaflets.[26] Those NGOs that have used the Internet in their outreach have used websites to transmit their proposals, but have not generated a significant following, nor been able to use social media to create a more interactive debate, let alone "go viral," and have lacked sufficient real-world field support to gain traction.[27]

---

26   Interview, Sarajevo, May 2011.
27   In addition to the various project web sites, an additional web site—www. ustavnareforma.ba—developed by EURAC, the Konrad Adenauer Stiftung and the Council of Europe provides a useful archive of relevant documents, but it primarily is a potential resource for experts and lawyers, and is not a tool for any broader citizen outreach. In 2012

Further, rigorous, sustained and long-term advocacy and outreach plans were not always built into NGO plans. For example, while Analitika has noted that it would welcome other NGOs taking up their proposals, it has not taken steps to build a constituency that might in fact seek to move these ideas forward. This lack of grassroots constituency building is consistent, as initiatives confuse "roundtables" with building a real civic support base, and rush to brief Parliament on their ideas (often required by donors) where parties quickly kill or stifle discussion before they can point to sizable support. (This is made even more difficult when NGOs develop a "soup to nuts" package of reform proposals that lacks any immediate cohesive civic constituency.) The lack of ability for state level civic legislative initiatives means that NGOs must identify a "sponsor" MP to put their proposals into parliamentary procedure. Further, the outreach that did happen failed to create a strong link between the constitution and practical concerns of citizens—such as jobs, the economy, and education. Their message did not resonate. As a result, in the public sphere there is still no aggressive and consistent call for change.

Fourth, there has been a general lack of coordination among NGOs and initiatives. On the one hand, this has resulted in a variety of ideas that provides fertile ground for discussion. On the other hand, this has segmented civic voices that in many cases share many interests regarding constitutional reform. There is also uneven interest among various donors to coordinate their efforts, resulting in multiple and even concurrent projects with nearly the same goal and often targeting the same NGO partners.[28] However, this is not unique to BiH, as coordination should always be a result of recognized need, rather than an imposed project deliverable, if it is to be genuine.

Political/Policy Challenges

The political challenges facing civil society actors in constitutional reform initiative are more daunting—and will be more difficult to remedy—than the technical challenges.

First, the general political and reform environment in BiH has deteriorated steadily since 2006, affecting reform progress in *all* sectors. The confluence of a number of factors—including progressive disengagement in BiH affairs by the Office of the High Representative, the failure of the April Package, and the general elections that entrenched Milorad Dodik and Haris Silajdžić into diametrically-opposite, zero-sum negotiation postures regarding the future of BiH—led to

---

the NGO *Zašto Ne?* received USAID funding via CCI, and built a website intended to crowdsource reform ideas (www.boljiustav.ba). This site has to date never been consistently promoted or used.

28   The PILPG project included a Consultation Group consisting of past and present relevant donors and other interested international parties to seek to remedy this weakness.

the stalling of reform, and even some signs of reversal of reform.[29] Regional developments, most notably Montenegro's independence referendum in 2006, and Kosovo's unilateral declaration of independence (UDI) in 2008, did not contribute to creating conditions for compromise in BiH on a political issue as fundamental as the constitution (McMahon and Western 2009; Chivvis 2010; Bassuener and Weber 2010).

Second, while civil society may be called on to participate by the international community, NGOs are not viewed as serious players by either domestic or international actors. The lack of trust between government and independent NGOs results in an antagonistic relationship, which minimizes civil society's opportunities to have an effect on legislation of any kind, let alone constitutional reform. Efforts have focused on establishing "coordination offices" and strategies for the government to ensure procedures for civic discussion on legislation of all kinds. In 2012–13, the UN Department of Political Affairs has supported an effort to support "dialogue" and "processes" for constitutional reform discussion between MPs and NGOs, bringing in global experts to share good practice. While potentially well-intended, these efforts—and the perceived need—reflect the country's essential democratic deficit: in a functioning democracy officials listen to civil society because *they know they need to* if they want to be viewed as accountable, and if they want to secure re-election. In BiH, this basic democratic connection is missing.

Participation in reform via European enlargement is also cosmetic at best. One specific area in which there is a lack of any meaningful institutionalized dialogue is related to BiH's Directorate for European Integration (DEI); it is an issue of concern as future constitutional reform efforts may very likely be pursued within the context of EU integration processes. In 2011 several NGOs and NGO networks sent formal written requests to the DEI for meetings, to request information or to seek ways to be included in BiH's European accession path. These requests were simply ignored. A subsequent letter sent to the EUSR received an email response, including the statement, "I would like to draw your attention to the fact that the Directorate for European Integration of Bosnia and Herzegovina is in charge for the programming exercise. I can inform you that the systematic participation of CS [civil society] in the work of the working groups is not foreseen. However, there is an overview presentation planned for civil society at the end of the identification

---

29 The "structured dialogue" on the BiH justice sector was launched in response to threats from the RS to pull out of state justice institutions (the BiH Court and High Judicial and Prosecutorial Council). There are some concerns that the dialogue could have the result of weakened state structures in this sector, though the process is ongoing (Hadžović 2011).

phase."[30] No further suggestions for how civil society might be institutionalized into BiH's accession processes were offered.[31]

NGOs also have difficulty getting their ideas and messages out to the international community in general. They either fail to foresee the benefit of doing so, or allow their interaction with embassies and other actors to be limited to unfocussed meetings or press opportunities with little follow up. More effective advocacy towards the international community could provide NGOs with a tool for public pressure; however to date this has not materialized.

As a result, NGO work is ghettoized into discrete projects that are kept on one track, while high-level political talks move forward on another track. The tracks never cross. It is ironic that donors have spent such considerable sums on supporting civil society initiatives, yet are either unaware of the disconnection between their work and track one politics, or are disinclined to bridge the gap, preferring to limit their genuine "partners" to officials and political party leaders. This dysfunctional relationship with both the government and the international community leads to a perception among advocacy NGOs that it is often not worth going out on a limb in support of reform if, in fact, their role will be primarily cosmetic. This has led some civic actors to opt out of certain opportunities to develop proposals and advocate for reform, either due to concerns about retribution in their communities or a lack of faith that such involvement would be worth it in the end. One very specific example that illustrates this dynamic—and the country's democratic deficit—is related to the Sejdić-Finci reform effort.

Following the formation of the Parliamentary Commission in autumn 2011, PILPG sought to support NGOs with proposals for reform to ensure that their ideas would be included in discussions. In addition to the NGOs with concrete relevant proposals, this offered an opportunity for other reform-minded groups to show their support for reform. However, numerous NGOs—in spite of their stated interest in constitutional reform—had no interest in being involved, noting that they did not want to give legitimacy to a process in which they had little faith. Their lack of trust in the Parliamentary Commission, the political parties behind the Commission members, and the international community led them to conclude they would have more to lose than to gain by participating. In the end, this choice is depressingly understandable. At the start of the Commission's work in October 2011, upon receiving the suggestion that civil society be involved in the work of the Commission, the majority of the 13 Commission members were adamant that

---

30   Email correspondence from the European Union Delegation to BiH, to the Peacebuilding Network Coordinator, November 29, 2011.

31   It should be noted that the EUSR is supporting a number of civil society initiatives, including the TACSO initiative, Citizens for Europe and Generation BiH for Europe. While some of these efforts offer interesting opportunities to participating NGOs, there are concerns by some that the relationship between the EU (as the donor) and participating/ funds-receiving NGOs is clientelistic to the point where criticisms are unwelcome, and controversial policy discussions absent.

this was inappropriate and unnecessary, stating that they were the democratically elected and legitimate representatives of the people, and that they themselves were expert enough to be sufficient for the process. Ultimately, as a compromise it was agreed that NGOs would have the opportunity to present their ideas for reform in one 90-minute session (Second Session 2011). This was far from the working-level consultative process initially hoped for by some, but (perhaps?) was better than nothing.

The NGO consultation was scheduled for November 4, 2011 with an open call in the press explaining that requests to participate should be sent in advance together with proposals. Four NGOs followed this procedure (ACIPS, FGT, the LI and the Citizens Front of the Others, an NGO from Mostar). On that day, these four NGOs had the opportunity to present their concrete proposals, which they did. The format of the meeting was a one-way transmission of information, with no questions coming from the Commission members for clarification or further information. Following these four, three other civic representatives spoke; these individuals were not offering specific proposed amendments or principles (and had not sent their intent to participate in advance), and the conversation shifted to politics and opinions on the genocide in BiH in a way that negatively affected the tone of the event. The press coverage following the session did not mention any of the specific proposals made, but focused on the bombast.

There is nothing to suggest that *any* of the civil society proposals were considered by the Commission. Other than being mentioned in the report in December 2011, which summarized the work process and acknowledged failure to reach agreement, the ideas do not show up in any of the party proposals. Even more worrisome, there has been no sustained reference to these civil society ideas by any of the international interlocutors who have been pressuring the Commission for reform; no statements reminding the parties—but also the citizenry in general—that solutions do exist, are homegrown and are being ignored. The fact that the process has become a litmus test among the parties representing the three constituent peoples—who have little interest in reform—has led many civic observers to view the work of the Commission as reform theater. A statement from the European Parliament in March 2012 warmly praising the work of the Commission, citing in particular the involvement of civil society, is viewed as evidence that the NGOs who did participate lent legitimacy to a process that was not—and was never going to be—meaningful (European Parliament 2012). The scrambling by the European Union throughout 2013 to achieve any signs of "credible effort" towards reform simply amplifies civic cynicism. Activists see that obstruction not only works, but is rewarded.

In the absence of domestic political will or internal incentives for reform, there is a heightened reliance on reform expectations among *external* actors; in particular, as the organization with the biggest carrot, the EU. A third challenge is related to the "post-Dayton, pre-Europe" shift; from Dayton implementation to EU enlargement. The EU has consistently shown itself willing to bend over backwards to ensure a suitable margin of appreciation for BiH as it prepares various reforms (Perry 2012). A writer for *The Economist* has referenced the EU accession standards as applied in BiH, noting, "The European Union, for example, has set the bar deliberately low for Bosnia to apply for candidate status, in recognition of its unique complexity." The 2012 adoption of two long-contested laws—the Law on Census and the Law on State Aid—was only possible once the Laws' level of "stateness" had been whittled down to an absolute minimum, so that some law—of any quality—could be adopted. [32]

In fact, any hopes that EU accession might provide a platform for broader constitutional reform have been misplaced. The EU's role in comprehensive constitutional reform efforts to date have been limited (Perry 2015). A review of annual EU Progress Reports demonstrates a steady decline in references to or recommendations for constitutional reform efforts (Dick 2012). There is an increasing sense that anything is negotiable, that conditionality is flexible and that any notion that EU membership might force politicians to make uncomfortable reforms is misplaced. The jury is still out on the transformative power of Europe in BiH (Džihić and Wieser 2011). It will be hard to convince civic actors to become active in constitutional reform if it appears that the forward motion of the BiH-EU juggernaut will render them irrelevant.

Conclusion

State-level constitutional reform is not impossible, though the challenges to it can seem daunting. There are many political parties and politicians in BiH with a vested interest in the current system as it is they who will fight tooth and nail to preserve the status quo. The international community no longer has the will to use available carrots or sticks to force reform. Until BiH politicians feel that they have something to lose by avoiding reform, it is unlikely they will be at the forefront for change. Unless there are incentives for them to make choices that run counter to their natural political instincts, they will simply not do so. The system—and the conflict—will at best remain frozen, and at worst continue to degenerate towards collapse.

It is reasonable to suspect that the best chance for constitutional reform will not consist of a quick impact "package" of comprehensive reform, but instead a possible long-term slog that tweaks the constitution in a piecemeal fashion. While even such an incremental approach would be vigorously opposed by some politicians, it may prove more difficult to wiggle out of targeted reform requirements. However, such an incremental approach would have to take place in an environment in which there was visible and active enforcement of the terms

---

32   The Law on Census was adopted after much pressure (Perry 2012). The Law on State Aid meets minimal requirements by establishing an unwieldy body that should oversee the Law in a way that the state actually has a negligible role in its implementation. The effectiveness of this law remains to be seen.

of the Dayton Peace Agreement if the country is to avoid a stability vacuum; this critical point is likely to remain contentious in light of the view of many in the EU on the need to close OHR with or without meaningful progress.[33]

Strategic litigation along the lines of the Sejdić-Finci and Pilav cases are likely to be the most effective weapon that can be wielded, particularly with regard to fighting constitutionally-based discrimination claims. One can imagine a plethora of additional possible cases, by a Serb in Mostar challenging the need to choose between a Bosniak or Croat school curriculum, or a Brčko resident challenging the need to "pick" an entity citizenship, for example. If domestic remedies prove to be unavailable, then as with Sejdić-Finci and Pilav, the ECtHR may prove to be involved in BiH for some years to come. The Council of Europe and the Venice Commission could also play a role in this longer-term game.

The Dayton constitution was built quite simply to end a war, and was not intended to provide an eternal blueprint for the structure of the country. However, in the absence of an effort to address the constitutional weaknesses in the late 1990s, the hoped for "interim nature" of the constitution has in fact solidified in order to protect and preserve a status quo favored by the ideological descendants of the wartime parties who were involved in the negotiations. As such, dysfunctionality is virtually built into the system. Hope that political will could make this workable has been proven false over nearly two decades. A vigorous bottom-up (grassroots) and top-down (international) constituency for reform is needed to put pressure on the political leaders; one that transcends the territorial debates that inevitably stoke fear and division, and which is instead based on a system that ensures for accountability by official electoral or prosecutorial measures. Until that happens, and until the civic voices for reform are consolidated around constituencies of real support for needed constitutional reforms, and are magnified by powerful external actors, the system will continue to exist as a pseudo-democracy that serves not the citizens of the country, but the parties who seek to preserve it.

Bibliography

Appeal of Stranka Za Bosnu i Hercegovinu and Mr. Ilijaz Pilav (2006) Party for Bosnia and Herzegovina. *case No. AP-2678/06*, Paragraph 7. Available from: http://www.ccbh.ba/eng/odluke/povuci_html.php?pid=67930.

April Package of Amendments (2006).

Arslanagić, S. (2010) Bosnia Poll Results: Bosniaks Vote for Change. *Balkan Insight*, October 4, 2010. Available from: http://www.balkaninsight.com/ en/article/bosniaks-vote-for-change-serbs-and-croats-remain-loyal-to-nationalists.

——. (2010) Bosnia's New Presidency Pledges End to Confrontation. *Balkan Insight*, November 10, 2010. Available from: http://www.balkaninsight.com/

---

33   See Mateja Peter's chapter in this volume on this issue.

en/article/bosnia-s-new-tri-member-presidency-sworn-in-leaders-pledge-to-foster-consensus.

Azinović, V., Bassuener, K. and Weber, B. (2011) *Assessing the Potential for Renewed Ethnic Violence in Bosnia and Herzegovina: A Security Risk Analysis.* Report by the Atlantic Initiative and Democratization Policy Council. Sarajevo, 2011.

Bahtić-Kunrath, B. (2011) Of Veto Players and Entity-Voting: Institutional Gridlock in the Bosnian Reform Process. *Nationalities Papers,* Vol. 39, No. 6, November 2011, pp. 899–923.

BCSDN (Balkan Civil Society Development Network) Civil Society: Lost in Translation? Donors' Strategies and Practices in Civil Society Development in the Balkans. *Balkan Civic Practices,* No. 8, January 2012.

Barnes, C. et. al. (2004) Civil Society Assessment in Bosnia and Herzegovina. Available from: pdf.usaid.gov/pdf_docs/PNACY559.pdf.

Bassuener, K. and Weber, B. (2010) Are We There Yet? *Democratization Policy Council Policy Brief,* May 2010. Available from: http://democratizationpolicy. org/images/policybriefs/policybrief1.pdf.

Belloni, R. (2001) Civil Society and Peacebuilding in Bosnia and Herzegovina. *Journal of Peace Research,* March 2001, 38(2), pp. 178 (163–180).

——. (2007) *Statebuilding and International Intervention in Bosnia.* London: Routlegde, pp. 118–121.

——. (2009) Dayton is Dead! Long Live Dayton! *Nationalism and Ethnic Politics,* 15(3–4), pp. 355–375.

Belloni, R. and Hemmer, B. (2010), *Bosnia-Herzegovina: Civil Society in a Semi-Protectorate,* In: Paffenholz, T. (ed.) *Civil Society and Peacebuilding: A Critical Assessment,* Boulder: Lynne Rienner, pp. 129–152.

Bieber, F. (2002) Aid Dependency in Bosnian Politics and Civil Society: Failures and Successes of Post-War Peacebuilding in Bosnia-Herzegovina. *Croatian International Relations Review,* January–June 2002, pp. 25–29.

——. (2006) After Dayton, Dayton? The Evolution of an Unpopular Peace. 5 *Ethnopolitics,* 25.

Bilefsky, D. (2009) Tensions Rise in Fragile Bosnia as Country's Serbs Threaten to Seek Independence. *New York Times,* February 27.

Biščević, H. (2010) "Bosnia Stalemate Turning into 'Frozen Conflict." *EurActiv. com,* September 24, 2011.

Carothers, T. (1999) Aiding Democracy Abroad: The Learning Curve. Washington, DC: Carnegie Endowment for International Peace.

Case of Sejdić And Finci V. Bosnia And Herzegovina (2009) European Court of Human Rights. *Judgment 9,* December 22, 2009. Available from: http:// cmiskp.echr.coe.int/tkp197/view.asp?action=html&documentId=860268&por tal=hbkm&source=externalbydocnumber&table=F69A27FD8FB86142BF01 C1166DEA398649.

Case U 5/98 Partial Decision III 1(A), 1(B) (2000) Constitutional Court of Bosnia and Herzegovina. July 1, 2000.

CCS (Centre For Security Studies) BiH (2003) Activity Report 2003. Available from: http://www.css.ba/images/docs/activity2003.pdf.

Chivvis, C. (2010) Back to the Brink in Bosnia? *Survival: Global Politics and Strategy,* 52(1), February–March 2010, pp. 97–110.

Constitutional Court of Bosnia and Herzegovina (n.d.) Decisions. *Case U-5/10.* Available from: http://ccbh.ba/eng/press/index.php?pid=4678&pkat=506&sta=3.

COE (Council of Europe) PA (Parliamentary Assembly) The Functioning of Democratic Institutions in Bosnia and Herzegovina. Vol. 3.1, Document. 12112, January 11, 2010. Available from: http://assembly.coe.int/Main.asp?link=/Documents/WorkingDocs/Doc10/EDOC12112.htm

COE (Council of Europe) SG (Secretary General) (2002) Bosnia and Herzegovina: Follow-up to Committee of Ministers Decisions Regarding Monitoring of Commitments and Implementation of Post-Accession Co-Operation Programme. *First Quarterly Report,* SG/Inf (2002) 27 § II(C), July 15, 2002. Available from: https://wcd.coe.int/wcd/ViewDoc.jsp?id=296231&Site=COE.

CPCS (Center for The Promotion Of Civil Society) (2010) Halfway There: Government Allocations for the Non-governmental Sector in Bosnia and Herzegovina. P. 15, Available from: http://www.cpcd.ba/v2/files/articles/20100929/5/na%20pola%20puta%20-%20izdvajanja%20za%20nevladin%20sektor%202010.pdf.

CSCE (Commission for Security and Cooperation in Europe) (2007) Bosnia-Herzegovina: Outstanding Issues in Post-Conflict Recovery and Reconciliation, Hearing Before the Commission for Security and Cooperation in Europe. *100th Congress 6, 2007.* Available from: csce.gov/index.cfm?FuseAction=Files.Download&FileStore_id=2012.

Dick, P. (2012) Requirements and Reforms, Cause and Effect: A Review of the European Union Progress Reports for Bosnia and Herzegovina for the Fulfillment of the Copenhagen Criteria. *Democratization Policy Council Policy Note,* November 2012.

Džihić, V. and Wieser, A. (2011) Incentives for Democratization? Effects of EU Conditionality on Democracy in Bosnia and Herzegovina. *Europe-Asia Studies,* Vol. 63, No. 10, December 2011, pp. 1803—1825.

The Economist (2012) Let's Stick Together. January 7, 2012.

European Parliament Resolution (March 14, 2012) Point 10 (2011/2888(RSP)). Available from: http://new.eur-lex.europa.eu/legal-content/EN/TXT/?uri=OJ:C:2013:251E:FULL

Fillmore-Patrick, H. (2009–2013) The Iceland Experiment: A Participatory Approach to Constitutional Reform. *Democratization Policy Council (DPC) Policy Note,* No. 2. August 2013.

FPI (Foreign Policy Initiative) (2007) Governance Structures in BiH: Capacity, Ownership, EU Integration, Functioning State, 14.

FPI (Foreign Policy Initiative) BiH (2009) Policy Analysis: Role of Civil Society in BiH Constitutional Reform 3. Available from: http://www.vpi.ba/eng/

content/documents/Role_Of_Civil_Society_in_BiH_Constitutional_Reform.
pdf.

Hadžović, E. (2011) Bosnia: Dodik Agrees to Drop Disputed Referendum. *Balkan Insight,* May 13, 2011.

Hays, D. and Crosby, J. (2006) From Dayton to Brussels: Constitutional Preparations for Bosnia's EU Accession 1. *Special Report 175,* October 2006. Available from: http://www.usip.org/publications/dayton-brussels-constitutional-preparations-bosnias-eu-accession.

ICG (International Crisis Group) Bosnia: State Institutions under Attack. *Europe Briefing,* No. 62, May 2011. Available from: http://www.crisisgroup.org/~/media/Files/europe/balkans/bosnia-herzegovina/B62%20Bosnia%20--%20 State%20Institutions%20under%20Attack.pdf.

——. (2011) Bosnia: What Does Republika Srpska Want? *Europe Report,* No.214, October 6.

——. (2009) Bosnia's Dual Crisis. *Europe Briefing,* No. 57, p. 7–8, November 12. Available from: http://www.crisisgroup.org/en/regions/europe/balkans/bosnia-herzegovina/b057-bosnias-dual-crisis.aspx.

——. (2010) Federation of Bosnia and Herzegovina—A Parallel Crisis. *Europe Report,* No.209, September 28.

——. (2002) Implementing Equality: The "Constituent Peoples" Decision in Bosnia and Herzegovina. *Balkans Report,* No. 128, April 16. Available from: http://reliefweb.int/sites/reliefweb.int/files/resources/6C1D3A9D91EC 29EC85256B9D00640396-icg-bos-16apr.pdf.

Jukić, E. (2012) Mostar's Unity Not in Danger, Inzko Says. *Balkan Insight,* March 19, 2012.

Keil, S. (2014) Building a Federation within a Federation-The Curious Case of the Federation of Bosnia and Herzegovina. *Le Europe en Formation,* Vol. 64, forthcoming 2014.

Mcmahon, P.C. and Western, J. (2009) The Death of Dayton: How to Stop Bosnia from Falling Apart. *Foreign Affairs,* September–October 2009, pp. 69–83.

Morrison, K. (2009) Dayton, Divisions and Constitutional Revisions: Bosnia & Herzegovina at the Crossroads 16. Available from: http://www.da.mod.uk/ colleges/arag/document-listings/balkan/09(11)%20KM2.pdf.

Mulabegović, B. (2010) Who is Bakir Izetbegović? *Globalia Magazine,* May 12. Available from: http://www.globaliamagazine.com/?id=1066.

Mustajbegović, S. (2007) Constitution Taken to Court. *Balkan Insight,* December 20, 2007. Available from: http://www.internal-displacement. org/8025708F004CE90B/(httpDocuments)/BF037A88F356A4D2C125741E0 051A98E/$file/BalkanInsight_com+-+Constitution+Taken+to+Court.htm.

NDI (National Democratic Institute for International Affairs) (2010) Public Opinion Poll Bosnia and Herzegovina. Available from: http://www.ndi.org/ files/NDI_Bosnia_Poll_Report_August_2010.pdf.

Olafsson, J. (2011) An Experiment in Iceland: Crowdsourcing a Constitution? Yale University, 2011. Available from: http://www.yale.edu/polisci/conferences/ epistemic_democracy/jOlafsson.pdf

OSCE Mission To Bosnia And Herzegovina (2009–2010) Municipal Funding of the Civil Society Sector in Bosnia and Herzegovina. *Unpublished report.*

OSCE/ODIHR (2004) Bosnia and Herzegovina Municipal Elections. *Election Observation Mission Report,* October 2. Available from: http://www.osce.org/ odihr/elections/bih/41178.

Ottaway, Marina and Thomas Carothers (2000) *Funding Virtue: Civil Society Aid and Democracy Promotion.* Washington, DC: Carnegie Endowment for International Peace, 2000.

Perry, V. (2012) Barriers to EU Conditionality in Bosnia and Herzegovina. *Working Paper V, The Working Group on the Western Balkans by Woodrow Wilson International Center for Scholars,* March 26, 2012. Available from: http://www.wilsoncenter.org/sites/default/files/Perry%20 Working%20Paper %20%237.pdf.

——. (2013) The Census in Bosnia and Herzegovina: A Basic Review. *Democratization Policy Council Policy Note,* No. 3, October 2013. Available from: http://democratizationpolicy.org/uimages/pdf/ dpcpolicynotebihnewseries3bihcensus.pdf.

Puljek-Shank, Randy And Tija Memišević (2013) Donor Support for Civil Society Advocacy in BiH. *Peace Academy.*

Quinn, A. (2010) Hillary Clinton Takes on Balkan Puzzle. *Reuters,* October 10, 2010. Available from: http://www.reuters.com/article/2010/10/10/us-balkans-clinton-preview-idUSTRE6991MW20101010.

Reich, H.A. (2006) Local Ownership' in Conflict Transformation Projects: Partnership, Participation or Patronage? *Berghof Occasional Paper,* No. 27, September 2006, p. 7. Available at http://www.berghof-conflictresearch.org/ documents/publications/boc27e.pdf.

Sebastian, S. (2007) Leaving Dayton Behind: Constitutional Reform in Bosnia and Herzegovina. *FRIDE Working Paper* 46, November 2007.

——. (2011) Breaking the Impasse: Constitutional Reform in Bosnia. *FRIDE Policy Brief,* No. 68, March 2011. Available from: www.fride.org/download/ PB_69_Bosnia_Eng.pdf.

——. (2012) Assessing Democracy Assistance: Bosnia." *FRIDE Project Report,* May 2012.

Second Session of the Joint Ad Hoc Committee for the Implementation of the Judgment of the European Court of Human Rights in the Case of Sejdić and Finci vs. Bosnia and Herzegovina, October 18, 2011.

SDC (Swiss Development Cooperation Office in Bosnia and Herzegovina) (2010) Contribution to Constitutional Reform Project, Phase III: Final Report, 2010.

Sejfija, Ismet. "From the 'Civil Sector' to 'Civil Society? Progress and Prospects. *Peacebuilding and Civil Society in Bosnia Herzegovina: Ten Years After Dayton.* In: Fischer, M. (ed.). Munster: Lit Verlag, 2006, pp. 125–140.

Available at http://www.berghof-conflictresearch.org/documents/publications/daytone_sejfira_civilsoc.pdf

UNV (United Nations Volunteer Program) (UNV) (2011) Civil Society in Bosnia and Herzegovina: Seeking the Way Forward.

USAID (United States Agency for International Development) (2004) Civil Society Assessment in Bosnia and Herzegovina. June 25, 2004.

——. (2009) NGO Sustainability Index for Central and Eastern Europe and Eurasia 74 (13th edn 2009) Available from: http://www.usaid.gov/locations/europe_eurasia/dem_gov/ngoindex/2009/.

Venice Commission (European Commission for Democracy through Law) (2004) Opinion on the Constitutional Situation in Bosnia and Herzegovina and the Powers of the High Representative. *CDL-AD (2005) 004 2*, March 11, 2004. Available from: http://www.venice.coe.int/docs/2005/CDL-AD(2005)004-e.pdf.

Verkoren, W. and Leeuwen, W. (2012) Complexities and Challenges for Civil Society Building in Post-Conflict Settings. *Journal of Peacebuilding and Development*, Vol. 7, pp. 81–94.

World Bank Social Development Department (2006) Civil Society and Peacebuilding: Potential, Limitations and Critical Factors. *Report No. 36445-GLB*, December 20, 2006.

Zuvela, M. (2013) Bosnia Passes ID Law, Ending Row that Cost a Baby's Life. *Reuters*, November 5, 2013. Available from: http://www.reuters.com/article/2013/11/05/us-bosnia-identity-idUSBRE9A40SG20131105.

Chapter 2

Party Politics in Bosnia and Herzegovina

John Hulsey

Introduction

Citizens exercise power in democratic elections through their choices at the ballot box. Political parties play a crucial role in structuring those choices and realizing the will of the people in governance both in the way that they inform voters' choices and in the ways that political parties bridge branches and levels of government through both competition and cooperation. The efficacy of the Bosnian party system, both in terms of its electoral and governance functions, has been powerfully influenced by the impact of the Bosnian war and the Dayton Peace Agreement in ways that exacerbate the patterns found in other East European states that democratized during the 1990s.

The Dayton Agreement that succeeded in bringing an end to violence in Bosnia and Herzegovina (BiH) puts in place incentives for candidates, parties and voters that privilege parties and politics based on ethnic difference and fails to create encouragements for compromise. These incentives are a result of the ways that Bosnia's consociational constitution segments power by both geographic region and by constituent people. In order to achieve an end to the war, the Dayton Agreement devolved power to Bosnia's entities, cantons and municipalities.[1] The boundaries of the entities and cantons reflect the front lines at the end of the war as well as the outcome of ethnic cleansing. The result is dramatic heterogeneity with regard to ethnic identification across most electoral units relative to homogeneity within electoral units. Consequently, the inducements that drive voter and party behavior at one level of government conflict with those at play at other levels. This chapter examines the impact of this conflict on attributes of Bosnia's party system as well as on the functioning of party politics between elections.

Considering the negative consequences of the structure of the Dayton Agreement (International Crisis Group 2003, Venice Commission 2005),[2] it is important not to divorce the Agreement from the context in which it was created. What are described here as disadvantages of the resulting system are the same features that made it palatable to the leaders of the warring groups. Consociationalism rests on the hope

---

1   See also Soeren Keil's chapter in this volume on the issue of territorial decentralization.

2   See also Valery Perry's chapter in this volume.

that broad representation, veto rights and decentralization will so lower the stakes of politics for both voters and parties that politics can proceed along democratic lines without a return to violence. Peaceful methods of conflict resolution can only take root when participants are secure in the knowledge that the loss of an election will not also bring marginalization or destruction. The complexity of the Dayton Agreement is a result of the need to lower the "costs of democracy" for signatories of the agreement (Bermeo 2003, p. 163).[3] This aspect of the Agreement is an undeniable success. However, the very mechanisms that reassured leaders of ethnic parties enough to lead them to lay down their arms have produced a Bosnia that routinely fails to govern itself. The political division of the country creates an extreme kind of consensus democracy.

By design, the Dayton institutions require cooperation across administrative boundaries that coincide with ethnic group boundaries, as well as across levels of government in order to achieve change or simply govern effectively in areas of concern for the country as a whole. This demand for cooperation is the inevitable outcome of shared power. However, a supply of politicians and parties willing or able to reach agreements and make compromises is not present. In particular, no party or set of parties has succeeded in winning parliamentary majorities at the state or entity level based on a compatible, much less a coherent, view of the direction of the country or the proper interpretation and implementation of the rules set out in the Dayton Agreement.

Bosnia's electoral rules and political structure are ill-suited to foster the election of parties that can reach such broad agreement, let alone the emergence of a single party that garners broad support in all regions and ethnic groups. In short, the demand for cooperation in governance is not reflected in electoral politics. There is no election in Bosnia in which all voters are choosing from the same candidates for the same seat or set of seats. The fragmentation of the electorate supports the political fragmentation of the country.

This chapter focuses on the role of electoral rules in producing political fragmentation, which is observed through the presence of abnormally large numbers of political parties. It is difficult to empirically disentangle the role of electoral rules and political structure from the role played by differences in what voters from different regions and groups prefer. Politics in Bosnia is hindered by the democratic election of officeholders with incompatible political programs and visions for the future of BiH. The simplest explanation focuses on the fundamental disagreement rooted in the identity politics of the war. However, the preferences held by voters both shape and are shaped by party politics. One appeal of an institutional explanation is that electoral rules are more readily changed than the ideals and life experiences of voters. The analysis based on comparative evidence presented here aims to show

---

3   Indeed, McCrudden and O'Leary call into question the use of international human rights law and courts to challenge and alter compromises between parties to the Dayton Agreement. They argue that such attempts undermine both the current compromise and the viability of power-sharing as a solution to future conflicts (2013, pp. xiv, 147–149).

reason to believe that different rules could produce more desirable outcomes, but that meaningful change would require rule changes that end the territorial allocation of seats and therefore fundamentally change the structure of the BiH political system.

The Dayton Constitutional Structure

In general elections held every four years, Bosnian voters choose parties and candidates in six parliamentary and presidential elections, although the segmentation of the political system means that any single voter votes in only four. Voters from the Republika Sprska (RS) vote in the BiH Presidency election for the Serb member of Bosnia's three-member presidency, the BiH Parliament, the Presidency of the RS and the National Assembly of the RS. Voters in the Federation vote for the Croat or Bosniak member of the BiH Presidency, the BiH Parliament, the Federation Parliament and the Assembly of their Canton. Residents of the District of Brčko who want to vote in general elections must declare in advance their chosen entity citizenship, to allow them to vote according to that electoral option. Elections for Bosnia's 143 municipal governments are also held every four years, but their cycle is offset two years from the general election cycle (GFAP 1995).[4]

The role of ethnicity varies across these elections depending on the groups present in the constituency and their relative size, so voters face different choices across elections even in a single trip to the ballot box. For example, a voter in the West Herzegovina Canton of the Federation votes first for the cantonal assembly for a region that is overwhelmingly populated by Croats. In the 2010 elections, no parties associated with Bosniaks or Serbs came close to receiving enough votes for representation in the cantonal assembly, so our example voter is choosing among several Croat parties.[5] It is to be expected that ethnic identity plays a reduced role in this kind of election, as there is no danger of being outvoted by members of another ethnicity. At the next level up, that same voter casts a vote in the Federation Parliament election. Within the Federation, Croats are a large minority of voters, while the three largest parties in the Federation Parliament are all associated with Bosniaks. In contrast to the cantonal election, a Croat voter must consider whether parties that engage in more aggressive rhetoric regarding Bosniaks are better suited to represent his or her interests. Prior research has shown that such considerations drive down support for parties with multi-ethnic or conciliatory programs in elections where other ethnicities participate relative to elections where only one ethnic group is represented. In other words, voters are more likely to choose multi-

---

4   The General Framework Agreement for Peace in Bosnia and Herzegovina ended the conflict in the country. It was negotiated in Dayton, Ohio in November 1995 and signed in Paris in December 1995. Annex IV of the GFAP contains Bosnia's current constitution.

5   All election results based on data from the Central Election Commission for Bosnia and Herzegovina (2013).

ethnic or non-nationalist parties when all of the competitive parties in the election are from one ethnicity or are non-nationalist (Hulsey 2010).[6] Voting for the BiH Parliament adds the consideration of a third ethnic group in that Serbs are also represented in the BiH Parliament, although exclusively through votes from the RS. Croats make up an even smaller proportion of the overall BiH electorate for a parliament in which there are fewer than half as many seats as for the Federation Parliament. Finally, voters in the Federation vote for either the Bosniak or Croat member of the BiH Presidency. In theory, this election should resemble the mono-ethnic elections to the West Herzegovina Cantonal Assembly elections; however, the presence of a Croat candidate who is popular among Bosniaks has led to large participation by Bosniaks in the election of the Croat member of the BiH Presidency. (This phenomenon will be discussed more fully below.) What is clear is that feelings of ethnic identification interact with the ethnic context of a particular election in order to shape voting behaviour and the party system.

While the voter from the West Herzegovina Canton votes in elections in each of which ethnicity plays a very different role, a general election voter in any district in the RS faces four similar elections in which only Serb parties are likely to gain seats. Elections for the RS Assembly, RS Presidency, the RS delegates to the BiH Parliament and the Serb member of the BiH Presidency are all dominated by Serb parties. Bosniak and Croat parties are dwarfed by even small Serb parties in RS elections. These two examples show the great variety in the role that ethnicity can play in Bosnian elections as well as the very divergent contexts of the two entities. Perhaps most significant is that the voter in West Herzegovina and the voter in the RS together cast eight votes in a general election, but can at no point vote for the same candidate or party list. The forms of party systems are influenced by the interaction of societal cleavages with incentives and constraints placed upon voters and parties by electoral rules. In Bosnia, the result is a party system that has a very high number of parties in the legislature, a high degree of stability despite that fragmentation, many parties that are excessively focused on one or a few leaders, and that continues to be made up primarily of parties that represent only one ethnic group.[7] The following section examines each of these characteristics in light of theories based on comparative evidence.

Why Does Bosnia Have So Many Parties?

General elections to the Parliament of BiH held on October 3, 2010 resulted in 12 parties gaining at least one seat in Bosnia's 42-seat legislature. One root of the dysfunction of party politics in Bosnia is this fragmentation of the party system

---

6   This effect may manifest both in terms of direct electoral competition and with an eye toward the canton, Federation and BiH Councils of Ministers, which are indirectly elected from their respective assemblies.

7   See also Tina Mavrikos-Adamou's contribution in this volume.

in the parliament, which, combined with the power-sharing requirements of the constitution, makes the creation of governing coalitions very difficult. The sheer numbers of parties involved across the three ethnic groups result in unstable coalitions without enough in common to jointly govern. Following the 2010 general elections, parties required more than 16 months to come to agreement on a coalition to form the Council of Ministers. The resulting coalition survived less than six months before it descended into crisis (Jukić 2012).

The sheer number of parties involved in the legislature played a role in causing this instability. A large number of parties makes it more difficult for voters to place themselves among competing ideological programs and makes it more difficult to build and maintain coalitions between elections. Comparatively, the most important factor determining the number of parties in the legislature is the design of the electoral institutions. The minimum level of support required to gain representation from a particular district depends on the number of mandates at stake in that district (Cox 1999). The Bosnian Parliament is elected through proportional representation from eight multimember districts nested within two entities. District magnitude ranges from three to six representatives elected within each district. The primary effect of the districts is to guarantee representation for parties that are very strong in a particular region. A total of 12 compensatory seats are distributed to parties in order to make the overall balance between parties in the legislature as close as possible to the overall proportion of votes received as well as to provide representation for those parties that receive a minimum level of support across the entire election without receiving enough votes in any district. However, the compensatory seats are allocated separately for the two entities, so votes cast in the Federation have no impact on seats allocated from the RS or vice versa (*Izborni Zakon Bosne i Hercegovine* 2001).

Compared to other post-communist countries, the BiH Parliament is highly fragmented. Of 88 elections in post-communist democracies between 1990 and 2008,[8] three of the 11 most fragmented elections were for the BiH Parliament. The effective number of parties by vote (ENPV) in the BiH Parliament for 2000, 2002 and 2006 was respectively 7.77, 8.77 and 8.91. The mean ENPV in all post-communist democracies for the time period between 1990 and 2008 is 5.37. The former Yugoslav republics show results similar to the full set of post-communist states with a mean ENPV of 5.4, despite the fact that Bosnia's very high results carry greater weight among the smaller set of countries. Bosnian elections stand out even more relative to the trend toward fewer parties as party systems consolidate. The mean ENPV for all post-communist democracies between 2000 and 2008 falls to 4.98 and falls to 5.17 for former Yugoslav republics. In contrast, the BiH Parliament is getting more fragmented and not less.

In isolation, the key factor in explaining the number of parties represented in a legislature is the district magnitude. However, as we have seen above, the

---

8   All comparative party system quantities generated from Dataset on Electoral and Party Systems in Post-Communist States (Bielasiak, 2012)

number of parties in the BiH Parliament is much higher than one would expect given the average district magnitude used in elections for the BiH Parliament. Cox's generalization of Duverger's Law[9] shows that incentives for coordination caused by district magnitude places a constraint on the number of parties equal to the magnitude of the district plus 1, known as the M+1 rule (Duverger, 1963, Cox 1999, pp. 151–152). However, the BiH Parliament's average district magnitude of 5.25[10] suggests an upper ENPV of 6.25 instead of the 7.77–8.91 that is observed. The cause of this discrepancy lies in the influence of ethnicity on the way that elections play out on different levels of elections and across districts.

The most important institutional characteristic of Bosnia's party system is the bifurcation of the electorate by entity for the purpose of elections to state-level institutions and the further subdivision of the Federation of Bosnia and Herzegovina into 10 cantons. In concert with the importance of elections to entity and canton-level legislatures, the sub-division of the electorate creates "local party systems"[11] that serve as seats of power for parties that would otherwise have an incentive to merge with similar parties in state-level elections. Bosnia's 42-seat lower house is tiny relative to the population of the country (Lijphart 2004, p. 106); however, its balance of regional districts and compensatory seats results in a reasonably proportional representation of the vote. The problems with the system emerge from poor "linkage" across election districts and across elections to different levels of government.

Strong linkage between district party systems describes situations in which elections in each district take the form of microcosms of the national party system, while no linkage describes the case in which the elections in each district do not include the same parties or are not at all about the same issues (Cox 1999, p. 155). Horizontal linkage refers to the degree of connection between electoral competitions in districts for the same body. So, there is higher horizontal linkage between House of Commons constituencies within England, where the same parties and programmatic choices are important in each district, than between English constituencies and constituencies in Northern Ireland. In contrast to the constituencies in the England, voting in the Northern Ireland constituencies

---

9   Duverger (1963) is the seminal work that identified the link between plurality elections in single member districts and two-party systems. Duverger argues that, since plurality elections in single member districts provide no representation for losing candidates, parties have a strong incentive to coordinate before elections such that two strong parties emerge. Cox (1997, 1999) builds on Duverger's logic to show the link between a large variety of different electoral rules and the number of parties. He finds that districts tend to support one more party than the number of representatives elected from that district (M+1).

10   In comparison, the median value for average district magnitude in the dataset is 9.18. So, based on the most established cause of fragmentation, the BiH Parliament should have *fewer* parties than the median country.

11   Cox (1999, 1997) uses "local party system" to describe each district's party system. Local party systems are linked to varying degrees to other party systems at the same level as well as to a national party system.

is based less on left-right economic distinctions and more on identity politics. Vertical linkage refers to the degree of connection between lower and higher level elections in federal systems. The US displays very high vertical linkage in that elections for state legislatures involve the same parties and similar programs to elections for Congress.

Bochsler's analysis of post-communist party systems finds that Bosnia's party system shows by far the least linkage[12] of the 20 countries he examines (Bochsler 2010, p. 818). His results show that territorially-defined social divisions, including ethnic divisions, are the most important cause of poor party system linkage, particularly when combined with electoral rules that do not create incentives for the creation of parties that compete in all districts. These conclusions map clearly onto observed patterns in Bosnian voting behavior, whereby the effects of ethnic cleansing have created a political geography in which most areas, and therefore most electoral districts, are dominated by one of the three constituent peoples (Keil 2013, pp. 78, 92). The distribution of people and the structure of the political system interact to dramatically inflate the number of parties.

The mechanism that produces poor linkage has both a horizontal and a vertical component. The horizontal component is the most direct and can be shown by the dramatic difference in voting outcomes across the eight voting districts. Table 2.1 and Table 2.2 summarize election results for 2006 and 2010. The dramatic difference in the overall election results for the BiH parliament between the RS and the Federation is apparent. The district-level results from the RS are effectively a microcosm of the entity-wide results. Competition is overwhelmingly between the Alliance of Independent Social Democrats (SNSD) and the Serb Democratic Party (SDS) with no other parties able to gain direct mandates from the district-level elections. Compensatory seats are allocated to a few small parties, but none is a threat to win significant representation. This pattern can be seen clearly in Table 2.3, which shows the district breakdown of votes for the 2010 BiH Parliament elections. The same two parties come in first and second in all three districts. This high degree of horizontal linkage across districts within the Republika Srpska causes it to behave in a way consistent with Cox's M+1 prediction, with only four parties represented in the RS half of the legislature. In other words, the number of parties from the RS can be explained by the number of seats being elected from each district. However, district heterogeneity between the RS and the Federation as well as heterogeneity between the Federation's districts together lead to high fragmentation in the BiH Parliament. The two dominant parties from the RS failed to receive any direct or compensatory mandates from the Federation half of Bosnia. The explanation for this outcome is clear; SNSD and SDS are Serb parties and few Serbs live in the Federation. The difference in voter composition means that the voter choices in the RS districts are very poorly linked to the voter choices in the Federation.

---

12 Bochsler uses the term "nationalization" to capture both horizontal and vertical linkage in contrast to more regionalized party systems. "Linkage" is the preferable term in the Bosnian context to avoid confusion with the use of the word "nation" to describe ethnic groups.

Table 2.1 Summary of 2006 general election results

Party	Type	BiH Parliament	Federation Parliament	RS Assembly	Cantonal Elections
Parties Elected from Republika Srpska					
Savez Nezavisnih Socijaldemokrata (SNSD)	Serb ethnic party	46.93% (7)		43.31% (41)	
Srpska Demokratska Stranka (SDS)	Serb ethnic party	19.44% (3)		18.27% (17)	
Partija Demokratskog Progresa (PDP)	Serb ethnic party	5.08% (1)		6.86 % (8)	
Stranka za Bosnu i Hercegovinu (SBiH)	Bosniak ethnic party	4.16% (1)		4.01% (4)	
Stranka Demokratske Akcije (SDA)	Bosniak ethnic party	3.67% (1)		3.39% (3)	
Demokratski Narodni Savez (DNS)	Serb ethnic party	3.56% (1)		4.04% (4)	
Socijalistička Partija (SP)	Leftist Party	2.25%		3.55% (3)	
Srpska Radikalna Stranka (SRS)	Serb ethnic party	2.83%		2.92% (2)	
Socijaldemokratska Partija (SDP)	Multiethnic party	2.12%		2.50% (1)	
Parties Elected from the Federation					
Stranka Demokratske Akcije (SDA)	Bosniak ethnic party	25.54% (8)	25.45% (28)		25.5% (74)
Stranka za Bosnu i Hercegovinu (SBiH)	Bosniak ethnic party	22.99% (7)	22.16% (24)		21.39% (59)
Socijaldemokratska Partija (SDP)	Multiethnic party	15.40% (5)	15.17% (17)		14.35% (43)
Hrvatska Demokratska Zajednica (HDZ) Coalition with HNZ	Croat party	7.99% (3)	7.56% (8)		7.3% (36)
Hrvatsko Zajedništvo (HDZ 1990 HZ-HSS-HKDU-HDU-DEMOKRŠĆANI)	Croat party	6.10% (2)	6.32% (7)		5.69% (29)
Bosanskohercegovačka Patriotska Stranka (BPS)	Bosniak ethnic party	4.41% (1)	4.10% (4)		3.63% (8)
Narodna Stranka Radom za Boljitak (NSRzB)	Multiethnic party	3.22% (1)	3.16% (3)		3.31% (10)
Patriotski Blok BOSS-SDU	Multiethnic party	2.77%	3.17% (3)		2.31% (5)
Hrvatska Stranka Prava (HSP) in Coalition with NHI	Croat ethnic party	2.28%	2.46% (1)		1.98% (14)
Demokratska Narodna Zajednica (DNZ)	Multiethnic party	1.90% (1)	1.87% (2)		1.9% (6)
Savez Nezavisnih Socijaldemokrata (SNSD)	Serb ethnic party	0.85%	1.46% (1)		1.49% (5)

Table 2.2 Summary of 2010 general election results*

Party[a]	Type	BiH Parliament[b]	Federation Parliament	RS Assembly	Cantonal Elections[c]
Parties Elected from Republika Srpska					
Savez Nezavisnih Socijaldemokrata (SNSD)	Serb ethnic party	43.3% (8)		38.0% (37)	
Srpska Demokratska Stranka (SDS)	Serb ethnic party	22.2% (4)		19.0% (18)	
Partija Demokratskog Progresa (PDP)	Serb ethnic party	6.5% (1)		7.6% (7)	
Demokratski Narodni Savez (DNS)	Serb ethnic party	4.6% (1)		6.1% (6)	
Socijalistička Partija i Partija Ujedinjenih Penzionera (SP-PUP)	Leftist party	2.4% (0)		4.2% S(4)	
Demokratska Partija (DP)	Serb ethnic party	2.4% (0)		3.4% (3)	
Srpska Radikalna Stranka (SRS)	Serb ethnic party	2.3% (0)		2.4% (1)	
Narodna Demokratska Stranka (NDS)	Conservative Party	1.1% (0)		2.0% (2)	
Parties elected from the Federation					
Socijaldemokratska Partija (SDP)	Multiethnic party	26.1% (8)	24.5% (28)	3.1% (3)	22.5% (61)
Stranka Demokratske Akcije (SDA)	Bosniak ethnic party	19.4% (7)	20.2% (23)	2.7% (2)	20.0% (55)
Savez za Bolju Budućnost (SBB)	Bosniak ethnic party	12.2% (4)	11.9% (13)		11.3% (29)
Hrvatska Demokratska Zajednica (HDZ)	Croat ethnic party	11.0% (3)	10.6% (12)		10.2% (48)
Stranka za Bosnu i Hercegovinu (SBiH)	Bosniak ethnic party	7.3% (2)	7.6% (9)		7.8% (23)
Hrvatska Koalicija HDZ 1990-Hrvatska Stranka Prava (HDZ-1990 & HSP)[d]	Croat ethnic parties	4.9% (2)	4.7% (5)		4.8% (26)
Narodna Stranka Radom za Boljitak (NSRzB)[e]	Multiethnic party	4.8% (1)	4.7% (5)		5.2% (20)
Demokratska Narodna Zajednica (DNZ)	Multiethnic party	1.5% (1)	1.5% (1)		1.5% (4)
Stranka Demokratske Aktivnosti (A-sda)	Bosniak ethnic party	1.7% (0)	1.5% (1)		2.2% (4)

Notes to Table 2.2

* *Note:* All election data from the BiH Election Commission (www.izbori.ba).
a Parties who did not win mandates at the BiH or Entity Level are excluded.
b All percentages are within RS and within the Federation, respectively. Mandates are in parentheses.
c Percentages for Cantonal Elections is the percentage of total votes across all 10 Cantonal elections. The number in parenthesis is the total number of seats won for all ten cantonal legislatures.
d Coalition between HDZ-1990, a splinter party from the HDZ and the HSP. They appear as separate parties in Entity and Canton elections. For consistency, I have combined the totals of the two parties in Entity and Canton elections.
e NSRzB runs in coalition with a set of smaller, multiethnic parties in some cantonal elections.

Table 2.3 2010 BiH Parliament votes by district

Party[a]	Total	RS District 1	RS District 2	RS District 3		
Parties Elected from Republika Srpska						
Savez Nezavisnih Socijaldemokrata (SNSD)	43.3% (8)	49.0%	36.9%	41.4%		
Srpska Demokratska Stranka (SDS)	22.2% (4)	15.2%	28.7%	26.1%		
Partija Demokratskog Progresa (PDP)	6.5% (1)	7.8%	4.7%	6.4%		
Demokratski Narodni Savez (DNS)	4.6% (1)	6.4%	2.9%	3.6%		
Socijalistička Partija i Partija Ujedinjenih Penzionera (SP-PUP)	2.4% (0)	1.8%	3.5%	1.8%		
Demokratska Partija (DP)	2.4% (0)	3.1%	2.0%	1.8%		
Srpska Radikalna Stranka (SRS)	2.3% (0)	1.8%	2.7%	3.4%		
Narodna Demokratska Stranka (NDS)	1.1% (0)	1.6%	1.1%	0.3%		
Socijaldemokratska Partija (SDP)	3.0% (0)	2.6%	4.8%	1.3%		

Parties elected from the Federation		Fed District 1	Fed District 2	Fed District 3	Fed District 4	Fed District 5
Socijaldemokratska Partija (SDP)	26.1% (8)	23.9%	11.4%	28.2%	24.0%	35.9%
Stranka Demokratske Akcije (SDA)	19.4% (7)	20.4%	12.5%	15.7%	22.6%	22.3%
Savez za Bolju Budućnost (SBB)	12.2% (4)	6.5%	6.4%	17.8%	14.1%	11.1%
Hrvatska Demokratska Zajednica (HDZ)	11.0% (3)	7.9%	37.5%	1.0%	11.7%	6.5%
Stranka za Bosnu i Hercegovinu (SBiH)	7.3% (2)	5.9%	3.8%	11.8%	7.3%	5.8%
Hrvatska Koalicija HDZ 1990-Hrvatska Stranka Prava (HDZ-1990 & HSP)	4.9% (2)	5.2%	18.8%	0.4%	3.9%	2.2%
Narodna Stranka Radom za Boljitak (NSRzB)	4.8% (1)	5.2%	6.5%	3.7%	6.3%	2.9%
Demokratska Narodna Zajednica (DNZ)	1.5% (1)	10.4%	0.0%	0.1%	0.1%	0.0%
Stranka Demokratske Aktivnosti (A-sda)	1.7% (0)	7.5%	0.0%	0.7%	0.8%	1.3%

Note: a Parties who did not win mandates at the BiH or Entity Level are excluded.

In contrast to the RS vote for the BiH Parliament, the number of parties representing the Federation is driven up by weak linkage across districts within the Federation. Whereas all three districts in the RS are dominated by the same two Serb parties, the Federation districts vary in interesting ways, owing both to differences in ethnic composition across districts as well as regional differences in support for parties within ethnic blocs. The difference in ethnic composition can be clearly seen when you compare Federation District 2 to the other four Federation districts in the bottom half of Table 2.3. Federation District 2 (which comprises much of the Herzegovina region, including Mostar) has the highest concentration of Croat voters, which gives a large boost to Croat-oriented parties like the Croatian Democratic Union (HDZ), HDZ 1990 and the People's Party—Work for Betterment (NSRzB) relative to the other districts.

There is also regional variation within ethnic blocs. For example, the vast majority of the Democratic People's Union's (DNZ) support comes from the northwest corner of Bosnia (the Bihać region). This geographic concentration affords the DNZ a direct mandate from Federation District 1, which is why the

DNZ, a Bosniak party, manages to gain representation in the Parliament despite receiving less than 2 percent of the vote from the Federation. In short, districts in the Federation are not a microcosm of the Federation as a whole and no electoral district in either entity is a microcosm of the country as a whole. These differences across voting districts are captured by the maps of vote share in Figure 2.1, which depicts the percentage vote received by the top parties in the Federation half of the election to the BiH Parliament. Results have been aggregated to the municipal level for the purpose of mapping. Far from being a microcosm of the whole, local party systems take different forms depending on the region. Much of this variation is due to concentrations of particular ethnic groups. For example, the two large Croat parties, HDZ and HDZ 1990 both perform best in Herzegovina. However, there is also clear heterogeneity across districts in the performance of parties associated with the same ethnic group, as can be seen with regard to the Social Democratic Party of Bosnia and Herzegovina (SDP), DNZ, Party for Bosnia and Herzegovina (SBiH) and the Party of Democratic Action (SDA).

Fragmentation of the BiH Parliament is also increased due to poor linkage with lower-level elections. Regional parties remain, in part, because their geographic concentration makes them viable parties in canton and entity elections even as incentives at the BiH Parliament level push toward electoral coalitions with other parties. In the example of the DNZ above, they are on the cusp of maintaining representation to the BiH Assembly, which suggests that they should enter into coalition with other parties or that voters should begin to shy away from the DNZ out of fear that their vote will be wasted. However, the incentives are different for the elections for the Una-Sana Canton assembly, where DNZ is a major power. The DNZ is the clearest example of a regional party, but other smaller parties like SBiH and HDZ 1990 also benefit from regional concentration in Sarajevo and Herzegovina, respectively. These pressures are also evident in the way that parties like HDZ and HDZ 1990 enter into coalitions with related Croat-oriented parties in BiH Parliament elections while running alone at lower levels. Were it not for the power bases afforded by lower level Canton and Entity elections, smaller parties like Croatian Party of Rights (HSP) would be forced to either merge with larger parties or lose representation. The same might be true even for larger parties like HDZ-1990. The same poor vertical linkage also works in reverse, as national parties without a strong regional center of power like Union for a Better Future of BiH (SBB) face the same set of choices, resulting in higher fragmentation in lower-level legislatures.

The sum total of these factors is a party system that is defined more by electoral competition among parties that represent a single ethnic group rather than explicit electoral competition between parties representing different ethnic groups. As a result, it makes more sense to think of Bosnia's party system as three distinct party systems each organized around an ethnic group, each characterized by significant pluralism, including parties that seek voters across ethnic group boundaries. Since parties in different ethnic blocs are hardly competing for voters with parties of other blocs, they have no incentive to create party programs that can appeal beyond their own ethnic bloc and may, in fact, be punished for doing so.

Party Vote Percent in 2010 Parliamentary Election by Municipality

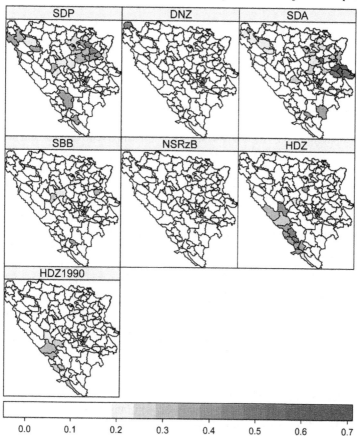

Figure 2.1 2010 vote shares by municipality for the Federation elections to the BiH Assembly

Party fragmentation also plays a role in the degree of personalism in Bosnian party politics, resulting in weakly institutionalized parties dominated by strong leaders. The same factors that make a larger number of parties possible also lower the barriers to the creation of new parties. As a result, intra-party conflict frequently ends in splinter parties as opposed to shared power within parties, as can be seen in the examples of HDZ-1990 splitting from HDZ and Željko Komšić's split from the SDP. In both cases, the newly-split parties are more leader-dominated than if they had stayed together. If there were stronger incentives toward party amalgamation, ideologically similar parties would also be much more likely to join together for electoral advantage. This permissiveness allowed more personalized parties like

SBiH and SNSD to resist pressure to merge with ideologically similar parties in the 1990s.

The next section discusses the development of the Bosnian party system in order to draw out similarities and differences in the way the parties and electoral rules have interacted to create the current system.

The Development of the BiH Party System

The development of the BiH party system is intertwined with the war and attempts to end and manage the conflict after the war. The war began, in part, from the shape that the Bosnian party system took during the first free elections in the Republic of Bosnia and Herzegovina while it was still part of a crumbling Yugoslavia. The first free elections in 1990 saw nationalist parties representing the three large ethnic groups in Bosnia effectively challenging the more ethnically diverse socialist successor party. Despite strong support for the multi-ethnic socialist party leading up to the election, nationalist parties, acting at times like a coalition despite the exclusivity of their programs, succeeded in the elections and won control of Bosnia's political institutions. The resulting coalition of nationalists was one of several crucial factors that led to war in Bosnia (Burg and Shoup 2000, p. 56).

Perhaps the key challenge in understanding BiH politics is reconciling Bosnia's traditions of tolerance and the continued commitment to those traditions of many Bosnians with the record of nationalist parties in elections both before and after the war. The victory of the nationalists may not have been inevitable. Indeed, the immediate context of the elections strongly influenced the choices voters faced. Rising nationalism in neighboring countries raised the stakes of the election and increased citizens' fears of falling under the dominance of political institutions controlled by other ethnic groups. These fears led voters to view the election as a kind of ethnic census in which support for multi-ethnic parties could increase the chance of domination of other groups (Burg and Shoup 2000, p. 57). Indeed, the broader pattern of initial post-communist elections favors parties that emphasize religious identity and nationalism over communist and socialist parties. It could serve as the grounds for electoral cooperation, but did not imply a shared vision for the country among the victorious nationalist parties.[13]

Even if the turn toward nationalism and war was not inevitable, the experience of war ultimately strengthened the position of the nationalist parties. As the leading organizers of the fight, the strongest nationalist parties for each ethnic group, SDA, HDZ and SDS governed and waged war. Doing so required the creation of strong formal organizations and informal structures and practices (that is, patronage systems) that penetrated to the local level, giving nationalist parties

---

13   This account focuses on Bosnia's internal path to war at the expense of the role played by neighboring countries in bringing war to Bosnia. The role of external forces is at least as important as the domestic failures but falls beyond the focus of this chapter.

control not only of military forces but of common resources such as housing and employment. The character of the war also reinforced the nationalist message that portrayed ethnic-based identity and organization as the path toward personal security. Fears about the threat from other ethnic groups were confirmed and ingrained by the horrors perpetrated in the name of ethnicity. Ethnic cleansing succeeded in transforming heterogeneous areas into ethnically homogenous areas. The Dayton Agreement, negotiated by these same parties, formalized and further strengthened them and the system they designed.

These factors led to the dominance of the SDA, HDZ and SDS immediately after the war, which continued for approximately five years. However, the factors used above to explain fragmentation in Bosnia's party system did so by creating incentives for challenger parties within mono-ethnic constituencies. While the SDA, HDZ and SDS remain important, their period of dominance was followed by increasing pluralization. This broad pattern has played out in very different ways in the three ethnic groups.

The international community played a key role in the emergence of opposition parties. Powerful international organizations operating in Bosnia attempted to both undermine nationalist parties and support the work of multi-ethnic parties and nationalist parties with more conciliatory programs. In the case of the SDS, the High Representative banned elected officials and party leaders and blocked funding sources. HDZ experienced less stringent sanctions. The OHR and other organizations provided direct assistance to multi-ethnic parties, such as the SDP, in the form of campaign assistance and open public support. The impact of the support provided to multi-ethnic parties was dwarfed by the impact of the recent war and the structure of the Dayton Agreement. While these efforts had a limited effect that fell short of the hoped outcome, they did have consequences, intended and unintended, on the party systems associated with each ethnic group (Manning and Antić 2003; Nenadović 2010).

The Serb party system in Bosnia is perhaps the simplest to explain and shows both the influence of international intervention on party politics, and the limits of that influence in the face of the continuing appeal of nationalist discourse and a centralized, quasi-state entity that exists as its own unique electoral unit. The dominance of the SDS established before the war was broken by a combination of international efforts to cut financing for the party and ban party leaders and the emergence of a new party, SNSD, and its charismatic leader, Milorad Dodik. During the period of more aggressive OHR intervention in electoral politics, Dodik was held up as a moderate Serb politician and alternative to the SDS (Majstorović 2013, Toal 2013). In addition to verbal support, Dodik and the SNSD received party assistance (Nenadović 2010, p. 1159). The attempted constitutional reforms of 2006, supported by SNSD though they would have weakened the entities, provided a political opening for Dodik to shift to the right (Toal 2013, p. 167). This shift carried the SNSD to its first victory over the SDS and Dodik has not looked back. The period since 2006 has been characterized by a solidification of SNSD power at the BiH and entity level. The SDS's organizational strength at the municipal level has allowed them to slow this process in lower-level elections in RS. The path of the SNSD shows the challenges in providing incentives for moderation with electorates that still respond to rhetoric from the war period and within an electoral structure that provides no incentive for compromise. The split between SNSD and SDS is less ideological than factional.

A similar factional split can be seen in the Croat party system in Bosnia in 2006, where the HDZ split into two parties, creating the HDZ-1990 alongside HDZ-BiH. Again this split focused on which group of elites would lead with the HDZ-1990 built around leaders with weaker connections to the HDZ in Croatia (Nenadović 2010, p. 1159). The primary outcome of the split between HDZ-BiH and HDZ-1990 is the opportunity it created in the 2006 elections for the Croat member of the BiH Presidency. The split in the HDZ vote played a role in the election of an SDP candidate, Željko Komšić, to the presidency. This election will be considered in more detail below. A more ideological alternative is offered by the NSRzB, which is a small, but growing, non-nationalist party. NSRzB goes so far as to caucus with the SDP within the BiH Parliament.

The Bosniak party system is the most difficult to characterize. Much like the Serb and Croat systems, the wartime Bosniak party, the SDA, no longer dominates. Challenges to the SDA have come from alternative nationalist parties with charismatic leaders but weaker party organizations as well as from the SDP, the largest multiethnic party in Bosnia, which draws most of its voters from among Bosniaks. SBiH, was the strongest challenger in the 2006 election after its leader, Haris Silajdžić, took advantage of opportunities created by international intervention in much the same way as Dodik and the SNSD, in that both initially presented themselves as more moderate alternatives that would be more palatable than the wartime nationalist parties. While the SDA never suffered from the international sanctions in the way that the SDS did, Silajdžić was able to initially position himself as a more moderate alternative in the years leading up to the failure of constitutional reform, which raised his profile and that of his party. By turning against constitutional reform in 2006, Silajdžić was able to partially outflank the SDA and win the Bosniak member of the BiH Presidency as well as become the second-largest party from the Federation in the BiH Assembly. In the 2010 elections, SBiH fell dramatically in the polls and was overtaken not only by the SDP but by a new Bosniak party, SBB, headed by a prominent businessman and newspaper publisher. The SBB continues the pattern of challenger parties to the SDA that are centered on a popular leader with relatively weak party institutions. If the SDP is considered a part of the Bosniak party system, then it is clearly the most competitive and ideologically diverse of the party systems. In the 2010 general elections, the SDP overtook the SDA as the largest party in both the BiH and Federation Parliaments.

The SDP is unique among the parties of BiH in that it combines broad electoral success with serious efforts to field candidates of more than one ethnicity while seeking and receiving votes from multiple ethnic groups.[14] For this reason, the party is very often categorized as a multiethnic party despite the fact that it receives the vast majority of its votes from Bosniaks (Bieber 2006, p. 105, Pickering 2009, Pugh and Cobble 2001). The SDP is the only party to receive votes in more than 75 percent of precincts, an indicator of the breadth of its support. Nevertheless, the SDP behaves like a Bosniak party in some ways. The goals of the SDP and the SDA frequently coincide in that they push for centralization of power at the expense of federal units, which are strongholds for Serb and Croat parties. This is consistent with the SDP's long-term commitment toward the rejection of ethnic categories in favor of social democratic ideology; however, the coincidence of goals with Bosniak national parties is a threat to Croat and Serb national parties. It is understandable both why all national parties would perceive the SDP as a threat, as well as why they would seek to bolster support among their own ethnicity by painting the SDP as an ethnic party.

Aside from the parliamentary victory in 2010, the greatest victory for the SDP was the election of the SDP candidate as the Croat member of the BiH Presidency in 2006 and 2010. Although most of Komšić's supporters were Bosniaks, they were also SDP voters, which suggests that their support was ideologically motivated in favor of a social-democratic candidate (Hulsey 2012).[15] The SDPs struggle to maintain a governing coalition in the Council of Ministers and Komšić's departure from the party in 2012 suggests that the party will have difficulty repeating its success in the 2014 elections. It will be interesting to see the degree to which Komšić's constituency differs from that of the established leadership of the SDP.

Conclusion: The BiH Party System and Prospects for State-building

Party systems are an essential part of democratic state-building, in that creating effective governance requires a coalition of elected leaders who can work together based on shared goals and shared legitimacy. The two primary obstacles to the creation of such coalitions in BiH are the continued segmentation of politics along ethnic lines and the fragmentation of the party system, both of which make

---

14   Other multi-ethnic parties, such as *Naša Stranka*, have emerged to offer an alternative to ethnic politics that is neither burdened by the socialist past of the SDP nor the history of Bosniak support. However, they have yet to gain wide support.

15   In the absence of reliable demographic data, it is impossible to say with certainty what proportion of Komšić's voters in 2006 and 2010 were Bosniaks. However, an analysis based on comparing precinct-level results in BiH Presidency, BiH Parliament and Federation Parliament elections estimates that more than 80 percent of the voters who chose Komšić voted for a party associated with Bosniaks in the BiH Parliament election. The analysis also estimates that the vast majority of the Bosniaks that voted for Komšić supported SDP as opposed to a more traditionally ethnic Bosniak party. In empirical terms, Komšić did well where the SDP did well in other elections. The full analysis, including a discussion of ecological inference methods can be found in Hulsey (2012).

coalition formation and stabilization difficult. The roots of the problem lay in the continued effectiveness of the rhetoric of ethnic identity and exclusion as well as electoral rules that privilege ethnic and regional identification.

The dominant political worldview in BiH continues to focus on ethnicity, which cannot lead to unity because of the mutual incompatibility of the aspirations at the core of each group's vision of the proper role and shape of the state. Two possible paths forward would be the emergence of a party or group of parties with a coherent vision for Bosnia; or, at the very least an atmosphere where officeholders could regularly compromise across ethnic boundaries—and were inclined to do so. Both of these paths to effective governance are made less likely because of the political and electoral structure currently in place. Given the fragmentation of the electorate and power in the political system, political parties are the political organizations that must build coalitions for reform. However, the electoral law and constitutional structure discourage the development of parties that cross ethnic group boundaries. This pattern is reinforced by the leader-centric and personalized internal structure of the parties, adding to the difficulties of building coalitions across ethnic lines.

At the same time, the large number of parties supported by distinct electorates encourages parties to split, favoring parties characterized by strong leaders rather than programmatic differences with other parties. More institutionalized parties would ease compromise by reigning in more extreme elements while leader-dominated parties fear that compromise only weakens them relative to leaders of ideologically-indistinguishable competitor parties.

Perhaps continued failures of governance will lead to popular demand for fundamental change (Bieber 2013). Indeed, the JMBG protests of 2013 and the demonstrations and citizen plenums in the spring of 2014 at the very least show an increase in activism and may represent a growing constituency for broad change in the BiH political system. However, demand for change must be met by supply of political organizations and coalitions to gain office and enact legislation. The analysis presented here makes clear the high barriers to such broad coalitions presented by the current electoral laws and political structure of Bosnia. Although institutions may shape and constrain voters' choices, they do not determine them. Nevertheless, the failure of previous attempts to build multiethnic coalitions for reform or promote strongly multiethnic parties can only lead to skepticism about the likelihood of change within the current constitutional and electoral rules and with the observed pattern of support for politicians with national agendas.

Bibliography

Bermeo, N. (2003) What the Democratization Literature Says—or Doesn't Say—About Postwar Democratization. *Global Governance*, Vol. 9, pp 159-177.

Bieber, F. (2006) *Post-War Bosnia: Ethnicity, Inequality and Public Sector Governance.* Basingstoke: Palgrave.

——. (2013) Is Change Coming to Bosnia? *Balkan Insight* [Online], Available from: http://www.balkaninsight.com/en/blog/is-change-coming-to-bosnia. [Accessed: July 29, 2013]

Bielasiak, J. (2012) *Dataset on Electoral and Party Systems in Post-Communist States.* Available from author.

Bochsler, D. (2010) The Nationalization of Post-Communist Party Systems. *Europe-Asia Studies.* Vol. 62, pp. 807–827.

Burg, S.L. and Shoup, P.S. (2000) *The War in Bosnia-Herzegovina: Ethnic Conflict and International Intervention.* New York: M.E. Sharpe.

Centralna Izborna Komisija Bosne I Hercegovine (2013) Statistike i Rezultati Izbora, Available from www.izbori.ba.

Cox, G. (1999) Electoral Rules and Electoral Coordination. *Annual Review of Political Science* Vol. 2, pp. 145–161.

Cox, G.W. (1997) *Making Votes Count: Strategic Coordination in the World's Electoral Systems.* Cambridge: Cambridge University Press.

Dayton Framework Agreement for Peace in Bosnia and Herzegovina, (1995).

Duverger, M. (1963) *Political Parties: Their Organization and Activity in the Modern State.* New York: Wiley.

Hulsey, J.W. (2012) Bucking Ethnic Representation: Election-Jumping and Ticket-Splitting in Bosnian Elections. Presented at the Annual Meeting of the Midwest Political Science Association, Chicago.

——. (2010) "Why did they vote for those guys again?" Challenges and contradictions in the promotion of political moderation in post-war Bosnia and Herzegovina. *Democratization,* Vol. 17, pp. 1132-1152.

International Crisis Group (2003) Bosnia's' Nationalist Governments: Paddy Ashdown and the Paradoxes of State Building. International Crisis Group, Sarajevo.

Izborni Zakon Bosne i Hercegovine (2001) Službeni glasnik BiH.

Jukić, E.M. (2012) Bosnia SDP Forces Out SDA Ministers at Last [online] *Balkan Insight.* Available from: http://www.balkaninsight.com/en/article/bosnia-sdp-forces-out-sda-ministers-at-last [Accessed June 26, 2013].

Keil, S. (2013) *Multinational Federalism in Bosnia and Herzegovina.* Farnham: Ashgate Publishing, Ltd.

Lijphart, A. (2004) Constitutional Design for Divided Societies. *Journal of Democracy.* Vol. 15, pp. 96–109.

Majstorović, D. (2013) Comments on Gerard Toal's "'Republika Srpska will have a referendum': the rhetorical politics of Milorad Dodik." *Nationalities Papers.* Vol. 41, pp. 209–213.

Manning, C. and Antić, M. (2003) The Limits of Electoral Engineering. *Journal of Democracy.* Vol. 14, pp. 45–59.

Mccrudden, C. and O'Leary, B. (2013) *Courts and Consociations Human Rights versus Power-sharing.* Oxford: Oxford University Press.

Nenadović, M. (2010) An uneasy symbiosis: the impact of international administrations on political parties in post-conflict countries. *Democratization*, Vol. 17, pp. 1153–1175.

Pickering, P.M. (2009) Explaining Support for Non-nationalist Parties in Post-conflict Societies in the Balkans. *Europe-Asia Studies* Vol. 61, pp. 565–591.

Pugh, M. and Cobble, M. (2001) Non-Nationalist Voting in Bosnian Municipal Elections: Implications for Democracy and Peacebuilding. *Journal of Peace Research*. Vol. 38, pp. 27–47.

Toal, G. (2013) Republika Srpska will have a referendum": the rhetorical politics of Milorad Dodik. *Nationalities Papers*. Vol. 41, pp. 166–204.

Venice Commission (2005) Opinion on the Constitutional Situation in Bosnia and Herzegovina and the Powers of the High Representative (No. 004), *CDL-A*

Chapter 3

Building the Rule of Law: Judicial Reform in Bosnia and Herzegovina

Meagan Smith Hrle

Introduction

Re-building an impaired and distressed justice sector is one of the basic building blocks in a post-conflict reconstruction process and a prerequisite to establishing the rule of law (UN Security Council, 2011). Despite the fundamental nature of the task, and the very apparent needs, the justice sector was not an immediate post-war priority in Bosnia and Herzegovina (BiH) (as was the case for elections and property return). Within the justice sector, the police were first to come under the spotlight of reform. Nevertheless, by the late 1990s, the international community turned its attention to the judiciary. This chapter will look at the process of rebuilding the judiciary and fostering the rule of law in BiH. As with the other efforts described in this book, this is a story without an end in sight. Significant progress has been made, despite numerous challenges, and at times, attempts to undo reforms on the part of the political elites.

This chapter will examine some of the more noteworthy interventions impacting the past 10 years of judicial reform efforts, the interplay between international and national efforts, and the particular resistance to strengthening state judicial institutions (also referred to as BiH judicial institutions) in some quarters. It will show that the hostile political environment in the Republika Srpska (RS), and the indifferent political environment in the Federation of Bosnia and Herzegovina (FBiH), both negatively impact judicial reform. Most concerning, however, is the politicization of judicial reform efforts, and attempts to challenge the authority and jurisdiction of BiH judicial institutions. As a result, judicial reform stakeholders—both national and international— are forced to focus on preservation of past reforms, instead of moving towards greater consolidation of the rule of law. Although data is scant, these developments negatively affect the public's perception of the judiciary, and serve to weaken overall public trust in judicial institutions.[1]

---

1   A 2010 United Nations Development Programme (UNDP) public survey found that only 15 percent of Bosniaks, 8 percent Croats and less than 4 percent of Serbs "fully trust" the judiciary in BiH (UNDP, 2011).

The term judicial reform will be used extensively, which refers to a process of improving the quality of justice, the efficiency, independence and accountability of the judiciary. Since the fall of one party rule in South East Europe, all countries have engaged in judicial reform efforts with largely similar aims of creating an independent and efficient judiciary, capable of ensuring the rule of law in newly formed democracies. The region has been guided by the broad notions set forth in the Copenhagen Criteria, as formulated by the European Council's Presidency in June 1993 which requires the candidate country to have achieved "stability of institutions guaranteeing democracy, the rule of law, human rights and respect for and protection of minorities" (European Council 1993a).

Added to this background of post-authoritarian transition, the judiciary in BiH was ransacked during the nearly four years of war. The judiciary had the enormous task of assisting BiH to recover from the bloodiest and most destructive conflict in Europe since World War II. Ironically, the same European Council's Presidency Conclusions which detail the Copenhagen Criteria also include, in Annex III, a resolution on BiH supporting the call for a cease fire, and calling for respect for UN safe havens and tightening of sanctions (European Council 1993b). Indeed, when the Copenhagen Criteria were issued in 1993, with a war ravaging BiH, the notion of these Criteria applying in BiH was far from any reality. The creation of an independent judiciary, able to process cases efficiently and in line with human rights standards established in the Dayton Constitution while at the same time capable of navigating the muddy waters of ethnic and political alliances, presented a monumental undertaking. While judicial reform efforts have yielded significant progress, and there are institutions and procedures in place which support independence, BiH has yet to fully consolidate the required elements of judicial independence (Venice Commission 2012; European Commission 2012).

This chapter will examine the judicial reform process and trace the contested political agendas which emerged in response to efforts to strengthen BiH judicial institutions. It will be argued that the consolidation of reform efforts, meant to enhance the independence of the judiciary and strengthen the rule of law, has been hampered by political agendas. The trajectory of justice sector reform can be divided into three broad periods: international led judicial reforms from 1998–2003; consolidation of reforms and integration of local authorities in the process from 2004–2008; and the period from 2009 to the present, characterized by a divisive political environment which adversely impacts judicial reform efforts, and the engagement of the European Union (EU). Significant interventions affecting overall reform will be noted during each period, with a focus on the most recent past.

Background: BiH Justice Sector after the War

Surprisingly, the judiciary was given no special attention in the Dayton Peace Accord (DPA). Annex 6 on Human Rights established both an Ombudsman for

Human Rights, and the Human Rights Chamber, a specialized court to examine cases alleging violations of human rights. Annex 11 authorized the UN to establish interventionist support to the police via the International Police Task Force. But there is no mention of the judiciary as a whole, which may be one reason reforming the judiciary was not prioritized in the immediate post-conflict period.

In places not directly affected by conflict, the judiciary continued to function to some degree. As a consequence of the displacement and conflict, there was a high turnover of judicial personnel, and political powers used these openings to fill sought after positions within the judiciary (Independent Judicial Commission, 2004). Upon the signing of the DPA, the judiciary slowly resumed functioning throughout the country, with some changes given the new post-war constellation of power and ethnic groupings. Despite obvious problems, there were many other priorities facing the international community that seemed more immediate to attend to, such as property return and security issues.

The judicial structures in BiH are highly fragmented, mirroring the complex constitutional structure. The RS and the FBiH have courts of first instance (Basic/ Municipal Courts) and courts of second instance (Cantonal/District Courts), a Supreme Court and a Constitutional Court. Brčko District has a first and second instance court.[2] Annex 4 of the DPA, the Constitution of BiH, established a BiH Constitutional Court, and specifies that BiH has responsibility for "international and inter-Entity criminal law enforcement." The Court of BiH and the BiH Prosecutor's Office were later established to provide judicial remedies and criminal investigations in matters within the competence of BiH.[3] Unlike most countries, even complex federal ones, there is no pyramid-like structure which provides uniformity in application and interpretation of law. Each jurisdiction (State, RS, the FBiH and Brčko District) is self-contained with its own procedural and substantive laws. The administration of justice is equally complex: there are 14 Ministries of Justice (State, entity, cantonal and Brčko District). Many experts conclude that BiH has a highly fragmented judicial system lacking some of the traditional features of judiciaries in federal systems (Venice Commission 2012).

---

2   A visual overview of the organizational structure of the BiH judiciary is available on the website of the European Commission for Efficiency of Justice (CEPEJ), within the country profile on Bosnia and Herzegovina: http://www.coe.int/t/dghl/cooperation/cepej/ profiles/CourtSystemBIH_en.pdf [Accessed April 10 2015].

3   The Law on the Court of BiH, imposed by the High Representative in 2000 and adopted by the BiH Parliament in 2002, provided jurisdiction over crimes defined in the laws of the State of BiH and for administrative jurisdiction over State administrative decisions. The criminal jurisdiction only became a reality with the adoption of the BiH Criminal Code in 2003 which includes war crimes, organized crime, economic crime and corruption, and terrorism. The processing of war crimes and related cases began in 2005 with the opening of the War Crimes Section within the Court of BiH.

Jump-Starting Reform Efforts 1998–2003

The period beginning in 1998 was characterized by incremental steps towards judicial reform, but by 2001, a more pro-active and comprehensive approach emerged. The Office of the High Representative (OHR), in its role of support to the Peace Implementation Council (PIC), was in a position to have the most information early on about the deficits in the judiciary. In 1998, OHR created a Judicial Reform Working Group to coordinate the activities of the international community. Other organizations engaged in monitoring or offered concrete assistance (Independent Judicial Commission, 2004).

In July 1998, the UN Security Council adopted Resolution 1184 which called on the UN Mission in BiH to establish a judicial monitoring program (UN Security Council, 1998). In November, the Judicial System Assessment Program (JSAP) was initiated to monitor, assess and document concerns countrywide. The same year, at its December meeting, the PIC called for building the rule of law as a priority in 1999 and laid out a series of proposed reforms, including the development of new state judicial institutions (PIC 1998). The PIC Declaration of May 2000, which focused on many aspects of state-building, also called for the establishment of a State Court (PIC 2000). Local authorities began taking steps to address deficiencies, although the main drivers of change remained the international community. Findings from JSAP reports and other sources indicated an overwhelming number of areas in need of attention, including lack of independent judges and prosecutors, outdated legislation, and an enormous backlog of cases (UNMIBH 2000).

State Level Judicial Bodies

One of the first significant reforms was the establishment of a new judicial institution—a trial court at the state level. The proposed jurisdiction was limited to administrative decisions of state institutions, and criminal offences committed by public officials in the course of their duties within state institutions, in line with the 1998 Madrid Declaration which called for "an institution to deal with criminal offences by BiH public officials in the course of their duties" (PIC 1998). The draft Law was introduced in Parliament but was not considered before Parliament was dissolved ahead of November elections (Aitchison 2011). On November 12, 2000, the High Representative imposed the Law on the Court of BiH, which gave the Court jurisdiction over "crimes defined in the Laws of the State of Bosnia and Herzegovina." The decision explains that the Court of BiH is necessary to provide judicial remedies for matters within the competence of BiH (OHR 2000). Two years later, the BiH Parliamentary Assembly adopted the Law on the Court of BiH Act in 2002 in keeping with the *post facto* adoption of laws imposed by the High Representative. In August 2002, the High Representative imposed the Law on the BiH Prosecutor's Office, an institution designed to investigate and prosecute crimes falling within the jurisdiction of the State as a "pre-condition for the establishment of the rule of law in the State of Bosnia and Herzegovina" (OHR 2002). The Prosecutor's Office included a special division for the prosecution of organized crime and corruption. The jurisdiction of the BiH Court and Prosecutor's Office was greatly expanded with the imposition of the BiH Criminal Code in January 2003 by the High Representative (Aitchison 2011). A BiH Ministry of Justice was also established in 2003 to provide executive support to the new judicial bodies.

Twenty-five representatives from the RS National Assembly almost immediately challenged the Law on the Court of BiH before the BiH Constitutional Court as having no basis in the BiH Constitution. In September 2001, the Court found that the Law is not a violation of the division of competences between the state and entity as provided for in the Constitution. Rather, the Constitutional Court found that BiH was authorized to establish additional institutions to exercise its responsibilities, including a court to strengthen the legal protection of its citizens and to ensure respect for the European Convention. The decision was reached with 5 votes in favor by two Bosniak and three international judges, and four votes against by two Serb and two Croat judges (BiH Constitutional Court, September 28, 2001). Nevertheless, this legal defeat would not deter representatives from the RS, who would continue to chip away at the legitimacy of this institution in other ways. Other expert institutions have also agreed with the BiH Constitutional Court's ruling. The Venice Commission, even in 1998, established that the BiH Constitution allowed for the development of state judicial institutions not specifically enumerated in the Constitution, as long as they responded to a specific need (Venice Commission 1998). In subsequent opinions, the Venice Commission acknowledged the constitutionality of the Court of BiH (Venice Commission 2012) and also endorsed the development of an Appellate Court within the Court of BiH (Venice Commission 2013).

These newly formed institutions-the Court of BiH and BiH Prosecutor's Office-served as the locus of attention during discussions about the International Criminal Tribunal for the former Yugoslavia's (ICTY) completion strategy and eventual transfer of cases from the ICTY to BiH. [4] More broadly, this coincided with the ICTY's strategy of supporting domestic prosecutions of war crime cases in the region. At the same time, the dismal state of affairs with respect to war crimes prosecutions in BiH came into sharp focus (Amnesty International 2003). Eventually, these discussions led to an agreement in 2003 on the need to establish a War Crimes Chamber within the Court of BiH and a Special Department for War Crimes within the BiH Prosecutor's Office as an *"essential part of the establishment of the rule of law and fundamental to the reconciliation process, creating necessary conditions to secure a lasting peace in BiH"* (OHR-ICTY 2003). These specialized divisions within the Court of BiH and BiH Prosecutor's Office began to function as of 2005.

The Court of BiH and Prosecutor' Office are the hallmarks of the international community's more interventionist days in BiH; bold new institutions hastily

---

4   See also Iva Vukosic's chapter in this volume.

developed largely without the involvement of local stakeholders.[5] The international community determined that these institutions were vital components for the effective processing of the most serious and sensitive cases facing BiH (Aitchison 2011), and in this way, linked their success to enhancement of the rule of law and stability in BiH. An enormous amount of resources were to be invested in them over the next decade, at times at the expense of entity judicial improvement projects. On the whole, these institutions have played an important role in the processing of war crimes and related crimes (OSCE Mission to BiH, 2011), while their track record in tackling organized crime and corruption remains weaker (Transparency International 2013).

Establishment of Single High Judicial and Prosecutorial Council (HJPC)

In February 2002, the PIC called for a reinvigorated judicial reform strategy, which included the establishment of a unified HJPC[6] and a comprehensive re-appointment process. As it was deemed important to move the re-appointment process forward quickly, the High Representative imposed legislation establishing three HJPCs (FBiH, RS and BiH[7]) in May 2002, pending political agreement on a transfer of powers from the entities towards the establishment of a single BiH HJPC. As a step towards greater independence, instead of the legislature and executive, now the entity Councils were in charge of the re-appointment process.

Upon imposition of the entity Councils, the High Representative directed the entity Prime Ministers to submit proposals for ceding authority over the entity HJPCs to a unified BiH HJPC (High Representative Decision, 2002). In its 2003 Feasibility Study, the European Commission outlined the adoption of legislation to create a single HJPC as one of the priority areas of reform to strengthen judicial independence (European Commission 2003). Further supporting this, the EC Council Decision of June 2004 called for BiH to establish a "single High Judicial and Prosecutorial Council for BiH with the aim of consolidating appointment authority over the Entity judiciaries and strengthening the independence of the judiciary throughout BiH" (European Commission 2004).

Armed with this clear EU demand, the High Representative began discussing the mechanism and contours to make this a reality. In August 2003, a draft Agreement on transfer of authority was submitted to the entities for consideration.

---

5   Except for select national experts involved in the drafting process.

6   Judicial/prosecutorial councils are common in Europe, and other civil law traditions. They are independent institutions distinct from the legislative and executive powers responsible for the independent delivery of justice. Although models vary, their core functions usually include: 1) appointment and promotion; 2) discipline; 3) administration/ IT; 4) financing. Councils are made up primarily of members of the judiciary, and thus are considered to be 'self-governing' bodies.

7   The BiH HJPC encompassed Brčko District, but was otherwise a shell awaiting the merger of the two entity HJPCs.

While the FBiH was a willing partner, negotiations with the RS took longer, and involved pressure from both the international community and the BiH Council of Ministers. In one of the most significant developments for the BiH judiciary, both entity governments agreed to transfer their powers over judicial councils to a state institution through the Agreement on Transfer signed in March 2004. The Law on the BiH HJPC was adopted by the BiH Parliament in May 2004. The HJPC is responsible for the appointment of judges and prosecutors, disciplinary proceedings, training, and judicial administration. The HJPC is widely viewed as the cornerstone of judicial reform and a key safeguard of judicial independence. Resistance to its formation was visible from the start, and the RS has continued to challenge its authority and powers.

Appointment Process

Also in 2002, the newly formed HJPCs, with considerable assistance from the Independent Judicial Commission which served as the Secretariat to the Councils,[8] undertook the enormous task of re-appointing all judges and prosecutors in BiH (except for Brčko District). This process, where more than 1000 positions were advertised, and all sitting judges and prosecutors were required to re-apply for their position, dramatically changed the composition of the judiciary. Around 30 percent of sitting judges were not reappointed (Urke 2012). One of the goals was to have the ethnic structure in the judiciary reflect the 1991 census. The number of Serb judges in the RS was reduced from 91 percent to 65 percent, and the number of Bosniak judges in the Federation was reduced from 65 percent to 56 percent (Independent Judicial Commission 2004, p.64). While political parties reacted harshly to this process, given the unified approach of the international community, the involvement of internationals in the Independent Judicial Commission and entity HJPCs, and the complete exclusion of the executive and parliaments, there was little space to hamper the process (Mayer-Rieckh 2007).

Consolidation of Major Changes, 2004–2008

This period continued to be fraught with challenges and a difficult operating environment for governmental and judicial stakeholders. Nevertheless, it was also a period where compromise was seen. The international community played a supportive and highly involved role, but use of the High Representative's powers lessened. The international community began looking for exit strategies. There was an increasing appetite among local stakeholders to engage on judicial reform.

---

8   The Independent Judicial Commission had nearly 100 international and national staff persons assisting the entity HJPCs through the lengthy process of "verification" of candidates and "investigation" into candidates. These findings were handed over to the Councils for their use during the selection process.

This was particularly the case with the development of the Justice Sector Reform Strategy, a process which began in 2006.

In February 2008, the PIC Steering Board agreed on a transition plan for the closure of OHR, which involved the fulfillment of certain conditions - often referred to as the "5+2 agenda."[9] "Entrenchment of the rule of law" was identified as one of the conditions. At the time, this referred to several concrete measures including adoption of the Justice Sector Reform Strategy and National War Crimes Processing Strategy. The 5+2 conditions served as that extra push to move political leaders towards adoption of these Strategies which had been in the drafting phase for some time. While politically oriented objections emerged during the development of these Strategies, final documents were nevertheless agreed upon, and core concerns addressed or mutually agreed to not include (Atos Consulting 2010, OSCE Mission, 2011). This was a period where a vision for judicial reform seemed to be developing, and the international community took less of an overt role. The following sections will describe judicial reform efforts with respect to developing a national justice sector reform strategy and the processing of war crimes.

Justice Sector Reform Strategy

In 2006 at a donor conference on the BiH justice sector in Brussels, the BiH Council of Ministers agreed to develop a national justice sector strategy. The newly formed BiH Ministry of Justice took the lead on facilitating the development of the Strategy, with the support of the UK government and local consultants. An organizing structure for the Strategy was quickly developed which included a Steering Board composed of entity, cantonal and Brčko District Ministers of Justice, and five working groups,[10] each with significant leadership from the entity Ministries of Justice and the judiciary (Atos Consulting 2010). The Justice Sector Reform Strategy was developed during numerous consultative meetings with stakeholders within the government, judiciary and civil society. Representatives from the entity and Brčko District Ministries of Justice attended nearly every meeting and actively engaged. The involvement of civil society in the development of the Strategy was beneficial, and represented the first steps in a stronger role for civil society in the justice sector (Atos Consulting 2010).

Three contentious issues emerged, and while many participants agreed on the way forward, due to objections from the RS, it was decided to "set aside" these issues. These included: consolidating the financing of the judiciary, harmonization of substantive and procedural civil and criminal laws, and harmonization of court practice. These elements were rejected as the solutions would have consolidated

---

9   See on the topic of exit strategies the contribution of Mateja Peter in this volume.

10   The working groups correspond to the five pillars of the Strategy: 1) judicial system; 2) execution of criminal sanctions; 3) access to justice; 4) support to the economic sector; and 5) coordinated, well managed and accountable sector.

power at the central level in the form of a single source of funding through the BiH Ministry of Justice, single substantive and procedural laws at the State level, and a BiH Supreme Court. By way of concession, these issues are included in the Strategy in the section "Key unresolved strategic issues of the Justice Sector," and it is noted that solutions should be found through the process of constitutional reform (BiH Justice Sector Reform Strategy 2008, 2012, pp. 45–48).

The Strategy was adopted by all Ministers of Justice in June 2008, a major feat in an increasingly polarized environment. The Strategy's implementation involved regular meetings with the participation of all 14 Ministries of Justice. An accompanying Action Plan was developed, as well as a Communication Strategy. In the future, a common justice sector donor basket was also envisioned. At the time of adoption, there were many reasons to hope that the justice sector reform had taken another huge step forward, and unlike earlier reforms, local stakeholders were in charge of the process this time, albeit with funding and support from the international community.

National War Crimes Processing Strategy

The adoption of the National War Crimes Processing Strategy in December 2008 was another critical moment, and a much needed measure to help BiH to more efficiently address its overwhelming backlog of war crimes related cases. The National War Crimes Processing Strategy called for the effective investigation and prosecution of the most complex cases by 2015 and of all cases by 2023. Prior to the development of the Strategy, even the size of the outstanding war crimes cases was unknown; some estimated between 13,000–17,000 suspects. An extensive case mapping exercise revealed approximately 8,200 suspects in 1,380 war crime case files (OSCE Mission 2011, p. 22).

The Strategy's key contribution was to set forth the parameters for the effective use of criminal justice resources to process these cases. The drafters opted for a "coordinated and centralized one," with the burden of processing the cases shared among all 14 jurisdictions (OSCE Mission 2011, p.19). According to the criteria defined in the Strategy, the BiH judicial institutions retain jurisdiction over the most complex cases, and allocate other cases to the entities and Brčko District depending on the *gravity* and *complexity of the case*. This process of transfer of cases from the state-level to the other jurisdictions only began in earnest in 2010. According to the OSCE Mission, approximately half of the backlog will be processed by the BiH judicial institutions, and the other half in the entities and Brčko District. In 2013 the donor community, the EU[11] and OSCE Mission partnered to inject a sizable amount of staff resources into the cantonal and district Prosecutor's Offices to support completion of this caseload (OSCE Mission 2013).

---

11   Further, through IPA 2012 the EU will donate 7.5 million Euros towards processing of war crimes cases during the period 2014–2016.

Authorities in the RS, the FBiH and Brčko District are active participants in implementation of the National War Crimes Processing Strategy with respect to ensuring the investigation and prosecution of cases within their respective jurisdictions (OSCE Mission 2011). At the same time, rhetoric and actions by RS political leaders undermine the work of the Court of BiH and Prosecutor's Office, which play a key role in overall implementation of the Strategy. The RS asserts that the BiH judicial institutions are biased against Serbs, as evidenced by the low number of crimes against Serbs prosecuted. Further, leaders in the RS, particularly President Dodik, deny crimes proven by the Court of BiH (and the ICTY).[12] According to data obtained by the OSCE Mission, these actions undermine trust in the judiciary and public support for the processing of war crimes cases (OSCE Mission 2011, p. 86). Despite massive amounts of donor funds poured into the Court of BiH and BiH Prosecutor's Office, the international community has no particular strategy in place to counter the negative messaging that has gained ground in the RS.

Cooperation Breaks Down 2009–2013

Although there were objections from authorities in the RS to creating and later strengthening state judicial institutions from the beginning, significant progress was made until 2009. The piecemeal development of these institutions, the extensive involvement of internationals initially, and substantive legal and procedural problems[13] would all be exploited by the RS authorities in the upcoming period. Experts point to a preliminary investigation by international prosecutors in the BiH Prosecutor's Office in 2008 for alleged misconduct against then Prime Minister Dodik as an important turning point (OSCE Mission 2009).

In the fall of 2008, the RS government formally refused to provide requested documentation to the BiH Prosecutor's Office on the grounds that the Prosecutor's Office does not have the competence to investigate the alleged crime. After more back and forth about submission of documents during the fall 2008, in December Dodik stated in the media that it was "unacceptable for the Republika Srpska that

---

12   In 2009, then Prime Minister Dodik denied the nature of war crimes which took place in Tuzla in May 1995 and in Markale market in Sarajevo in February 1994 (OHR/EUSR/OSCE/CoE, 2009). In 2010, Dodik denied the genocide in Srebrenica during the pre-election campaign (Halimović, 2010).

13   A recent example of this includes the European Court for Human Rights' July 2013 decision in *Maktouf v. Damjanović* which held that the Court of BiH violated Article 7(2) of the European Convention on Human Rights (ECHR) in applying the 2003 BiH Criminal Code in connection with the conviction and sentencing of the applicants, as the SFRY Criminal Code, which was in force at the time, provided for more lenient sanctions. Article 7 of the ECHR prohibits the retroactive application of criminal legislation. This verdict has created an avalanche of questions and concerns about legal certainty, equality of citizens before the law, fairness in sentencing, and justice for victims.

Muslim judges try us and throw out complaints that are legally founded. And we think that it is only because they are Muslims, Bosniaks and that they have a negative orientation towards the Republika Srpska, and we see the conspiracy that has been created" (B92 2008). In 2009, the State Investigation and Protection Agency (SIPA) filed a formal criminal report to the BiH Prosecutor's Office against Dodik and other high ranking RS officials for alleged abuse of office in connection with the construction of the RS government building, parts of a new highway, and other related allegations. This brought on an onslaught of rhetoric and posturing against BiH institutions and the international community (ICG 2011). On the grounds of lack of jurisdiction, in June 2011 the investigation was transferred from the BiH Prosecutor's Office to the RS Special Prosecutor's Office.

Also of note, by this time international prosecutors were no longer in charge of this case following the termination of their mandate in December 2009. As of January 2010 only a few internationals remained in the office as advisors. In December 2011, the RS Special Prosecutor's Office closed the investigation against Dodik, officially due to lack of sufficient evidence (Jukić 2011). On the same day, BiH political leaders reached an agreement on formation of the state level government, after a 15-month stalemate. In a press conference, President Dodik stated, "We did not get what we thought we should, but no one got everything they wanted" (The Economist, 2011).

Justice Sector Reform Strategy

After a successful initial Ministerial Conference involving all 14 Ministers of Justice in 2008, there were high hopes that the Justice Sector Reform Strategy would consolidate ongoing efforts, create cooperation among Ministries of Justice, and galvanize international community support. The international community financially supported the process, but was not directly involved in the development or implementation. Unfortunately, fairly early on, implementation of the Strategy began to lag. Although there are various factors involved, in sum, lack of political will struck again.[14] Ministers failed to appear for key Ministerial Conferences. Working level officials, mainly from the RS, failed to attend meetings to track the Strategy's progress. The RS and cantonal Ministries of Justice back-tracked on previous commitments, such as towards the establishment of a state penitentiary and the adoption of a single Law on Prosecutor's Offices at the federal level (Association of Democratic Initiatives et al. 2012). The FBiH Ministry of Justice suffered from a lack of authority, and at times, lack of sufficient dedication to the process, while the cantonal Ministries of Justice lacked personnel and planning capacity. Activities which fell under the purview of the HJPC progressed, as the HJPC immediately enmeshed the Strategy's demands into its annual work plans. The international community tried to spur on implementation through meetings,

---

14   On the role of political elites in blocking reform processes, see Tina Mavrikos-Adamou's chapter in this volume.

coaxing and reminders, but with little success. For example, two joint letters sent to all Ministries of Justice in 2010 appeared to be received without any palpable reaction.[15] On a positive note, the development, and later monitoring of the Strategy involved the participation of civil society, which was a novel approach.

Attacks on BiH Judicial Institutions

Beginning in 2008, systematic and targeted attacks against the state judicial institutions, particularly the Court of BiH and BiH Prosecutor's Office began, largely initiated by political powers in the RS. These attacks are well-documented in a number of reports issued by international organizations, researchers, and analysts (OSCE Mission 2009, Azinović, Bassuener and Weber 2011, Hunček Pita, 2012). The SNSD, the leading Bosnian Serb party, pre-election campaign document, "Steps for the Future" also calls for the reduced role of the BiH Court and Prosecutors Office, or their abolishment (SNSD, 2010). Thus these attacks are more than just scoring points, but reflect a clearly defined political goal.

In 2009, Prime Minister Dodik initiated the submission of reports to the UN Security Council, coinciding with the High Representative's official report and presentation on the situation in BiH. These submissions often focus on issues within the justice sector. For example, the second submission of November 2009 decried the presence of internationals in the judiciary: "This arrangement has resulted in political manipulation of the criminal justice system. Foreign judges in BiH have strong incentives to obey the OHR and other foreign officials who have been involved in setting their terms of work and compensation" (RS Government 2009). The RS's Eighth Report to the UN in November 2012 includes an extensive list of needed reforms to the BiH judiciary and detailed claims regarding alleged bias of BiH institutions in the investigation and prosecution of Serb war crime victims (RS Government 2012). The 2013 Reports repeat similar claims (RS Government May and November 2013).

In 2011 and 2012, the BiH Court and Prosecutor's Office remained under constant attack, and even their existence was formally called into question. The European Commission Progress Report for 2011 (p. 12) noted, "Political pressure and verbal attacks on the judiciary have intensified. In particular, the legitimacy and role of the High Judicial and Prosecutorial Council (HJPC), the Court and the Prosecutor's Office of Bosnia and Herzegovina have been challenged by political representatives, particularly from Republika Srpska. The attempt to undermine the independence of the judicial system remains an issue of serious concern." In an exaggerated legislative initiative in January 2012, a member of the RS National Assembly introduced a bill in the BiH Parliament which called for the BiH Court and Prosecutor's Office to cease to exist within 30 days of the entry into force of

---

15   A letter sent in January 2010 was signed off by OHR, the EU, OSCE, USAID and CoE, while a letter sent in June 2010 was signed off by OHR, OSCE, USAID and CoE.

the law. By May the adoption procedure had been halted (European Commission, 2012, p. 13).

Along with such formal initiatives, there is a constant barrage of negative press about the work of these institutions, primarily in the RS media (Hunček Pita 2012). The attacks are with such severity that the overall independence of the judiciary is called into question. The international community, other than an occasional press release or remark in an annual report, has done little to address this rising problem.

Call for a Referendum

In February 2010, Dodik succeeded in pressing the RS National Assembly to adopt a Law on Referendum and Citizen Initiatives (Toal 2013). In what has become, in retrospect a decisive move for the future of judicial reform, in April 2011 Dodik decided to make good on use of this newly-minted tool. Dodik called for a referendum to address: 1) the legality of the BiH Court and Prosecutor's Office; 2) the legality of decisions taken by the BiH Parliamentary Assembly; and, 3) the authority of the High Representative. On April 13, 2011, President Dodik made an inflammatory speech in the RS National Assembly addressing all manner of concerns, such as the lack of prosecution of Serb victims of the war, allegations that the war was a "jihad against infidels—non-Muslims in BiH," and an allegation of development of an Islamic state in Sarajevo (ICG 2011, p. 7). He also discussed at length the illegality of the Court and Prosecutor's Office of BiH due to their lack of constitutional basis.

Following his speech, the Assembly passed a decision to hold a referendum with the question: "Do you support the laws imposed by the High Representative of the International Community in Bosnia and Herzegovina, especially those pertaining to the Court of Bosnia and Herzegovina and the Bosnia and Herzegovina Prosecutor's Office, as well as their unconstitutional verification in the Bosnia and Herzegovina Parliamentary Assembly?" The inherent bias was obvious and the over-the-top nature of the question had come to be expected. Still, the fact that it was formally debated and agreed upon in the RS National Assembly seemed to justify a sharp response from the international community.

High Representative Inzko called this the most serious violation of the Peace Agreement since its signing. The international community was united in its concern about the issue, but how to resolve the matter was a point of contention. Inzko thought that he would have the support of the PIC in using his Bonn powers to annul the referendum (Azinović, Bassuener and Weber 2011). In the end, the EU took the lead without the involvement of the High Representative. A high level EU official, Miroslav Lajčak, met with Dodik in late April in Banja Luka, while Doris Pack, a European Parliament member and rapporteur on BiH, met with RS Parliament Speaker Igor Radojičić in Brussels in early May.

Despite all of this, Dodik persisted. On May 13, 2011, the EU High Representative Ashton flew to Banja Luka for a meeting with Dodik which resulted in an oral agreement that the RS government will annul the referendum decision and will review the conclusions purportedly in exchange for a structured dialogue with the European Commission on Justice and Home Affairs. Ashton's press statement released following her talks with Dodik, in a surprising affirmation of his concerns, noted: "Mr. President, you presented four particular concerns and we reassured then that those and many more issues will be discussed in the structured dialogue that presents a comprehensive overview of the whole judiciary" (European Union 2011b). Following Ashton's message and the media attention on her flight to Banja Luka prior to Sarajevo, there was much commentary that the EU indeed bowed to Dodik's demands, and even affirmed his leadership role (Bieber 2011).

On May 31, 2011 President Dodik made a speech at the RS National Assembly explaining the agreement with Ashton and the way forward with respect to judicial reform. The RS National Assembly adopted revised conclusions noting that "for the time being" it is not necessary to organize the referendum. Further, the RS National Assembly expressed its support for the Structured Dialogue to give way, in the long term, to "fundamental reconstruction of the judiciary" (RS National Assembly Conclusions 2011). On June 1, 2011, the RS National Assembly adopted a series of recommendations for conducting the Structured Dialogue which includes, among other things: creating entity judicial and prosecutorial councils (essentially doing away with the BiH HJPC), taking away the BiH Constitutional Court review of entity Constitutional Court decisions, and establishing a different "system, structure and competences of the judiciary at the BiH level" (RS National Assembly Recommendations, 2011). All the recommendations sought to limit or remove the BiH judicial institutions' sphere of influence and would undo many of the significant judicial reforms achieved in the last 10 years.

Dodik's show of brinkmanship was a successful gamble. He succeeded in luring one of the top EU leaders to Banja Luka, and he created a spin in the media that the EU agrees that the judicial system requires a major overhaul (in seeming disregard for the reforms undertaken to date). While all tried to claim a political victory, some analysts have asserted that the EU's approach sent the wrong message to local authorities by rewarding nationalistic and obstructionist rhetoric (Sebastian 2011). The impact of the stronger EU political involvement (versus technical support, which was ongoing) in judicial reform will be examined in the following section.

European Union Led Reform

The first Structured Dialogue on Justice, hurriedly held in June 2011 in Banja Luka, ushered in a new era for judicial reform in BiH. Despite its origins as a political deal, the EU insisted that the Structured Dialogue is part of the new strategy of frontloading justice and home affairs issues. Lessons learned in other countries show that justice reforms often take the longest and are among the most important areas tackled in the EU accession process. The EU Delegation admits that this is a new mechanism, and BiH is the "first enlargement country to benefit from this new methodology" (EU Delegation, n.d.). The 2011 EC Progress Report (p. 11) notes that the goal is to "facilitate the revision of legislation and functioning of institutions in line with relevant European standards and aiming at ensuring an independent, effective, impartial and accountable judicial system."

Plenary sessions of the Structured Dialogue, involving the key judicial stakeholders from all jurisdictions, take place two times a year. The EU emphasizes that this is an important exercise between the EU and BiH premised on ownership and responsibility. One of the ground rules is that any reform initiative must be channeled through the Structured Dialogue process. Following each meeting, the EU Delegation publishes the agreed upon recommendations on its website. No other information is publicly available from the process. Civil society is not represented, with the explanation that the Dialogue is a process between the institutions of BiH and the EU. Nevertheless, representatives from EU member state embassies may attend. Civil society organizations confirm that they are informed about developments, although after-the-fact briefings place them in a reactive, instead of proactive role (Association for Democratic Initiatives et al. 2012).

In many ways, the Structured Dialogue has replaced the central role the Justice Sector Reform Strategy was to play. At a time when this Strategy was reaching a low in terms of cooperation among Ministries of Justice, the Structured Dialogue emerged as the new EU-led platform to support the justice sector's progress towards greater respect for the rule of law and EU standards. Unfortunately, it seems that stakeholders perceived that the arrival of the Structured Dialogue provided yet another reason to let progress on the Justice Sector Reform Strategy fall to the wayside. The EC's 2012 Progress Report (p. 12), however, notes that the Structured Dialogue has had a "positive effect" on implementation of the Justice Sector Reform Strategy. Indeed, most of the issues taken up in the Structured Dialogue are non-implemented activities in the Justice Sector Reform Strategy or the War Crimes Processing Strategy.

Republika Srpska Law on Courts

The debacle over amendments to the RS Law on Courts initially was touted as a success in terms of the role of the Structured Dialogue. In December 2011, the RS National Assembly adopted amendments to the RS Law on Courts despite several provisions violating the competencies of the HJPC. In the months preceding this, the HJPC, the High Representative, the EU Special Representative, and the OSCE Mission had made numerous interventions with the RS government to secure a version of the Law which would respect the role of the HJPC. Even Structured Dialogue recommendations in November 2011 called for "close coordination" between the RS and the HJPC on the finalization of the draft law, and the EU underlined that it expects the law to be "mindful of the independence of the judiciary and fully coherent with the prerogatives and recommendations of the HJPC" (p. 8). In the month between the Structured Dialogue and the Law's adoption, the HJPC made several attempts to coordinate with the RS Ministry of Justice, but to no avail. The RS National Assembly adopted amendments which infringed on the competencies of the HJPC (Weber 2012). Following more behind the scenes interventions by the international community, the RS government agreed that once these changes enter into force, further amendments will be made in parliamentary proceedings to comply with the HJPC's concerns. The fact that the RS was able to draw the HJPC and others into spending time and effort arguing about established competencies, and thereby preventing more pressing aspects of judicial reform to move forward, seems far from progress. Rather, this is just one example of how the authorities in the RS are managing to dictate the shape and pace of judicial reform; law by law, dispute by dispute. Further, it is concerning that as of July 2014, the promised amendments have only been adopted in first reading. It seems the RS continues to shape the agenda.

Conclusion

After over 10 years of a significant judicial reform process in BiH, much progress has been made and many developments could be highlighted and praised. However, the hostile political climate in the past few years threatens to undo, or weaken, some of the significant reforms. The ability of the Structured Dialogue process to manage negative political influences, and in particular, the demands of the RS to overhaul the BiH judicial institutions, remains unclear. Politicians in all jurisdictions have little interest in a genuine reform process; rather they are looking for opportunities to maximize their influence within the judiciary.

With respect to the judiciary in the Federation, the Structured Dialogue has had limited impact. The Federation continues to limp along, neither actively using the Dialogue process, nor resisting it. The fragmentation of the funding of the judiciary across 10 cantons in the Federation, one of the fundamental problems influencing independence of the judiciary in this jurisdiction, has proven too intractable to resolve.

Although still early to draw a firm conclusion, the Structured Dialogue seems to have, in the short term, lessened the impact of the Justice Sector Reform Strategy. The adoption of a revised Justice Sector Reform Strategy for 2014–2018 may reinvigorate the implementation process; this remains to be seen. The EU has made clear that resolving the outstanding war crimes cases is a priority and a requirement towards EU integration. While slow going, it seems that progress is being made on this front.

So where does this leave the state of BiH's judiciary? One result of the political elites' strategies towards the justice sector, charaterized by attempts to undo state level reforms and/or maintain control of financial and human resources, is that the important role of the judiciary in tackling corruption has been given short shrift. Effective processing of high stakes corruption cases could be a game changer on BiH's political scene, boost public confidence in the judiciary, and bolster the rule of law. Of course, creating a justice system which can effectively process high profile corruption cases is the result of numerous contributing factors, such as an independent appointment process, an independent budget, and enforceable ethical standards, transparency in decision-making, a judiciary free from political influence, and others. Although the international community is attempting to address these issues, the political elites have no interest in supporting an independent judiciary which could jeopardize their positions, and as in other policy areas, politicians largely act without accountability towards their electorate or regard for the few civil society voices active in this domain.

The continual undermining of BiH judicial institutions does not bode well for the long-term consolidation of the rule of law. In particular, the HJPC plays a vital role in ensuring independence through the appointment process, disciplinary proceedings, and setting nationwide standards for the administration of justice. The BiH Court and Prosecutor's Office were designed to play a key role in tackling some of the most serious and sensitive crimes facing BiH: war crimes, organized crime and corruption. Granting constitutional status to the HJPC, and the BiH Court and Prosecutor's Office are important measures that would secure their institutional independence. The international community (both on the ground and in world capitals) should develop a more unified and strategic approach on judicial reform that supports the consolidation of the rule of law in the face of political opposition. Judicial independence should be upheld and promoted through every intervention and measure of support. Attempts to undo reforms should be vociferously challenged. Moving forward, the judicial reform process pace and priorities should not be set exclusively by the political elites. More voices are needed in these debates.

Bibliography

Aitchison, Andy. *Making the Transition: International Intervention, State-building and Criminal Justice Reform in Bosnia and Herzegovina*. Cambridge: Intersentia, 2011.

Amnesty International (2003), *Shelving Justice War Crimes Prosecutions in Paralysis*, November 2003.

Association For Democratic Initiatives et al. (2012) *Godišnji Izvještaj organizacija civilnog društva (OCD) o provedbi Akcijskog plana za provedbu strategije za reformu sektora pravde (SRSP) u BiH*, January 30, 2013.

Atos Consulting (2010) Bosnia and Herzegovina: Development of the Justice Sector Reform Strategy. Available from: http://atos.net/content/dam/global/case-study/case-study-uk-government.pdf [Accessed October 14, 2013].

Azinović, V., Bassuener, K. and Weber, B. (2011). *Assessing the potential for renewed ethnic violence in Bosnia and Herzegovina: A security risk analysis*, October 2011.

Bieber, F. (2011) See you at the next crisis! Available from: http://fbieber. wordpress.com/2011/05/13/see-you-at-the-next-crisis/ [Accessed September 17, 2013].

BiH Ministry of Justice (2008) Justice Sector Reform Strategy 2008–2012.

BiH Constitutional Court (2001) Decision Case No. U 26/01, September 28, 2001.

BiH Constitutional Court (2004) Decision Case no. U56/02, January 30, 2004.

BiH Constitutional Court (2009) Digest of the Case Law of the Constitutional Court of BiH. P. 231.

B92 (2008) Dodik's Statement Stir New Controversy. Available from: http://www.b92.net/eng/news/region.php?yyyy=2008&mm=12&dd=12&nav_id=55686 [Accessed December 12, 2008].

European Commission for Democracy through Law (Venice Commission) (1998) Opinion on the need for a judicial institution at the level of the state of Bosnia and Herzegovina, November 3, 1998.

European Commission for Democracy through Law (Venice Commission) (2012) Opinion on Legal Certainty and the Independence of the Judiciary in Bosnia and Herzegovina, June 18, 2012.

European Commission for Democracy through Law (Venice Commission) (2013) Opinion on the draft Law on the Courts of Bosnia And Herzegovina, June 15, 2013.

CEPEJ (European Commission for the Efficiency of Justice) (2012) Efficiency and Quality of Justice: An Overview. *European Judicial Systems*, Edition 2012. Council of Europe, 2012.

European Commission (2003) Report from the Commission to the Council on the preparedness of Bosnia and Herzegovina to negotiate a Stabilisation and Association Agreement with the European Union ("Feasibility Study") Available from: http://www.delbih.ec.europa.eu/documents/delegacijaEU_20 11121403014088eng.pdf [Accessed November 18, 2013].

European Commission (2011) Bosnia and Herzegovina 2011 Progress Report.

European Council (1993a) Presidency Conclusions. *Copenhagen European Council –June 21–22, 1993*. Available from: http://www.europarl.europa.eu/enlargement/ec/pdf/cop_en.pdf._[Accessed July 16, 2013].

European Council (1993b) Presidency Conclusions. *Copenhagen European Council –June 21–22, 1993, Annex III Declaration on Bosnia-Herzegovina.* Available from: http://europa.eu/rapid/press-release_DOC-93-3_en.htm. [Accessed July 16, 2014].

European Council (2004) Decision on the principles, priorities and conditions contained in the European Partnership with Bosnia and Herzegovina. *2004/515/EC: Council Decision of June 14, 2004.* Available from: http://eur-lex.europa.eu/LexUriServ/LexUriServ.do?uri=CELEX:32004D0515:EN:H TML. [Accessed July 16, 2014].

European Union (2011a) European Union-BiH Structured Dialogue Recommendations, November 2011.

European Union (2011b) Statement by High Representative Catherine Ashton at the press point with the President of Republika Srpska, Milorad Dodik, May 13, 2011. Available from: http://www.consilium.europa.eu/uedocs/cms_Data/docs/pressdata/EN/foraff/121984.pdf, [Accessed July 16, 2014].

European Union (2012) European Union-BiH Structured Dialogue Recommendations, April 2012.

European Union Delegation to BiH (n.d.) 10 facts to know about the EU-BiH Structured Dialogue on Justice. Available from: http://europa.ba/Download. aspx?id=736&lang=EN [Accessed July 16, 2014].

European Union Delegation To BiH (2012) Speech by Ambassador Peter Sorensen on the occasion of the Signing Ceremony on Judicial Co-operation and on the EU Grant to the HJPC "Strengthening the Judiciary in BiH. Available here: http://www.europa.ba/News.aspx?newsid=5482&lang=EN [Accessed November 2, 2012].

Halimović, Dž. (2010) Institute for War and Peace Reporting. *Genocide Denial Concern in Bosnia*, October 1, 2010. Available from: http://iwpr.net/report-news/genocide-denial-concern-bosnia. [Accessed October 14, 2013].

High Judicial and Prosecutorial Council (2012) Letter from President Novković to Commissioner Fule, November 9, 2012. Available from: http://www. pravosudje.ba/vstv/faces/pdfservlet?p_id_doc=20198 [Accessed July 16, 2014].

Hunček P.A. (2012) Prava (ne) utemeljenost medijskih kampanja iz Republike Srske. In: Šarčević, E. (ed.) *Pravosuđe u medijima*.

Independent Judicial Commission (2004) *Final Report January 2001–March 31, 2004.*

International Crisis Group (2002) Courting Disaster: The Misrule of Law in BiH, March 25, 2002.

International Crisis Group (2009) Bosnia's Incomplete Transition: Between Dayton and Europe, March 9, 2009.

International Crisis Group (2011) Bosnia: State Institutions under Attack, November 5, 2011.

International Tribunal for the Former Yugoslavia (2003) Press release: Working Group on Development of BiH Capacity for War-crimes Trial Successfully Completed, February 21, 2003.

Judah, T. (2011) A new Bosnian government, Bosnia's December surprise, *The Economist*, December 30. Available from: http://www.economist.com/blogs/ easternapproaches/2011/12/new-bosnian-government. [Accessed August 31, 2013].

Jukić, E. (2013) Bosnia:—And Turbulence—On The Horizon—Analysis, January 2, 2013. Available from: http://www.eurasiareview.com/02012013-bosnia-stagnation-and-turbulence-on-the-horizon-analysis/ [Accessed October 10, 2013].

——. (2011) Corruption Probe Dropped Against Bosnian Serb Leader. *Balkan Insight*, December 29, 2011.

Mayer Reickh, A. (2007) Vetting to Prevent future Abuses: Reforming the Police, Courts, and Prosecutor's Offices in Bosnia and Herzegovina. In: Mayer-Rieckh, A. and De Greiff, P. (eds) *Justice as Prevention: Vetting Public*

Employees in Transitional Societies. New York: Social Science Research Council, pp. 201–204.

Office of the High Representative –International Tribunal for The Former Yugoslavia Experts Conference (2003) Joint Preliminary Conclusions on Scope of BiH War Crimes Prosecutions, January 15, 2003.

Office of the High Representative (2000) Decision Imposing the Law on the State Court of BiH, November 12, 2000.

Office of The High Representative (2001) Decision providing the Independent Judicial Commission (IJC) with a comprehensive mandate, March 14, 2001.

Office of the High Representative (2002a) Decision enacting the Law on the BiH Prosecutor's Office, August 6, 2002.

Office of the High Representative (2002b) Decision Enacting the Law on the High Judicial and Prosecutorial Council of the Federation of Bosnia and Herzegovina, May 23, 2002.

Office of the High Representative (2002c) Decision Enacting the Law on the High Judicial and Prosecutorial Council of the Republika Srpska, May 23, 2002.

Office of the High Representative (2011) Special Report by the High Representative to the Secretary General of the United Nations on the implementation of the Peace Agreement in Bosnia and Herzegovina, May 6, 2011.

Organisation for Security and Cooperation in Europe Mission to Bosnia and Herzegovina (2004) OSCE Trial Monitoring Report on the New Criminal Procedure Code in the Courts of Bosnia and Herzegovina, December 2004.

Office of the High Representative, European Union Special Representative, Organisation For Security and Cooperation in Europe, Mission to Mission to Bosnia and Herzegovina, Council of Europe (2009) Press Release: Denial of War Crimes Inexcusable, September 15, 2009. Available from: http://www.ohr.int/ohr-dept/presso/pressr/default.asp?content_id=43944 . [Accessed October 10, 2013].

Organisation for Security and Cooperation in Europe, Mission to Mission to Bosnia and Herzegovina (2009) Independence of the Judiciary: Under Pressure on BiH Judicial Institutions, December 2009.

Organisation for Security and Cooperation in Europe Mission to Bosnia and Herzegovina (2011) Delivering Justice in Bosnia and Herzegovina, An Overview of War Crimes Processing from 2005–2010, May 2011.

Organisation for Security and Cooperation in Europe Mission to Bosnia and Herzegovina (n.d), *War Crimes Processing Project*. Available from: http://www.oscebih.org/documents/osce_bih_doc_20130325125313594eng.pdf. [Accessed October 10, 2013].

Peace Implementation Council (1998) Madrid Declaration, December 16, 1998. Available from: http://www.ohr.int/pic/default.asp?content_id=5190 [Accessed July 16, 2014].

Peace Implementation Council, Declaration, May 24, 2000. Available from: http://www.ohr.int/pic/default.asp?content_id=5200. [Accessed July 16, 2014].

Republika Srpska National Assembly (2011) Republika Srpska National Assembly Recommendations for Structured Dialogue on the Judicial System. *Republika Srpska Official Gazette* no. 61/11.

Republika Srpska National Assembly (2011) Conclusions no. 01–868/11. *Republika Srpska Official Gazette* no. 61/11. Available from: http://www.narodnaskupstinars.net/?q=la/akti/zaklju%C4%8Dci/zaklju%C4%8Dci-broj-01-86811 . [Accessed July 16, 2014].

Republika Srpska Government (2011) Work Plan 2011–2014.

Republika Srpska Government (2009) Second report of Republika Srpska to the Security Council on the situation in Bosnia and Herzegovina. November 2009, Paragraph. 99.

Republika Srpska Government (2012) Eighth report of Republika Srpska to the Security Council on the situation in Bosnia and Herzegovina, November 2012.

Republika Srpska Government (2013) Ninth report of Republika Srpska to the Security Council on the situation in Bosnia and Herzegovina, May 2013. *Republika.*

Republika Srpska Government (2013) Tenth report of Republika Srpska to the Security Council on the situation in Bosnia and Herzegovina, November 2013.

Savez Nezavisnih Socijaldemokrata (2010) (In English: Alliance of Independent Social Democrats). *Steps for the Future*, October 3, 2010. Available from: http://istinomjer.ba/im2/wp-content/uploads/2011/06/SNSD.pdf [Accessed October 10, 2013].

Sebastian, S. (2011) A New Start in the Balkans? *FRIDE. Policy Brief*, Vol. no. 89, August 2011. Available from: http://www.fride.org/download/PB_89_A_new_start_in_the_Balkans.pdf [Accessed October 10, 2013].

SRNA (2012) Agreement on Programme-Project Cooperation Reached. Available from: http://www.srna.rs/novosti/49064/agreement-on-programme-project-cooperation-reached.htm [Accessed October 12, 2013].

Toal, G. (2013) Republika Srpska will have a referendum: the rhetorical politics of Milorad Dodik, Nationalities Papers. *The Journal of Nationalism and Ethnicity*, Vol. 41:1, pp. 166–204.

Transparency International Bosnia And Herzegovina (2013) Procesuiranje korupcije pred sudovima i tužilaštvima u Bosni i Hercegovini (2011–2012), July 2013.

United Nations Mission in Bosnia and Herzegovina (1999) Report for the Period November 1998—January 1999.

United Nations Security Council Resolution (1998) The situation concerning conflicts in the former Yugoslavia. *Resolution 1184 (1998), July 16, 1998, S/RES/1184.* Available from: http://www.refworld.org/docid/3b00f15860.html. [Accessed September 20, 2013].

United Nations Development Programme (2011) Facing the Past and Access to Justice from a Public Perspective. *Special Report.* Available from: http://www.undp.org/content/dam/bosnia_and_herzegovina/docs/Research&Publications/Crises%20Prevention%20and%20Recovery/Facing%20the%20Past%20

and%20Access%20to%20Justice/BiH_facing_the_past_and_access_to_
justice.pdf [Accessed April 20, 2011].

United Nations Mission In Bosnia And Herzegovina-Judicial System Assessment
Programme (2000) Thematic Report IX. *Political Influence: The independence
of the judiciary*. United Nations Security Council (2011) The rule of law
and transitional justice in conflict and post-conflict societies—Report of the
Secretary General. UN Doc no. S/2011/634, October 12, 2011.

Urke, S. (2012) Establishment of an Independent and Accountable Judiciary in
Countries in Transition: Bosnia and Herzegovina as a Case Study. In: Engstad,
E., Frøseth, A., Tønder, B. (eds.) *Judicial Independence—100 years of the
Norwegian Judges' Association*, pp. 347–372.

Weber, B. (2012) It's the EU's Turn Now. Available from: http://istinomjer.
ba/13/01/2012/its-the-eus-turn-now/ [Accessed September 17, 2013].

Chapter 4

Virtual Deterrence—BiH's Institutionalized Insecurity and the International Flight from Responsibility

Kurt W. Bassuener

Introduction

In 2005, the average citizen of Bosnia and Herzegovina (BiH) saw little reason to worry about the potential political renewal of violence or state collapse. The prevailing assumption was such developments would be prevented by the international community which had driven progress and state-building over the course of the previous decade. In the eight years since, this comfortable certainty has all but evaporated as the country's political and security environments have been weakened. Since 2005, the EU has assumed the pre-eminent international role in the country, and the prospect of eventual membership has been assumed to be the primary driver for progress. The EU, due to its willful de-emphasis of hard-power deterrence and willingness to let institutions be co-opted for tactical reasons, has allowed fear to become the most potent political currency in BiH once again.

This chapter is based upon the author's empirical observations in 17 years of work on international Bosnia policy. It begins with a review of the country's security situation and structures immediately after the war. The narrative then follows the trajectory of defense and wider security sector reform beginning in the late 1990s and running through 2005. The development of recent stagnation, regression, and enumeration of potential security risks and implications follows.

Background

The security situation in Bosnia and Herzegovina (BiH) at the time of writing (mid-2014) is fundamentally different than it was nearly 18 years ago, when the 1992–1995 war was brought to an end by the Dayton Peace Accords (DPA) (or, General Framework Agreement for Peace, GFAP). At that time, hundreds of thousands of Bosnians were under arms, over 100,000 had been killed and 2 million people—half the prewar population—were refugees or internally displaced. The war was by far the largest and bloodiest in Europe since the Second World War. Before hostilities began, the republic was already awash with arms as military production was the keystone of the Yugoslav defense strategy, which was designed to resist a Warsaw Pact-armored thrust through Vojvodina and Slavonija (Johnson 1971).

For these reasons, NATO's Implementation Force (IFOR) consisted of three reinforced divisions, totaling 54,000 troops in all (Bowman 1996). Its task was to implement the military/security elements of the DPA, encapsulated in Annex 1A of the treaty (GFAP 1995). These included creating a three-mile/five kilometer Zone of Separation (ZOS) between the Bosnian Serb and Federation forces along the Inter-Entity Boundary Line (IEBL). It also was to ensure that heavy weapons were collected in cantonment areas where they were under IFOR control. The relative importance these tasks held for the drafters of the Accords is clear—the Constitution of BiH was Annex 4, refugee return was encapsulated in Annex 7, the role of the civilian international High Representative came in Annex 10 (GFAP 1995). It is also worth noting the initial timelines for the deployment of NATO forces (20,000 of them American) were incredibly ambitious; the authorization for the deployment of US troops was a single year, after which they were supposed to be withdrawn (Clinton 1995). The rules of engagement were also restrictive. Fear of sustaining casualties was paramount for the Clinton administration; therefore "force protection" trumped achieving mission goals. Also regularly touted was the fact that US forces were for the first time in a joint operation with Russian troops, which deployed a contingent to IFOR.

Not high on the list of priorities was the arrest of persons indicted for war crimes (PIFWCs) by the International Criminal Tribunal for the former Yugoslavia (ICTY) at The Hague; there were no forcible arrests in 1996 in Bosnia. Another manifestation of the pronounced political objective to maintain what was termed a "permissive environment" for the NATO force, and the civilian police element of the international presence, the UN's International Police Task Force (IPTF), which was tasked with vetting local police forces for war crimes suspects and training them, was not allowed an executive mandate. It was feared that if the IPTF got into trouble attempting to conduct an arrest, for example, IFOR would be called upon to bail them out, which could incur casualties—a major fear for the Americans. So the IPTF was made impotent by design. There was no end-state strategy pursued by the international community in Bosnia.

Slowly, it became clear to Western policymakers that the civilian aspects of the Dayton Agreement would be harder to implement than the raw military elements. The Clinton administration extended its force deployment for six months in 1997, then another. By the end of the second year after the signature of the Dayton Accords, the reality that forces and political attention would have to be maintained far longer than hoped became undeniable. President Clinton announced in December 1997 on a visit to Bosnia that American forces would remain as long as necessary (Clinton 1997). The civilian elements of peace enforcement were also reinforced. The Peace Implementation Council (PIC), established in the Dayton

Accords to oversee their implementation, stated in its December 1997 meeting that its High Representative was empowered as "final authority in theatre" to enforce Dayton to take executive actions to that end—including imposing and rescinding laws and removing public officials (PIC, 1997)

Following the election of United Kingdom Prime Minister Tony Blair in 1997, forces began the forcible arrest of PIFWCs in Britain's zone of responsibility, Multinational Division (MND) North, based in Banja Luka. Bosnian Serb indictee Simo Drljača unwisely drew a pistol on the Special Air Service unit detailed to capture him in July 1997. He was shot dead (*The Economist* 1997). The new robustness of the British interpretation of its Annex 1A mandate, to "maintain a safe and secure environment," led to increased minority returns in the British zone, in particular the area around Prijedor, in the coming years. The American and French zones both had a much more restrained approach; the weight of minority returns tended to reflect this as well (Bassuener and Witte 2003).

In 1998 and 1999, SFOR (NATO's Stabilization Force, replacing IFOR in late 1996, with 32,000 troops), ratcheted up its assertiveness, in ever greater coordination with the international High Representative (NATO, n.d.). This culminated in the deployment of SFOR troops to ensure the fulfillment of RS President Nikola Poplašen's dismissal by the High Representative. After some days of standoff, this was achieved (Solana 1999). This occurred immediately prior to the launch of NATO's Operation Allied Force in March 1999, which aimed to eject Serbian forces from Kosovo through an air campaign striking targets in Kosovo and Serbia proper.

New Horizons Open in the Region

The end of the Kosovo war in June 1999 opened up new horizons region-wide. With the Stability Pact for Southeastern Europe, announced in July 1999 at a conference in Sarajevo, NATO and the EU both announced they were open to eventual membership of all countries in the region, so long as they met the standards of these clubs (Stability Pact, n.d.). Prior to this point, aspirations for membership in these Euro-Atlantic institutions had far less traction.

In late 1999, Croatia's wartime nationalist President Franjo Tuđman died of cancer, triggering a scramble to succeed him. In the special presidential elections and parliamentary elections which followed in January 2000, Tuđman's Croatian Democratic Union (HDZ) was ejected from power by a convincing margin. His successor, Stjepan Mesić (who had left the HDZ over the war in Bosnia) announced early on an unequivocal break with Tuđman's policy toward its southern neighbor, with which it shares a 1,000 km frontier. In a visit to Sarajevo, he stated that while the Bosnian Croats could expect support for their rights from Zagreb, Sarajevo was their capital and they must see their future in that context (Bassuener and Weber 2012, p. 5). This statement earned him bilious enmity from BiH Croat nationalists, and helped trigger pursuit of a third entity.

In the immediate aftermath of Serbia's ejection from Kosovo in June 1999, war architect and leader Slobodan Milošević felt secure enough to call for an early presidential election in September 2000. This was a fatal error. The main political forces had aligned together in a broad coalition, the Democratic Opposition of Serbia (DOS). Regime attempts to steal the September 24 election backfired spectacularly, ending in massive demonstrations in Belgrade and the ouster of Milošević and his coterie. Parliamentary elections the following December gave the DOS coalition a commanding victory, making Zoran Đinđić prime minister.

By year's end, the two wartime leaders who had agreed on a predatory carve-up of Bosnia and Herzegovina during the war were dead, literally or politically. While the new democratic Serbian government and its successors never made a categorical statement to Bosnian Serbs parallel to Mesić's,[1] the fact remained that new possibilities were opened for building up the state of Bosnia and Herzegovina. This volume discusses many aspects of the state-building effort, which geared-up in 2000 and ran through 2005, in detail. The efforts, led by High Representatives Wolfgang Petritsch (1999–2002) and especially Paddy Ashdown (2002–2006), were also manifest in the security sector.

Despite the overwhelming force brought to bear in Bosnia by NATO with IFOR in 1996 the wartime security structures—armies, intelligence services, and police—remained intact. There were no comprehensive strategies or plans on how to unify them, only piecemeal efforts to regulate them and periodically reduce them.[2] The persistence of these structures, and the sway of political parties over them, posed both security threats and plentiful avenues for corruption and abuse of power. In the meantime, NATO forces in BiH were progressively reduced to roughly 12,000 by the end of 2002 and 7,000 by the end of the mission in 2004 (NATO 2004).

However, the forces increasingly engaged in operations supporting political objectives. SFOR engaged in a high-profile operation in Mostar in 1999, Operation Westar, aimed at rolling up a Bosnian Croat covert intelligence network. In 2001, a subsequent raid on *Hercegovačka Banka* seized documentation of efforts to create a third, Croat, entity. HDZ BiH leader Ante Jelavić was later removed from office by High Representative Petritsch for his advocacy of a third entity (SFOR Informer Online 1999, Fletcher 2001).

But there were still evident limits to the deployment of SFOR. In the June 2001 cornerstone laying ceremony at the Ferhadija Mosque in Banja Luka, demolished

---

1   One wonders how much progress would have been feasible if they had. As the decade wore on, the role of Belgrade became more problematic, especially under Koštunica, who rarely acknowledged BiH's existence, but also under his nominally progressive successor, Boris Tadić. See Bassuener and Weber 2012.

2   The 1996 Florence Agreement set limits on how many forces Bosnia and Herzegovina's two armies, Croatia and Serbia could field. But these ceilings only pertained to the army, leaving out the heavily armed interior ministry forces which had been full combatants in the war. See http://www.osce.org/item/43725.

by Bosnian Serb authorities in 1993, several international dignitaries were trapped by a Serb nationalist mob protesting the reconstruction. SFOR did not intervene, to the consternation of many observers (CNN 2001).

Seizing the Opportunity—Accelerating Security Sector Reform in Bosnia

The State Border Service (SBS) (now renamed the State Border Police) was the first state security organ. "Negotiated" by Richard Holbrooke with the BiH Presidency, under threat of imposition by High Representative Wolfgang Petritsch in late 1999 (Bassuener 2009), the SBS had jurisdiction 10km into state territory, and filled a void. Prior to that, entities policed the borders and unmonitored cross-border activities were rife. The SBS' employees reflected the 1991 census results in every area where it operated.

In the gear-up for the war in Iraq, opportunity presented itself for more thoroughgoing and radical reform of the BiH security sector with the discovery of illicit conduct involving BiH structures. Arms were captured on a vessel in the Adriatic headed for Iraq. A company in Bijeljina, Orao, was found to be providing aviation components for the Iraqi air force. The evident lack of civilian control and oversight (or outright complicity) gave impetus to High Representative Ashdown to pursue a more integrated and comprehensive approach toward reforming the security sector, combined with strengthening the state (DPI, 2002).

The Defense Reform Commission was established in 2003 as a result of these scandals by High Representative Ashdown. The Commission, organized into 10 functional working groups, developed proposals on how to unify the Federation and Republika Srpska's armed forces. These recommendations led to a Defense Reform Law adopted by the BiH Parliamentary Assembly in October 2005 which eliminated the entity Ministries of Defense (MoDs) and armed forces.

Even prior to the passage of the law, BiH fielded ad hoc joint detachments for overseas peacekeeping deployments, such as a platoon-strength demining unit to Iraq (Alvarez 2006). The new unified force was targeted to have 10,000 troops, organized in functional units—nine infantry battalions and one armored battalion. The infantry units were allowed to remain ethnically composed and based in areas where they comprised a majority. The Armed Forces of BiH (AFBiH) also included an ethnic regimental system as an outlet for veterans of the antecedent (and opposing) military formations. But these were open to co-ethnics who joined the force subsequently as well. While not operational units, these forces often commemorate wartime events in uniform.

As a second pillar of the security system, a parallel Intelligence Reform Commission was created in 2003 to develop a plan to unify the entities' intelligence services. The OHR made the proposal directly to the BiH Parliamentary Assembly, which adopted the law in 2004. The Intelligence and Security Agency (OSA) was established in mid-2004. Cuts of 30 percent of combined entity intelligence service manpower followed unification of the entity services (Bassuener 2009).

Third, judicial and police reform were also viewed as integral to the restructuring of the security environment.[3] A new Criminal Code and Criminal Procedure Code were adopted in 2001–2002. The High Judicial and Prosecutorial Council (HJPC) was established in 2004 to appoint and discipline judges and prosecutors at all levels, statewide. The Court of Bosnia and Herzegovina was established at the same time to try cases in violation of state laws, with two specialized chambers—one for war crimes (many cases being handed down by the ICTY) and one for organized crime and corruption. The State Prosecutor possessed the ability to take on cases from lower levels if the crime in question posed sufficient concern for the state. Both the Court and the State Prosecutor's Office had international personnel in executive positions to both advise and take active roles in prosecutions of sensitive cases. The State Information and Protection Agency (SIPA), created to protect state institutions in 2002, took on the role of enforcing state laws.

The final piece in the architecture of the state security and justice sector was to be the most numerous and most problematic—the police. Police forces in BiH had been directly engaged in war crimes and ethnic cleansing. Despite the vetting by the UN's IPTF, numerous dubious personnel remained on the various forces. IPTF and the follow-on EU Police Mission (EUPM) worked within the confines of the Dayton structures to reduce the size of the forces, provide training and standardization. The fragmentation of the forces—RS police, Federation police, cantonal police forces and Brčko District police, in addition to the State Border Police and SIPA—reflected the constitutional structure of the state.

The European Commission funded a 2003 functional review of the police which found them too costly, inefficient, and insufficiently effective at essential crime-fighting tasks (Lindvall 2009). Pursuing organized crime, from human trafficking to car theft rings, required coordination and combined strategy; this was difficult to manage with so many jurisdictional borders. Police restructuring was therefore integral to security sector reform as conceived by Paddy Ashdown and his OHR staff. Ashdown thus launched the Martens Commission in 2003, with the full buy-in of EUPM, the EC and the US, to develop reform proposals and guidelines. The Commission articulated three principles for an integrated policing system in BiH:

No political interference with operational policing.
All legislative and budgetary competencies for police matters must rest solely at the state-level.
Functional local policing areas must be determined by technical policing criteria.

The last criterion was understood to mean cross-entity regions could (not must) be established. There was one additional, but unarticulated motive for the pursuit of police reform: the wish to eliminate the RS' capacity to command coercive force. This would also be correspondingly taken from the Federation. But the extent to

---

3   See Meagan Smith-Hrle's contribution to this volume.

which the RS Ministry of Interior forces (MUP) had been engaged in the war was well established through ICTY proceedings and the Srebrenica report ordered by the High Representative, through which RS authorities listed the forces involved in these operations (BBC 2005).

International Hope Meets the Ugly Reality of Dayton Incentives: The Stall and Collapse of Reform and State-Building

By mid-2005, the prevailing assumption of the international community was that BiH institutions had gathered sufficient capacity and its leaders had manifested the requisite will to propel the country into the Euro-Atlantic mainstream, represented by the EU and NATO. There had indeed been successes; in 1996 few would have imagined the establishment of a single Ministry of Defense, military, or intelligence service. While constitutional reform and police restructuring were generally accepted as required, they were not viewed as overly daunting goals at the time.

The need to maintain executive mandates was seen as past. The "push of Dayton" could be replaced by the more democratic "pull of Brussels." Central European countries that had less than a generation before been behind the Iron Curtain were now full members of the EU. Slovenia, a former Yugoslav republic a stone's throw away from Bosnia's northern frontier with Croatia, was among the new members inducted in 2004. Many, especially in continental Europe, believed it was long past time for Bosnians to take "ownership" of their country's development and reform.[4] It was also a time in which the EU saw a chance to demonstrate that the "European perspective" could be transformative in a postwar state—and that the EU no longer required embarrassing American engagement on the European continent. The EU became an increasingly visible factor in BiH, fielding not only a Commission Delegation, but also the EUPM beginning in 2002. In December 2004, it took on the role of enforcing Annex 1A of Dayton from NATO; SFOR made way for EUFOR. NATO maintained a small headquarters staff in BiH, primarily for defense reform, intelligence, and counterterrorism. It retained an executive Chapter 7 mandate from the UN Security Council (as EUFOR holds), which allows use of force, but without any operational capacity.

There was recognition that the constitutional structure of the state needed development and adaptation to allow for further progress.[5] To this end, the

---

4   The European Stability Initiative was—and remains—perhaps the most ardent proponent of this approach. Gerald Knaus and Marcus Cox argued in their 2003 *Journal of Democracy* article "Travails of the European Raj," that the international High Representative was impeding development of democracy and a culture of accountability in BiH. Available at   http://www.journalofdemocracy.org/article/lessons-bosnia-and-herzegovina-travails-european-raj (Accessed April 4, 2015) .

5   See Valery Perry's chapter in this volume.

Council of Europe's Venice Commission delivered an opinion in early 2005 on the constitutional structure of Bosnia and articulated that substantial changes were required. A high-profile but unofficial negotiation effort began soon afterward among the leading parties, and, the US Government became more directly involved following the 10th anniversary of the GFAP (Rice 2005). The process generated a set of reforms initially agreed upon by the major political parties and developed into a package of amendments to be passed in parliament. It failed to pass in April 2006 by a mere two votes.

After some failed attempts to agree upon the implementation of the police restructuring plan which the different parties agreed upon earlier, the issue remained as one of two requirements to begin talks on getting a Stabilization and Association Agreement (SAA) with the EU. In October 2005, RS President Dragan Čavić agreed to the three principles but not the international interpretation of them—particularly on the potential for cross-entity police regions. What emerged was in essence a deal to make a deal. The Police Restructuring Directorate was created to summon agreement from the parties on how to operationalize the three principles. For two years, efforts to achieve police reform were stymied by resistance at critical junctures by senior political figures from both entities—particularly then-RS Prime Minister Milorad Dodik and then-Bosniak member of the BiH Presidency Haris Silajdžić. Still, at the end of 2005, there was a sense of optimism and momentum; the two "leftovers" of constitutional reform and police restructuring were not seen as insurmountable obstacles. While widely held at the time, these prevailing assumptions set the stage for the curtailment of state-building and its subsequent unraveling to date.

The closure of the OHR and "transition" to an EU-led presence was considered inevitable; the "double hatting" of the HR and EU Special Representative, began in 2002, and made the selection of the next HR/EUSR a joint PIC Steering Board-EU enterprise. After months of speculation on who would succeed Ashdown, Christian Schwarz-Schilling was selected. Schwarz-Schilling saw his task as closing the OHR within a year; his opening statement on state television upon arrival in 2006 made clear his intent, and that he would cease to employ the Bonn Powers except *in extremis*.

Milorad Dodik became RS Prime Minister in March 2006 after the collapse of the RS government. Reform processes stalled across the board. While initially this was hoped to be simply collateral damage from a rapid and chaotic power shift, it became clear it was a command decision to cease the development of state institutions and attempt to regain competences already delegated to the center by inter-entity agreement.[6] The foundering of constitutional reform with the failure of the "April package" of constitutional amendments in April 2006 poisoned the political discourse. Finally, Dodik took a cue from the Montenegrin independence referendum in May 2006 and began to threaten to call a referendum in RS (Toal and Dahlmann, 2011). He never specified that this would be an independence

---

6   Author's personal recollections while working at OHR in 2006.

referendum; the implication was enough. These ingredients helped generate a perfect storm which drove the political situation of the country ever downward (Ashdown and Holbrooke, 2008). This continues to date.

Stunted at Birth: The Impact of Politics on the AFBiH

The degeneration in the overall political situation of the country since 2006 has inevitably had an impact on the function and development of the Armed Forces. The force's mandated strength is 10,000 active duty personnel, with 5,000 in reserves and 1,000 civilian employees.[7] In the 2011 research, interlocutors doubted the force approached that actual strength. Some estimated that the total force strength was about 8,500, with reserves inactive and without resources (Azinović, Bassuener and Weber 2011, p. 33).[8] In addition, "up-or-out" provisions applying to privates who never attained promotions to become noncommissioned officers led to thousands of personnel being pensioned-off, leaving holes in the force that remain unfilled. Even if fully staffed, the AFBiH would be among the smallest forces for a country of its size in Europe and the wider region. Macedonia, for example, has a force which is larger, despite the country having slightly more than half of BiH's estimated population.

Local political factors have limited the force's ability to evolve and develop. Development of state institutions stalled in 2006–2007; they have been progressively hollowed-out since. The AFBiH has been on a budgetary starvation diet for a number of years, driven by RS parties. In addition, up to one-quarter of the force's manpower remains tied-down in guard duty at scores of unneeded facilities due to unresolved property ownership between the state and the entities— e.g., the RS.[9] Resolution of this defense property issue—ownership of 69 "non-prospective" sites—is a requirement for BiH to be able to avail itself of the North

---

7 See Annex for the AFBiH's full organizational structure and basing locations.

8 The following facts and quotes on the security situation and military reform are all taken from , Bassuener and Weber (2011), which was a comprehensive examination of the security sector and its reform in BiH, in which the author was involved. The authors interviewed representatives of the BiH Armed Forces, EUFOR, EU member state military professionals in BiH, NATO member military professionals in BiH, representatives of the various police agencies (state, entity, canton), private security companies, as well as experts on the social situation, juvenile delinquency, religious and political extremism, etc. In addition, a quantitative and qualitative analysis on inflammatory statements and terminology in the media was conducted. Roughly 80 interviews were conducted overall. The full security study can be viewed at http://www.atlanticinitiative.org/research-projects-activities/42-rokstories/386-a-security-risk-analysis-assessing-the-potential-for-renewed-ethnic-violence-in-bosnia-and-herzegovina.html (Accessed April 4, 2015).

9 At any given time, 700 troops are guarding these sites. Factoring the rotations this comes to roughly 2,000 troops. Discussion with international military professionals, September 2011.

Atlantic Council's agreement to offer the country a Membership Action Plan (MAP) at Tallinn in 2010, as well as one of the five objectives and two conditions set by the PIC Steering Board in its "5+2" formula for closing OHR (PIC 2008). At the time of writing, no end is in sight to this stalemate.

AFBiH command appointments are reportedly deeply politicized, but this also cascades through the force structure to relatively junior levels. A foreign military observer told the author that political party affiliation was essential for promotion; AFBiH officers had told him "if you're not connected to a [political] party, you don't get on."[10] In addition, one interviewee noted that "officers are limited because of their constituent people identity. Sorry—this slot is for a Bosniak and you're a Croat—that sort of thing."[11] This was seen as simply a reflection of the Dayton constitutional order—true meritocracy in the AFBiH could only flow from a different state structure.

Meanwhile, the built-in dotted lines in the force leave it prone to stress fractures in the event of violent unrest. The structure of the force, arrived at through political compromise, made it inherently vulnerable (see Annex). The maintenance of mono-ethnic infantry battalions—the main repository of potential fighting ability—was seen by participants in the defense reform process as a necessary evil to get the deal done; "that was as far as we could go," as one senior foreign participant recently told the author.[12] Another interlocutor noted that it "was only the situation at the time; we didn't follow up (and keep pushing for deeper integration)."[13] The rest of the force consisted of multiethnic units (the armored battalion, based in Tuzla, for example—see annex at end of chapter for complete force structure).

The inclusion of an ethnic regimental system was also viewed as a necessary ingredient to achieving defense reform politically. The 1st Guards Regiment (Croat), 2nd Rangers (Bosniak) and 3rd Infantry Regiment (Serb) do not have operational character, but were to be a repository for the traditions of the forces which would cease to exist with defense reform. There were to be six other functional regiments established—membership is voluntary by design. But these regiments were never established (Azinović, Bassuener and Weber 2011, p. 35). There is an uncomfortable overlap between the regiments and the mono-ethnic infantry battalions and the regiments, whose members are concentrated in those operational units. New recruits tend to join—by choice or under pressure—the regimental system and to be posted to infantry units close to home, unlike the Yugoslav People's Army, which made a point of mixing troops and deploying them away from their home republics. As one interlocutor stated, "the problem

---

10 Discussion with international military professionals, September 2011.

11 Discussion with international military professional, June 2011.

12 Discussion with former senior Defense Reform Commission official, Sarajevo, August 2013.

13 Discussion with international organization officials, military professionals, and diplomats, June 2011.

is that they are under pressure to wear the ethnic badges. Infantry commanders are squeezed all the time to do ethnic regimental functions by politicians (and) veterans' organizations."[14] One foreign military professional saw the regimental system as the biggest threat to the AFBiH.[15]

Examples are rife of political leaders addressing serving soldiers at regimental functions and employing divisive, nationalist rhetoric. The lines between regimental events and commemorations undertaken by AFBiH personnel acting in their personal capacity can often be confusing.[16] Regimental functions often appear to blur the lines between ethnically polarized commemoration of wartime experience and the needs of a unified state-level force.

The architects of defense reform hoped that the AFBiH, once established, would increasingly participate in NATO structures and international military missions, spurring its evolution beyond the built-in compromises and further mixing and integrating the force organically. There is some evidence of this. Soldiers from the RS went on a NATO exercise in Georgia in 2009, one year after that country's war with Russia, despite then-RS Prime Minister Dodik's exhortation not to participate (SETimes 2009). "There was real pressure," one interviewee noted. "These guys know that they are under military law; they'd be disciplined and risk being sacked. They had to ask themselves 'would Dodik cover me if I lose my job?'" There also have been a number of rotations of platoon-strength AFBiH units deployed to Afghanistan, under Danish command (in the British southern sector in Kandahar and Helmand Provinces). These are generally seen to have gone well, but they cannot compensate for the inherent weaknesses in the AFBiH and the political and financial strictures which have impeded its development.

There are varying views on the AFBiH's capacity. Some interviewees rated the command highly; others noted that there was no vision for the force from the Chief of Staff or Minister of Defense—"this is a management problem.[17] Junior officers were seen as wanting "to make it work, but don't have the resources ... it's a social welfare organization."[18] The ever-tightening constraints on resources are viewed by some Bosniak officers as stealth demilitarization, driven by the RS. Not only do AFBiH forces not have a chance to develop capacity, they have too few resources to maintain the facilities and equipment that they already possess. None of the professionals interviewed believed the AFBiH was capable of conducting major operations. One stated that the AFBiH "is ill-equipped ... The battalions have no

---

14 Discussion with international military professional, May 2011.

15 Discussion with international organization officials, military professionals, and diplomats, June 2011.

16 One such event, held in Stolac in June 2010, was reported in the media as a regimental ceremony (see *Dnevni Avaz*, "BH vojnici postrojovani uz hrvatsku himnu," June 15, 2012). Yet one foreign military professional insisted the event was a veterans organization event, and therefore legal.

17 Discussion with international military professionals, September 2011.

18 Discussion with international military professional, June 2011.

capability to fight or move."[19] In foreign deployments, the AFBiH has had to rely on foreign funding, rather than follow the NATO standard practice of funding its own deployments.[20]

None of those interviewed by the author believe that the AFBiH command would initiate any violence or destabilization. One interlocutor remarked that "there is no initiative in this society; it would have to be organized from on-high, politically."[21] The consensus view was encapsulated in a statement by one foreign military professional "The (AFBiH) are not a major factor in destabilization. It's a quiet mess."[22]

But most professional observers interviewed by the author were far less sanguine about the potential impact of destabilization initiated outside the AFBiH on the force. The majority view among those familiar with the AFBiH and the defense reform process is that the force would crack into ethnic components under significant political pressure and social stress. AFBiH officers told US diplomats that they could envision troops under their command arming civilians in eastern Bosnia in the event of unrest there, for example (US Embassy Sarajevo). An interviewee expressed the view that the AFBiH could become "a fractured militia ... essentially a rifle brigade."[23] Still another professional with frequent interaction with the AFBiH told the author "if the balloon goes up, they'll go home and act—blow up telephone exchanges, or whatever."[24] While some interviewees were skeptical of sufficient stresses ever taking place, none expressed confidence the chain of command could withstand them. The general view is that the "AFBiH cannot retain cohesion beyond a yet unknown threshold of social and political polarization."

A minority of those interviewed by the author thought that the AFBiH could be called upon to make a "show of force" in the event of a public disturbance, only then followed by EUFOR. But the pronounced majority counseled against such a course of action; some stated outright such an order would be illegal. In any case, the order would have to come from the three-member BiH Presidency, and it was seen as highly unlikely that unanimity could be established in that forum. Even in the event that such an order was given, some noted that the AFBiH could legitimately refuse it, since there is no training or doctrine for such an eventuality; its role is strictly restricted to territorial defense.[25] A senior AFBiH officer told US diplomats that the force would "break" if called upon to act against an internal security challenge (US Embassy Sarajevo, 2008).

---

19   Interview with international military professionals, April 2011.

20   Discussion with international military professionals, September 2011.

21   Discussion with international military and security professionals, June 2011.

22   Discussion with international military professionals, June 2011.

23   Discussion with international military professionals, November 2008.

24   Discussion with international organization officials, military professionals, and diplomats, June 2011.

25   Discussion with international military professionals, September 2011.

The very existence of a unified Armed Forces of BiH was inconceivable at the time of the Dayton Accords; its very existence is an accomplishment. But the force was assembled with inherent weaknesses and brought into being just as the broader political and security reform came to a complete standstill and then shifted into reverse. The NATO connection never got sufficient traction due to the RS' ambiguity on whether BiH should *ever* join NATO, or even whether the AFBiH should exist at all. Even with its arrested development, the AFBiH is not seen as a source of potential instability but a potential casualty thereof. Yet "given the increasing political polarization of the environment, it could be an ingredient in a volatile 'cocktail' of factors: political actors, entity and cantonal security forces, veterans' organizations, and private security firms."[26] Its weapons and capabilities could provide a considerable accelerant to unrest. In the event of civil disturbances, the best that can be hoped is that the AFBiH would keep its troops in barracks, and its equipment under guard.

Brief Assessment of Other Security Threats in BiH

The Atlantic Initiative and Democratization Policy Council's security risk assessment[27] remains the most comprehensive attempt to analyze and document the spectrum of security risks in BiH. For the purposes of this volume, this chapter will summarize these findings. Since the study's publication in October 2011, there have been no developments which have affected the risk factors and trend lines. It is the author's view that the situation has deteriorated on nearly all fronts in the intervening two years.[28]

1. The International Community Role—Creating a Rules-Free Environment

The current political and social environment is a result of assumptions that have held sway in the international community since 2005 and the subsequent shift in posture. The unwillingness to maintain and employ Dayton implementation and enforcement mechanisms—the OHR and EUFOR—and a move to a "soft power" approach has generated a rules-free environment, in which political leaders feel free to pursue their unfulfilled agendas without restraint. There is no collective political will to revisit its foundations, despite the current approach's clear failure. The PIC Steering Board remains on bureaucratic autopilot with a course

---

26　Ibid.

27　The entire study is available on the www.atlanticinitiative.org and www. democratizationpolicy.org websites.

28　Ibid., pages 4–7.

set in 2005. This has increased the likelihood, and potential gravity, of political miscalculation by Bosnia's leaders—with potential security implications.[29]

2. Domestic Environmental Factors

An analysis of hate speech and political rhetoric clearly shows that the political and public discourse in Bosnia radicalized from 2009–2011, increasing sharply since the October 2010 elections (Azinović, Bassuener and Weber 2011, p. 35).[30] Political elites and most of the media in the country play an active role in this deterioration. The state of BiH itself is more frequently called into question. Discussion of political crisis precipitating violence is also on the rise among politicians and media commentators, including the Croat member of the state presidency, Željko Komšić. In response to a direct question of what would happen if the RS pursues secession, he answered that this would "lead to certain war." (Daily.tPortal.hr, 2013). Popular fears appear to be rising. Use of the term "war" inevitably harks back to 1992. Since the current circumstances and forces available for conflict are substantially different, this often leads to the conclusion that since war in the manner of 1992 is not possible, organized violence is also not possible. This second conclusion does not necessarily follow the first. This allows a false sense of security both domestically and internationally.

The political elites' confrontational relationship has hamstrung or gutted governing institutions, delivering poor results. This holds true at the state, entity, and cantonal levels (CCI 2010). Political leadership at all levels has been unwilling to compromise on policies that would serve the public good. Not only does this negatively affect citizens' ability to identify with their own state (and political elites), it also has a negative effect on citizens' perception of security—and their real security.

The global economic downturn hit Bosnia hard. The policy priorities of the ruling elites, who diverted new revenues from 2006 into transfer payments to preferred constituencies—war veterans (defined expansively) in particular—made the economy considerably more vulnerable. The onset of the recession—and reduction in remittances[31]—accelerated an already certain reckoning. Budgetary shortfalls, especially at the entity level, have ballooned (SWOT 2011). Political elites in BiH have increasing difficulty in dealing with the weak economy. The

---

29   Roland Kostić's comprehensive doctoral research, *Ambivalent Peace* (2007), was undertaken before the full impact of the international retrenchment which began in earnest in early 2006 was readily apparent to many Bosnians or international actors. Were the research undertaken later, it is likely there would be more apparent polarization, and it would be harder to attribute this to assertive external state-building efforts, as his research did.

30   See also "Strategija iskljucivanja: Govor mrznje u BH javnosti," Mediacentar Sarajevo, July 2010.

31   See Adnan Efendic's chapter in this volume on this issue.

global economic crisis has exacerbated the problem, but the patronage system that dominates the political system as well as the ruling elites' relationship with the economy is the main cause. BiH's governments face a stark choice: either depart from the existing political system and culture or face serious budgetary problems, and possibly insolvency.

3. Potential Sparks

Substantial interethnic violence can be generated either by design or could erupt spontaneously and then be instrumentalized by the various parties according to their various agendas.

A dysfunctional state, a poor economy, and nationalist indoctrination have all been visited upon BiH youth. Rising and increasingly violent juvenile delinquency represents an individualized, direct product of this situation. Football hooliganism adds ethnicity and organization to the mix. Hooligan and criminal groups have already been used for political exploits in the country, as they are semi-organized and relatively easy to mobilize (Katana 2011).

Minority return has lost the central political relevance it once had. Yet minority returnees remain a vulnerable social group and have recently been revived as a political focal point by the 1 Mart (March 1) movement.[32] They often have a difficult relationship with the ethnic majority population in their communities. While they face structural discrimination, relations between minority returnees and the dominant local populations have normalized considerably in the past decade. Yet the increasingly heated political environment has clearly added to a subjective feeling of insecurity among minority returnees, negatively affecting relations with the ethnic majority populations in their communities—not only, but especially, in the RS (Hina 2013). Given the current political context, some of the attacks on returnees clearly have the potential to spontaneously escalate into wider interethnic violent conflict (Jukić 2013).

Unsubstantiated allegations of an increased terrorism threat in Bosnia, based on the preposterous claim that some 100,000 Wahhabis reside in the country, are not aimed at deterring such a threat but rather at pigeonholing Bosniaks as terrorists and delegitimizing their political aims (Azinović, Bassuener and Weber 2011).[33] In response, the Bosniak "side," particularly the official Islamic Community, has long tended to deny by default any security threat that may be posed by the presence of dangerous individuals and ideologies associated with Islam, calling all such references hostile and "Islamophobic" (Ibid.). As demonstrated by the October 2011 attack on the US Embassy by lone gunman Mevlid Jašarević, there are real

---

32   Reflecting the date of the BiH Independence referendum in 1992, 1 Mart advocates the registration of citizens where they lived in 1992 for their participation in elections. See http://www.prvimart.ba/

33   The claim of 100,000 wahabbis was made in several Bosnian Serb and Serbian media outlets. For example, "Po Bosni vršlja 100.000 vehabija," *Vesti Online*, April 3, 2010.

threats (Associated Press 2011). Ongoing arguments on the numbers of Bosnians who are going to fight in Syria have become a new issue in this realm (Teodorović and Synovitz 2013). Political elites, through formal and informal ties, exert control over both law enforcement agencies and some militant groups. Effective deterrents remain few, while enablers of terrorism and political violence are many. They include a weak (failing) state, an abundance of readily available arms and ammunition, widespread corruption, weak border controls, and the mobilization of uncontested ideologies.

4. Public Security Setting

Since the war, police services in BiH have gone a long way towards re-professionalization, modernization and democratization (Lindvall 2009). But this professional evolution is far from complete, not least due to the remaining institutional-legal fragmentation of the numerous police agencies. Police in recent years have been subjected to increasing political pressure, both to relinquish their relatively new operational autonomy and to submit to ethnic political loyalties (Global 2010). This raises important questions about the capacity of the police agencies to successfully combat organized crime and corruption, particularly in cases where members of the political elite and representatives of state institutions are implicated. Police capacity to uphold public order and security in the event of violent inter-ethnic incidents is also in question.[34] All professionals interviewed in the AI-DPC study agreed that given sufficient pressure, the police forces would split along ethnic lines. The EU seems to have adopted a see no evil, hear no evil, speak no evil attitude toward BiH policing, having abandoned its three stated principles, signing the SAA in return for a mere declaration of local will to reform. It dismantled the EUPM in June 2012.

The judiciary in BiH has not effectively dealt with the biggest problem which most debilitates rule of law in the country—institutionalized corruption and organized and economic crime. It has also demonstrated that it is not immune to corruption itself. In spite of the presence of many courageous judges, prosecutors and attorneys investing their expertise and courage in upholding the rule of law, there is a clear, worrying trend of substantial erosion of the judiciary and the rule of law more generally. The undermining of the state, the political attacks and pressure on the judiciary and on the achievements of previous reforms, as well as a problematic general attitude and behavior of political elite's vis-à-vis the judiciary and the rule of law, all stem from the overarching political deterioration in BiH and the softening international posture. Contrary to its proclaimed aims to strengthen rule of law and fight organized crime and corruption, the international community has contributed to this rules-free environment. The failure of the judiciary to hold public officials accountable has contributed to the breakdown of a sense of limits.

---

34   Interviews with police officials from the Federation of BiH and international policing officials, 2011.

Thousands of tons of unstable munitions and explosives remain dispersed throughout BiH, along with surplus arms in varying states of repair. Included in the AFBiH's stockpile are thousands of heavy weapons (artillery, armor), tens of thousands of small arms, and thousands of tons of ammunition—this is a vast surplus. Of the surplus, 4,500 tons were already deemed unsafe by the joint international Expert Working Group (EWG) in 2011 (EWG 2011). The composite picture of control of arms and munitions by public authorities is cause for alarm—in terms of the volatility of the ordnance on hand (78 percent was assessed as unstable in mid-2011),[35] the security of the facilities in which it is housed, and the lack of professionalism or active criminality of some of those entrusted to protect these stockpiles (Ibid.).

The abundance of arms and ammunition remaining from the war and the relative ease with which they can be obtained continues to be a public security risk. In the immediate aftermath of the war, many of these weapons—mostly assault rifles, rocket-propelled grenades, handguns, and hand grenades—were stockpiled illegally out of a fear of renewed conflict, and for the protection of family and property. This practice was particularly widespread in the countryside. Of the estimated 1.2 million small arms and light weapons in BiH, an estimated 90 percent are in civilian possession (Center for Security Studies 2010). Of those, less than one-third are legally owned. This effectively means that, on average, nearly every household in the country owns a gun. In addition, every fifth citizen (19.5 percent) owns an illegal firearm (Ibid.). Screening procedures are questionable. The presence and easy availability of firearms is another unwelcome addition to an already complex security situation, with little or no effective deterrents to their sale or ownership.

Substantial consolidation and regulation in recent years have made the private security sector (PSC) less of a known unknown. But all international security officials in BiH who spoke to DPC-AI researchers believed that members of PSCs would be among the first to take up arms in case of a violent ethnic conflict (Azinović, Bassuener and Weber 2011). They consider PSC personnel—particularly special forces and intelligence veterans—to be among the best trained among the security agencies in BiH, public or private. Many also note they are well-equipped, having access and skill to use weapons that their firms do not (at least officially) possess. A company or even platoon-sized assemblage from one of the smaller (and less scrutinized) PSCs could have a major impact if activated in the early stages of a conflict.

Retreat from Responsibility—EUFOR's Shrinkage

When taking on the Dayton enforcement role from NATO in December 2004, the EU apparently believed it inherited a risk-free way to show the flag and demonstrate

---

35   Interview with international official, June 2011.

its peacekeeping capacity without American participation. Great efforts were made to proclaim that EUFOR would be a continuation of SFOR; promotional posters illustrated exactly this (Bassuener and Ferhatović 2007). The initial force strength was roughly 7,000, but the force was reduced radically in early 2007. The force has progressively shrunk, with corresponding diminution of operational capacity. Even with the capacity on hand, the posture and deployment of the force reflected reduced EU/member state appetite. Patrols were curtailed in 2007 on account of their being seen by the then-EUFOR Commander, Major General Ignacio Martin Villalain of Spain, as "provocative." (Azinović, Bassuener and Weber 2011, p. 73). By the end of the decade, EUFOR's operational capacity was all Sarajevo-based, and its strength had fallen well-below the 2,500 troops required as an absolute minimum to fulfill the mandate, according to the assessment conducted prior to its reduction in 2007 (Ibid.).

Frictions exist within the Union—with Britain leading a minority camp against German and French calls to withdraw the force—as to whether to maintain it at all. The compromise reached to maintain the force in 2012 was to leave it at a present strength of under 600 troops. Assessments of currently serving member state diplomats to the author have been quite clear that the most the force's operational elements could secure is the Sarajevo International Airport, into which reinforcements would arrive.[36] This is wholly consistent with AI-DPC's security risk assessment. But such deployment would not be automatic; they would depend on the disposition of the 28 member states of the EU.

With the reduction in forces has come a unilateral reinterpretation of the Annex 1A and Chapter 7 responsibilities of EUFOR by the EU. In June 2012, Deputy Secretary-General of the European External Action Service Maciej Popowski openly stated that despite the remaining Chapter 7 mandate, the EU wanted to move EUFOR into a capacity building role.[37] Later in the conference, the discussion in a subsequent panel made clear that many in the EU view the very existence of a Chapter 7 mandate existing in a country with a "European perspective" as a humiliation (EUPM 2012). In its 2013 Progress Report, the European Commission states the following (author emphasis):

"The EUFOR Althea military operation contributes to maintaining a safe and secure environment in the country. The UN Security Council has extended EUFOR's mandate until November 2013. The Operation was reconfigured and reduced to 600 troops in theatre, focusing on capacity building and training, *while maintaining the means to contribute to the Bosnia and Herzegovina authorities' deterrence capacity*." (European Commission 2013). As noted earlier in this chapter, the AFBiH's "deterrent capacity" is oriented to territorial defense, not internal security. The role of "maintaining a safe and secure environment" in BiH

---

36   Interview with international official, June 2011.

37   EUPM Legacy Seminar, June 7–8, 2012 at http://www.eupm.org/Legacy.aspx. The site contains the program and a number of the prepared statements of the speakers, but not questions and answers from the audience, which followed each panel.

is unequivocally that of EUFOR since December 2004. It is readily apparent that the EU is defining its mandate down to the posture and mission it would prefer to have, rather than the one it voluntarily took on.

At the time of writing (October 2013), the EU has just finished conducting the second of its "Rapid Response" (*Brzi Odgovor*) exercises, involving "over the horizon" troops brought in from Austria, Slovenia, Turkey, as well as the forces already based at the EUFOR base at Butmir. The exercise scenario apparently involved EUFOR forces working together with AFBiH forces on some internal security threat—an eventuality, as discussed earlier, which is highly problematic.[38] In addition, the main message that the highly publicized exercise (billboards are visible statewide) seems calibrated to convey is that there is no need for a standing EUFOR at all, since the EU and its partners can insert troops as needed. However, the likelihood that the response would be rapid in the event of a civil disturbance or other security threat is far from clear, as there would need to be a unanimous decision by the 28-member European Council to dispatch reserve troops. With its current posture and attitude, the EU has foresworn deterrence and diminished even its capacity to react to dangerous levels. The EU—and its individual members—is setting the Union's Common Security and Defense Policy (CSDP) up to fail with such a risky calibration of forces and capabilities to potential threats.

Conclusion

The security environment in Bosnia and Herzegovina is—due to the combination of domestic, regional, and international factors—much more volatile and vulnerable than is widely acknowledged or recognized. The civil unrest which took place in February 2014, though it manifested no ethnic character in its content, underscored this fact[39] (Weber and Bassuener 2014). During this unrest, EUFOR remain confined to barracks.[40]

The EU's aim to unilaterally confer the responsibility for maintaining internal security in BiH to the AFBiH (which was not designed for this role) and the police (which are certainly even more politicized than the military), thereby divesting itself of the responsibility that it enthusiastically adopted from NATO in 2004, is of a piece with this overall international retreat from engagement and responsibility, despite the ongoing rollback of political and structural reform.

The February 2014 civil unrest, which included incidents of violence and destruction of public buildings, should have served as a wake-up call for international actors. While there can be no certainty on the location, nature, timing

---

38   *Bosnia Daily*, "Change of Command in the Multinational Battalion of EUFOR," August 21, 2013.

39   Florian Bieber was among the many who noted this reality. See http://fbieber. wordpress.com/2014/02/09/is-change-coming-finally-thoughts-on-the-bosnian-protests/

40   Interview with EU member state military professional, April 2014.

or severity of a security breakdown, it seems likely that another will eventually occur, since the ingredients for the February 2014 unrest—popular dissatisfaction with political elites and lack of accountability mechanisms—have not dissipated.[41] When this happens, it is also probable that domestic factors will inflame it out of self-interest (and self-preservation). The lack of international coercive force readily at hand to deter, or if required, react, to such an eventuality increases the likelihood that such an event will escalate into a wider security issue in Bosnia and Herzegovina.

Annex on AFBiH Force Composition and Structure

The defense law that prescribes the force strength also determines the force composition. These quotas of "constituent peoples" are linked to the 1991 census, with some overrepresentation for Croats vis-à-vis their proportion of the population then:[42]

Bosniaks: 45.90 percent or 4,826 persons
Serbs: 33.60 percent or 3,533 persons
Croats: 19.80 percent or 2,084 persons, and
Other nationalities: 0.70 percent or 74 persons

The armed forces force structure is divided into operational and support commands. All command structures are multiethnic—even the mono-ethnic infantry battalions are subsumed into brigades that include battalions from all three constituent peoples. As of April 2011, the AFBiH is structured as follows[43]—the locations in which the commands and units are listed in parentheses:

Joint Staff AFBiH (Sarajevo)

Lt.Gen. Miladin Milojčić—Chief of Staff
Maj.Gen. Rizvo Pleh—Deputy Chief of Staff, Operations
Maj.Gen. Slavko Puljić—Deputy Chief of Staff, Resources

---

41 A public opinion poll conducted by the EU Delegation in Spring 2014 following the protests found public dissatisfaction with governance and the overall situation was high statewide, and support for the protests was pronounced in both the Federation (where the protests were concentrated) and the RS. Public pessimism about the future was also pronounced.

42 Azinović, Bassuener and Weber. Discussion with international military professional, November 2008

43 Brochure of the Ministry of Defense and Armed Forces of Bosnia and Herzegovina, p. 15 at http://www.mod.gov.ba/files/file/maj_2011/bosura%20eng%20mail.pdf

AFBiH Operational Command (Sarajevo)

4th Infantry Brigade (Čapljina)
5th Infantry Brigade (Tuzla)
6th Infantry Brigade (Banja Luka)

Artillery Battalions are located in Doboj, Mostar, and Žepče
Air Forces and Air Defense Brigade (Zalužani, outside Banja Luka):
- Air Defense Battalion (Sarajevo)
- Air Surveillance and Warning Battalion
(Zalužani, outside Banja Luka)
- Air Forces Support Battalion (elements in both Banja Luka and Sarajevo)
Tactical Support Brigade (Sarajevo)
- Armored Battalion (Tuzla)
- Communications Battalion (Pale)
- Engineering Battalion (Derventa)
- Military Intelligence Battalion (Sarajevo)
- Mine Clearance Battalion (Travnik)
- Military Police Battalion (Sarajevo)
- Nuclear, Biological and Chemical Warfare
Battalion (Tuzla)

AFBiH Support Command (Banja Luka)

Personnel Management Command (Banja Luka)
Training and Doctrine Command (Travnik)
Logistics Command (Doboj)
- Logistical Support Battalions (Banja Luka, Čapljina,Tuzla, Sarajevo)

Bibliography

Alvarez, S. (2006) Bosnian Soldiers Unite, Help Iraqis. *Armed Forces Press Service*, January 31. Available from: http://www.defense.gov/News/NewsArticle.aspx?ID=14483 [Accessed September 4, 2013].

Anastasijević, D. and Borden, A. (2000) Out of Time: Drašković, Đinđić and the Serbian Opposition Against Milošević. Institute for War and Peace Reporting.

Ashdown, P. and Holbrooke, R. (2008) A Bosnian powder keg. *The Guardian.* October 22.

Associated Press (2011) Gunman fires on US Embassy in Bosnia. October 28. Available from: http://www.theguardian.com/world/2011/oct/28/us-embassy-bosnia-gunman [Accessed September 5, 2013].

Azinović, V., Bassuener, K. and Weber, B. (2011) Assessing the Potential for Renewed Ethnic Violence in Bosnia and Herzegovina—A Security Risk Analysis. *Atlantic Initiative and Democratization Policy Council.*

Bassuener, K. (2009) SSR in Bosnia and Herzegovina, 1996 to present: An Overview, 2009. *PowerPoint Presentation for Chevening Lecture.*

Bassuener, K. and Ferhatović, E. (2007) The ESDP in Action—A View from the Consumer Side. European Security and Defense Policy—An Implementation Perspective. In: Merlingen, M. and Ostrauskaite, R. (eds) European Security and Defense Policy—An Implementation Perspective. Routledge.

Bassuener, K. and Weber, B. (2012) Croatian and Serbian Policy in Bosnia and Herzegovina: Help or Hindrance? *DPC Policy Study*, October 2012. Available from: www.democratizationpolicy.org.

Bassuener, K. and Witte, E.A. (2002) An Agenda for Bosnia's Next High Representative. *Democratization Policy Institute.*

——. (2003) U.S. Troops in Bosnia: Wimpier Even than the French. *Washington Monthly*. Available from: http://www.washingtonmonthly.com/features/2003/0303.bassuener.html. [Accessed April 4, 2015].

BBC News (March 31, 2005) RS Srebrenica probe names officials [online] BBC. Available from: http://www.bosnia.org.uk/news/news_body.cfm?newsid=2039 [Accessed September 4, 2013].

Bosnia Daily (August 21, 2013) Change of Command in the Multinational Battalion of EUFOR.

Bosnian Ministry of Defense (n.d) Brochure of the Ministry of Defense and Armed Forces of Bosnia and Herzegovina. p. 15. Available from:. http://www.mod.gov.ba/files/file/maj_2011/bosura%20eng%20mail.pdf. [Accessed April 4, 2015].

Bowman, S. (December 1996) Bosnia: US Military Operations. *CRS Issue Brief*, Available from: http://www.fas.org/man/crs/93–056.htm [Accessed October 9, 2013].

CCI (Center for Civic Initiatives) (2010) Monitoring rada Vijeća ministara BiH za period 01.01—31.08.2010.

CSS (Center for Security Studies) (2010) Study on Small Arms and Light Weapons in Bosnia and Herzegovina 2010. Sarajevo, 2010.

Clinton, W. (1995) Transcript of President Clinton's Speech on Bosnia. *CNN*, November 27. Available from: http://edition.cnn.com/US/9511/bosnia_speech/speech.html [Accessed September 9, 2013].

——. (1997) President Bill Clinton. *Statement,* December 18. Available from: http://edition.cnn.com/ALLPOLITICS/1997/12/18/clinton.bosnia/fdch.html [Accessed September 4, 2013].

CNN (2001) Violence Flares at Bosnia Ceremony, June 18. Available from: http://edition.cnn.com/2001/WORLD/europe/06/18/bosnia.riots.02/   [Accessed September 4, 2013].

Daily.tportal.hr (2013) Komšić: If RS attempts to secede, there will be war. *Daily. tPortal.*hr, August 17. Available from: http://daily.tportal.hr/280587/Komsic-If-RS-attempts-to-secede-there-will-be-war.html [Accessed October 9, 2013].

DPI (Democratization Policy Institute) (2002) An Agenda for Bosnia's Next High Representative. Washington, May 2002.

The Economist (July 17, 1997) Bosnia: Progress at Last? Available from: http://www.economist.com/node/151682 [Accessed October 9, 2013].

EPW (Expert Working Group) (2011) Expert Working Group Presentation on the Situation—Disposal of Surplus Weapons and Ammunition in AF BiH. *Management of Storage Sites*, July 6, 6. Available from: PowerPoint presentation made available to the author.

EUPM (2012) Eupm legacy seminar—June 7–8. Available from: http://www.eupm.org/Legacy.aspx [Accessed April 4, 2015].

European Commission Brussels (2013) Bosnia and Herzegovina 2013 Progress Report. Available from: http://ec.europa.eu/enlargement/pdf/key_documents/2013/package/ba_rapport_2013.pdf [Accessed October 16, 2013].

Fletcher, P. (2001) Bosnian Croats accuse West over bank funds. *Reuters*, April 20. Available from: http://iwpr.net/report-news/nato-westar-operation-reveals-bosnian-croat-spy-net [Accessed September 4, 2013].

GFAA (The General Framework Agreement Annex) 1A (December 14, 1995). Available from: http://www.ohr.int/dpa/default.asp?content_id=368 [Accessed September 4, 2013].

GFAP (General Framework Agreement for Peace) (December 14, 1995) Available from: http://www.ohr.int/dpa/default.asp?content_id=380 [Accessed October 6, 2013].

Global (2010) Lov na vještice u RS-u. pp. 14–16.

HINA (2013) Prijedor mayor calls commemoration of war victims gay parade. *HINA*, June 2. Available from: http://dalje.com/en-world/prijedor-mayor-calls-commemoration-of-war-victims-gay-parade/470516 [Accessed October 9, 2013].

Johnson, A.R. (1971) Total National Defense in Yugoslavia. *RAND Corporation—Santa Monica*. Available from: http://www.dtic.mil/dtic/tr/fulltext/u2/742397.pdf [Accessed September 4, 2013].

Jukić, E. (2013) Bosnian Serbs attack Zvornik Muslims on Eid. *BalkanInsight*, August 9. Available from: http://www.balkaninsight.com/en/article/bosnia-muslim-returnee-attacked-by-serb-in-zvornik-1 [Accessed October 9, 2013].

Katana, G. and Sito-Sučić, D. (2011) Violence halts Bosnian Premier League match. *Reuters*, September 2011. Available from: http://www.dnaindia.com/world/1591383/report-violence-halts-bosnian-premier-league-match [Accessed October 9, 2013].

Lindvall, D. (2009) The limits of the European vision in BiH—An analysis of the police reform negotiations. Stockholm, 2009.

NATO (n.d.) History of the NATO-led Stabilization Force (SFOR) in Bosnia and Herzegovina. Available from: http://www.nato.int/sfor/organisation/sfororg. htm [Accessed September 4, 2013].

NATO (2004) SFOR Organization. Available from: http://www.nato.int/sfor/ organisation/sfororg.htm [Accessed September 4, 2013].

OHR (2011) Decision removing Ante Jelavić from his position as the Croat member of the BiH Presidency. *OHR*, March 7. Available from: http:// www.ohr.int/decisions/removalssdec/default.asp?content_id=328 [Accessed September 4, 2013].

OSCE (n.d) Article IV. Available from: http://www.osce.org/item/43725 [Accessed October 9, 2013].

PIC (Peace Implementation Council) (1997) PIC Bonn Conclusions. December 10. Available from: http://www.ohr.int/pic/default.asp?content_id=5182#11 [Accessed September 4, 2013].

PIC (Peace Implementation Council) (2008) Declaration by the Steering Board of the Peace Implementation Council, February 27. Available from: http://www. ohr.int/pic/default.asp?content_id=41352 [Accessed October 9, 2013].

Rice, C. (2005) Remarks in Honor of the Tenth Anniversary of the Dayton Peace Accords in Washington DC, November 22. Available from: http://2001–2009. state.gov/secretary/rm/2005/57265.htm [Accessed October 9, 2013].

Setimes (2009) Dodik urges RS troops to boycott NATO exercises in Georgia, May 8. Available from: http://www.setimes.com/cocoon/setimes/xhtml/ en_GB/features/setimes/newsbriefs/2009/05/08/nb-11 [Accessed September 4, 2013].

SFOR Informer Online (1999) Findings in Operation Westar. *SFOR Informer Online*, 1999. Available from: http://www.nato.int/sfor/sfor-at-work/opwestar/ findings/t000215a.htm [Accessed September 4, 2013].

Solana, J. (1999) NATO Sec-Gen on Poplasen Removal and the Brcko Decision. *Official Statement by NATO Secretary General*, March 11 in Brussels. Available from: http://www.usembassy-israel.org.il/publish/press/security/archive/1999/ march/ds1312.htm [Accessed September 4, 2013].

Stability Pact for Southeastern Europe (n.d) About the Stability Pact. *Stability Pact for Southeastern Europe*. Available from: http://www.stabilitypact.org/ about/ [Accessed September 4, 2013].

Swot Kvartalni Ekonomski Monitor Nr. 4 (2011) I dalje bez snažnije ekonomskog oporavka. Banja Luka, July 2011, p. 8.

Teodorović, M. and Synovitz, R. (2013) Balkan Militants Join Syria's Rebel Cause. *Radio Free Europe/Radio Liberty*, June 8, 8. Available from: http:// www.rferl.org/content/syria-balkan-militants-join-rebel-cause/25011213.html [Accessed October 9, 2013].

Toal, G. and Dahlman, C.T. (2011) Bosnia Remade—Ethnic Cleansing and Its Reversal. Oxford University Press.

US Embassy Sarajevo (2008) Bosnia—Senior Military Commanders Concerned about Political Crisis Impact on Armed Forces. *Leaked US Diplomatic Cable*,

March 4, 4. Available at: http://wikileaks.org/cable/2008/03/08SARAJEVO414. html.

Valicon, d.o.o., (2014)—Protests in Bosnia and Herzegovina, Public Opinion Research. Poll commissioned by EU Delegation in BiH following February 2014 protests, obtained by the author.

Weber, B. and Bassuener, K. (2014) EU Policies Boomerang: Bosnia and Herzegovina's Social Unrest. *Policy Brief, Democratization Policy Council,* February 14. Available at: http://democratizationpolicy.org/eu-policies-boomerang--bosnia-and-herzegovina-s-social-unrest.

Chapter 5

Post-war Economic Transition in Bosnia and Herzegovina—A Challenging Transformation

Adnan Efendić and Azra Hadžiahmetović

Introduction

In this chapter, the economy of Bosnia and Herzegovina (BiH) is analyzed in three different periods: pre-war transition, post-war economic and institutional restructuring, and the current macroeconomic environment.

The chapter is structured as follows. In the first section, BiH's economic performance prior to the beginning of transition and the war (1992–95) is examined (that is, the late 1980s and early 1990s). This is followed by a discussion of the role of the international community and the international financial institutions (IFIs) in post-war BiH, and efforts to support BiH's development as a sustainable economy. In the third section, key macroeconomic aggregates and their behavior over time are reviewed, including indicators such as GDP, unemployment, fiscal indicators, and investment. The role of the Central Bank of BiH is presented, as this institution is rather unique as one of the strictest Currency Board arrangements in the world. In addition, the scope and role of remittances is examined, as a specific aspect of post-war BiH and the significant wartime displacement, which created a diaspora very often willing to send money back to the country. The penultimate section is focused on BiH's expressed intention to become a full member of the EU, including the key stages of this process, BiH's current position, and some of the key challenges remaining. The final section concludes by providing some policy recommendations based on the analysis presented.

BiH—From Early Transition to War

The late 1980s and early 1990s were characterized by the beginning of transition throughout South East Europe, and this process overwhelmed the territory of the former Yugoslavia with numerous unresolved internal political and economic issues. In a complex state structure with six republics, issues of the national statutes and ethnic relations were emphasized, and discussions on the need to strengthen the federation or to create a loose confederation were opened, with eventual disastrous results (Lampe 2000). While economic changes shook the country, it was also a time of new possibilities for introducing pluralism into the political scene, which would ultimately result in the rise of prominent ethnic and nationalist leaders and resulting social tensions.

At that time, the dominant political system in Yugoslavia was one of socialist self-management, where the economy was more open and market-oriented than in other socialist countries (World Bank 1996), and often treated as "something between" (that is, between socialism and capitalism). It was considered, according to its political and economic characteristics, to be a system that could more quickly and easily respond to the requirements of the transition to a market economy, and in that way, had the potential to provide solutions to open internal political and economic issues (Hadžiahmetović 2011).

The course of transition, which started with some high hopes, was defeated by the rise of political and national tensions and the subsequent side-lining of economic reform. The initial transition program within the Yugoslav framework was oriented towards strengthening economic growth and employment, transformation of the economic structure and privatization. In practice, this became a program with substantial heterogeneity among the former Yugoslav republics in terms of implementation and success, as the various republics each started from a different level of internal economic capacity and strength. This kind of economic program from the beginning was perhaps necessary medicine, but one that also fed into political and national conflicts. Reforms conceptualized with good intentions aimed at strengthening elements of internal cohesion and the general economic base instead became a constituent part of disintegration and the massive wartime destruction (Anđelić 2003).

In the geographic and political center of those events was BiH, one of the six former Yugoslav republics, covering an area of 51,129 km^2 (with approximately 20 km of coastline along the Adriatic Sea), a population of 4.1 million, $10.6 billion of GDP, and a $2,429 per capita income in 1990 (EC/WB 1999). As a part of the Yugoslav economy, BiH had a strong raw material base, natural resources, and was more open and market oriented, with a strong industrial sector (particularly in energy and the production of raw materials), and a developed construction sector (Savezni Zavod za Statistiku, 1991). However, it was one of the weaker republics (similar to the Federal Republic of Macedonia) in terms of its per capita national output (*"društveni proizvod"*), and was economically surpassed by Slovenia, Croatia, Serbia and Montenegro (Savezni Zavod za Statistiku 1991). Being at a lower starting point in transition generally affected success in transition reforms (Mickiewicz 2005), and, when combined with the war, this had a significant impact on BiH's economic development prospects.

In the early 1990s the dramatic political and economic situation in Yugoslavia put BiH in an extremely difficult position. In 1990 and 1991 there was an enormous decline of industrial production, export and import; market disintegration; and blockage of the commodity turnover and payment operations, as well as the monetary system (Hadžiahmetović 2011). Although "transitional recession"

(recession related to the beginning of transition reforms, primarily, liberalization) is often linked with the beginning of the transition period, Mickiewicz (2005) argues that almost all transition countries, including Yugoslavia, were in economic crisis even *before* they introduced transition reforms. He (2005) defines this downturn as a "post-Communist recession" that was related to the lack of reforms and the timing of core reforms before the transition had really started. However, the main result of this period in BiH was the decline of the standard of living (per capita income dropped from around $2,400 in 1990 to around $1,900 in 1991) and a rise in unemployment to around 27 percent (World Bank 1996).

As Yugoslavia disintegrated, with the declarations of independence of Slovenia and Croatia—and the war in Croatia—BiH's transition hopes were dashed. The difficult process was pushed aside as war raged for 3.5 years, destroying economic activity, infrastructure and lives. At the signing of the Dayton Peace Agreement (DPA)[1] in 1995, compared to 1991 BiH had around 23 percent fewer people, industrial production dropped more than 90 percent, and the unemployment rate was also around 90 percent. Estimated GDP per capita fell from $1,900 in 1991 to around $500 in 1995. The total war damage in terms of the replacement costs of productive capacities was estimated in the range of $15–20 billion, while the overall damage from the war was estimated to be in the range $50–70 billion (World Bank, 1996; 1997). Such an economic collapse in Europe was without precedent since the end of the Second World War.

Post-Dayton BiH—Economic Restructuring and International Community

The IMF, World Bank, and Debt

Immediately after signing the DPA that formally ended the war, BiH became a member of the IMF, and the door was then open for membership in the World Bank and its associated bodies (IBRD, IDA, IFCA, MIGA).[2] Since the beginning of its engagement, the IMF has been playing a key role in designing and assessing economic policy in BiH. The World Bank, European Commission, Office of the High Representative (OHR) and others followed the status of BiH in the IMF, defining measures in the areas of monetary and fiscal policy, structural and external sector measures. Enormous war damages, 1 million displaced persons, 1.2 million refugees, and 90 percent unemployment put three major challenges in front of BiH (World Bank 1996):

---

1   The Constitution of BiH was drawn up as part of The General Framework Agreement for Peace in BiH (GFAP) in 1995—Annex 4.

2   IBRD—International Bank for Reconstruction and Development; IDA—International Development Association; IFC—International Finance Corporation; MIGA- Multilateral Investment Guarantee Agency.

- Implementing the reconstruction and recovery program necessitated by the war damage.
- Developing the new governance structure and institutions for economic management.
- Managing the transition to a market economy.

The international community was ready to provide support to the country through a $5.1 billion reconstruction program. During the first three years after the war, close to $5 billion was provided through various mechanisms ($2.0 billion in 1996; $1.2 billion in 1997; and $1.5 billion in 1998) (World Bank 1998). Immediately after becoming a member of the IMF (with a proportional share of membership based on BiH's position in the former Yugoslavia), the IMF in addition approved $30 million of SDR (Special Drawing Rights) of emergency aid. However, this IMF initial support was partly spent on repayment of debts acquired before and during the war. It is important to note that this manner of accepting a country into the IMF based in large part on initial loans was the only case in the history of the IMF, reflecting the economic and political circumstances in BiH after Yugoslavia's dissolution and the 3.5 year-long war (Hadžiahmetović 2011). The IMF disbursed the remaining "emergency aid" in establishing budgets at different levels in BiH, and later on, through support to the Currency Board arrangement (Central Bank BiH). Since 1998 the IMF has been providing balance of payments support, budgetary support and support for monetary, fiscal and structural reforms through regular Stand-by arrangements (SBA). So far, there have been four SBAs with the IMF (1998, 2002, 2009, 2012), and the total amount drawn by BiH is close to 712 million[3] of the Special Drawing Rights (SDR) (that is, close to 1.1 billion USD[4]).

Of the total amount of funds invested in reconstruction programs, 25 percent were funded by the World Bank (directly or through other funds). The World Bank projects had substantial financial support of other national donors, who, together with the European Commission facilitated coordination and monitoring of the reconstruction and transition programs (World Bank BiH, 1998). During the first few years the aid funds were invested mostly in infrastructure programs and projects. Reconstruction of physical assets (over 50 percent of funds disbursed) was marked as the most successful aspect of the Priority Reconstruction Program by the end of 1998. These funds also fueled high economic growth, and, together with targeted economic programs (around 20 percent of funds) helped to restart economic activities in the country (European Commission/World Bank 1999). In the same report, the progress in building and strengthening institutions and initiating the policy reforms of transition were noted as fairly modest.

---

3 In January 2014 there was another SBA tranche of 42.3 million SDR bringing the total disbursements to just under 754 million SDR.

4 Calculations based on the exchange rate between SDR and USD (accessed on November 25, 2013). Source: IMF official web page: http://www.imf.org/external/np/fin/data/rms_sdrv.aspx

In addition to the reconstruction of infrastructure and housing, the priority engagements of the international community were to create possibilities for employment and to meet the requirements for external funding. With the substantial presence of foreign aid, BiH recorded extraordinary high rates of economic growth—over 80 percent in 1996, 34 percent in 1997, 16 percent in 1998 and 10 percent in 1999 (World Bank 2014). These growth rates were high primarily because of the low starting point immediately after the war. Unfortunately, these high percentages were not sustainable primarily because they were "aid driven" and did not support private investment and related growth; accordingly, the rates of growth deteriorated as donor support decreased (Efendić 2003).

Nearly solely as a result of this initially high foreign financial support, high levels of import, public spending, public investment and public expenditures were feasible. An average annual growth of around 30 percent, unemployment cut by half relative to the immediate post-war period, the reconstruction of basic infrastructure, and a twofold increase in production—these are just a part of the "impressive" results of reconstruction facilitated by macro-economic stability initiatives, including financial management and a strict monetary arrangement supported by the IMF Stand–by arrangement (Hadžiahmetović 2011). However, it still took 10 years to achieve a GDP similar to the pre-war level; only in 2005 was the total GDP registered at $10.9 billion. The most recent GDP has reached the level of $17.0 billion in 2012, although the highest level was recorded in 2011, at $18.2 billion (Central Bank BiH 2013). Unfortunately, BiH did not record a significant inflow of foreign investment during this immediate post-war reconstruction phase. In addition, internal sources of growth were not mobilized, there was little investment in or by the private sector, and growth fell to around 5 percent in 2000, and completely disappeared at the beginning of the global economic crisis from 2009–2012.

The recent global financial and economic crisis caused additional economic deterioration in BiH, leading to the agreement on a Stand-by arrangement with the IMF in 2009. A risk of further economic decline was reduced thanks to this additional funding, although public debt had increased, and the new financial assistance was not used in support of capital investments, but more generally to offset regular operating funds needed by the public administration. The arrangement was agreed for 36 months (July 2009–June 2012), amounting to about $1.1 billion with a broad set of aims: to protect the functioning of the Currency Board arrangement and the effects of an unfavorable external environment; to consolidate public finance and bring public spending to a sustainable level in the mid-term; to maintain an adequate level of liquidity and capitalization of banks; to secure a sufficient level of external financing; and to improve confidence (IMF 2012).

The first results of the implementation of this 2009–2012 Stand-by arrangement indicated that the program helped stabilize a difficult economic situation in 2009–2010, increased confidence, increased bank deposits, and stabilized foreign exchange reserves (IMF 2012). Still, it is difficult to measure causation in this case, in particular the real impact of this support on the economic system. However, the imperatives of fiscal consolidation within the context of "the fiscal anchor"—i.e., the Stand-by arrangement, would become inevitable. This additional consolidation led to pressure for better control of national consumption and further decrease of fiscal deficits in order to control the rising external debt. As an illustration of the consequences of the minimal structural economic and budgetary reform, the budgets of the BiH entities for 2013 (FBiH and RS) increased relative to 2012, but primarily due to the need to finance the public debt, and *not* as a consequence of expected (or desired) economic growth. Paying off these additional debts as well as the continuing need to reduce the total deficit of the general government will cause problems in the near future—over 80 percent from the disbursed 338.2 million of SDR (close to 518 million US$[5]) BiH obligations under the 2009 Stand-by Arrangement disbursed in February 2012 should be paid back in 2013–2014 (IMF 2012)[6]. It will lead to a real need to increase public revenues and further compress expenditures, in spite of the likelihood of less than desirable economic growth. Such a situation will be very likely resolved through new, additional fiscal burdens (depending on the level of government, such revenue raising mechanisms have been implemented for 2013 including an increase of excise taxes—for example, on tobacco), price increases in public services, increased prices for public sector energy products), but also re-allocation of public spending and certain budget items. These economic policies will be needed to meet IMF terms, but will be politically difficult; in fact there will be many incentives among current politicians to push off the difficult medicine into the future, so that their successors will bear the blame. This process of mortgaging the future to pay for current expenses will yield few significant positive long-term economic results because the main task for policy makers will be servicing liabilities towards its creditors, rather than focusing on internal sources of economic growth and development.

The external indebtedness of BiH in many ways mirrors general pessimistic economic trends, as in 2012 BiH's debt stood at over 7 billion BAM (Figure 5.1). The trend has been increasing since 2008, although the debt service rate remained more or less the same, suggesting the potential problem of "debt burden" that will be left to future generations. Compared to the 2008, external indebtedness has increased by almost 60 percent. Of BiH's total liabilities in terms of external debt, in 2012, the highest percentage of them—25 percent—is owed to the World Bank. Hence, the largest creditor in BiH remains the World Bank group (EC 2012).

---

5   Calculations based on the exchange rate between SDR and USD (accessed on November 25, 2013). Source: IMF official web page: http://www.imf.org/external/np/fin/data/rms_sdrv.aspx

6   Repayment of borrowed resources under the SBA are due within 3¼-5 years of disbursement, which means each disbursement is repaid in eight equal quarterly installments beginning 3¼ years after the date of each disbursement. Source: IMF official web page: http://www.imf.org/external/np/exr/facts/sba.htm

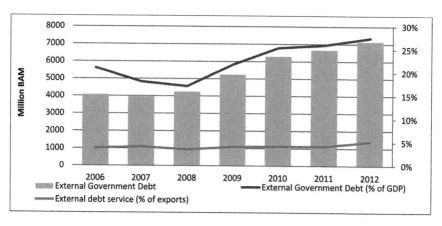

Figure 5.1 General government external debt and debt service 2006–2012
Source: CBBiH 2013.

BiH's Gray Economy

One of the characteristics of the BiH economy worth mentioning is the high participation of the informal sector ("gray economy") in the overall GDP. It is estimated that over a quarter of GDP is generated in this sector. For example, Tomas (2010) reports that in 2008 the estimated proportion of the gray economy was 27 percent of GDP. A positive side of the gray economy in BiH is that it increases the total disposable income of the population; having a partly positive impact on public revenues as well (for example, through additional VAT coming from more consumer spending). On the other side, it decreases expected total public revenue collection, putting pressure on the public sector to impose higher taxes on the formal sector than would otherwise be necessary. Simply said, the unpaid taxes are *de facto* an external (opportunity) cost paid by the formal sector in terms of higher taxation. In addition, the gray economy is very often linked with issues such as corruption, unfair competition and lower formal institutional efficiency.

Some institutional economists identify the gray economy and/or corruption as a possible way of measuring institutional (in)efficiency (for example Mauro 1995; Lane and Rohner 2004); that is, they consider the level of corruption/gray economy as a measure of the failure of society's formal institutions (Yeager 1999). The persistence of corruption and informal economy in a society means that the "rules of the game" are not respected; hence transaction costs are higher. In such situations, when informal economic activities take a large proportion in the market, as is the case in BiH, the informal institutional patterns are more likely to emerge and be an important part of the overall institutional environment. In the context of BiH, it seems that there is a consistent story, because some authors identify the presence and importance of informal institutional settings in the everyday life of BiH citizens and the business sector as well (for example, Efendić 2010; Efendić,

Mickiewicz and Rebmann 2014). Apparently, informal economic activities and informal institutions are nothing but substitutes for the lack of formal economic opportunities (job creation by the formal market) and lack of formal institutional efficiency (primarily caused by inefficient implementation mechanisms in different institutional fields).

The Impact of Political Fragmentation

Moreover, BiH is facing even more obstacles considering its small market, weak economic potential, fragmented political structure and lack of a single economic space. From the standpoint of universal criteria and principles of regionalization, the existing fragmented and asymmetric structure today shows the complexities, overlapping jurisdictions, costs and other deficiencies of the existing governmental structure (Hadžiahmetović 2011). One result is a lack of driving developmental mechanisms, an undeveloped state-wide infrastructure and a weak or non-existent network of developed urban centers. Even a shallow assessment of development effects indicates that the continued absence of a single economic space in BiH (meaning the absence of different sorts of barriers for economic activities within the country) and the resulting economic logic causes stagnation in terms of economic development, potential income increases, employment, investments, standard of living, competitiveness and integration in the internal EU market (Ibid.). The main problem related to the absence of a single economic space is primarily linked to the unique institutional structure of BiH in which the main economic policies (for example, industrial policy, agriculture, social policy, direct taxation) are located squarely at the entity levels—with little to no state level harmonization, strategy or coordination— which leads to different solutions, approaches, strategies, and regulations in the key areas relevant for the functioning of a single economic space. For example, the free movement of capital is noted by the EC (2012) as an area without any progress over the last years.

BiH is a unique example of over-institutionalization that has resulted in a lack of development. The dysfunctional structure, together with the gray economy, results in an inadequate system that prevents the dynamic implementation of crucial structural reforms in BiH. This kind of "a system without a system" is itself an obstacle to any serious economic progress, perpetuating the gray economy, crime and corruption. It specifically demonstrates and manifests the well-known *free rider problem*, implying that what has to be done for the social good will be done by someone else. A system which does not imply clear rules—subordination, coordination, responsibility, sanctions for non-performance—is a sum of different types of autism—political, entity, national; all closed systems which act on their own. Thanks to the engagement of the international community, primarily of the OHR and IMF (Hadžiahmetović 2011), results were achieved regarding basic economic stability (primarily monetary stability with the Currency Board arrangement—Central Bank BiH), but the issue of real economic and fiscal sustainability is now in question. In addition, it must be noted that the transformation from a socialist economy to a donor economy, to the current "waiting economy," has caused fatigue among the bulk of BiH society not personally profiting from this dysfunction. The root causes of these problems are not in the sphere of economy nor the culture, but in the political system.[7] The public sphere—which should be an important sphere for action—is so fragmented that is it unable to support the development of an economy that could reintegrate BiH. This too is a reflection of the political structure and its built-in dysfunction (Ibid.).

As a result, BiH still has a slower pace of economic activity than the other transition countries of Central and Eastern Europe. According to the European Bank for Reconstruction and Development (EBRD) indicators which measure structural and institutional performances, BiH is below both the average of 29 transition countries and the average of South East European countries, in particular the EU's transitional countries. The value of this aggregated index suggests that BiH has achieved just above 60 percent of its institutional progress which would equalize it with the more developed European market economies (Efendić;, Pugh and Adnett 2011).). In addition, the economic growth achieved by this transition country suggests that both processes, i.e., institutional and economic convergence towards EU standards, might take much more time than would be necessary if BiH was a more functional country.

BiH—Contemporary Macroeconomic Performance

After 2000, the economic progress of BiH was characterized by rather stable growth rates, averaging approximately 5 percent annually. Such growth rates, although not negligible for BiH, were insufficient, taking into account the economic potentials available in the country but not used, and the fact that the EU integration process should lead to faster economic progress. Unfortunately, even this growth was stopped in 2009 as a consequence of the global economic crisis.

The concerns regarding the sustainability of this economic growth were heightened by the domestic demand for rapid credit growth, as well as demands for salary increases, and the worsening fiscal position became very clear in 2009 when economic growth in BiH dropped for the first time in the post-Dayton period. The economic downturn was mainly caused by a drop in private domestic consumption, a decrease in private investments and a contraction of external demand. Consequently, trade volumes decreased drastically, and construction activity and industrial production also decreased, further contributing to a rise in the already high unemployment (EC 2010). However, the drop was mostly due to a 3.3 percent decrease in industrial production (Figure 5.3), which contributes around 20 percent to GDP (EC, 2010). This was itself caused by a 4.5 percent decrease of activity in the processing industry, as well as decreased export demand,

---

7   See Valery Perry's contribution in this volume.

foreign investment and remittances (CBBiH 2013). There was no significant recovery of GDP in 2010–2011; positive growth was achieved mostly as a result of recovery of the export markets. In 2012, the first available data again suggests negative growth and further problems for BiH's economic development prospects (Figure 5.2).

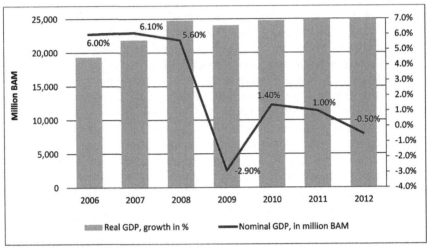

Figure 5.2 Nominal GDP in BAM and annual GDP growth in percentages
Source: CBBiH 2013.

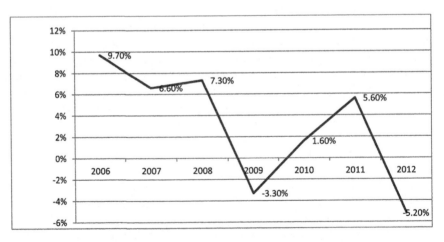

Figure 5.3 Growth of industrial production in percentages
Source: CBBiH, 2013.

Industrial production is closely linked to GDP, and registered a serious 5.2 percent drop in 2012, suggesting a decrease of all economic activity. One of the reasons for this negative growth rate is the weak external environment (EC 2012), including recession in the region (Serbia and Croatia) as well as broader recessionary tendencies in the Eurozone (Central Bank BiH 2013). However, internal political dysfunction—and the impact on new business development and non-investor confidence—cannot be ignored.

Unemployment

In a country with unreliable statistics and a non-functioning labor market characterized by a significant gray economy, one of the key macro-economic indicators—the unemployment rate—is a subject of estimation at best. It is also, however, an area of significant concern among analysts of the BiH economy. The complex administrative structure and fragmented labor market, inadequate institutions and a weak, patchwork regulatory framework are crucial barriers for the efficient functioning of the labor market in BiH. Additionally, it is characterized by significant structural rigidity—a low rate of labor force participation, significant deficiencies and discrepancy of skills, low salary flexibility, a high tax burden on the labor force and an increasing percentage of employment in the informal sector.

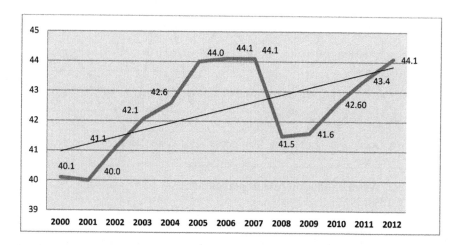

Figure 5.4 Unemployment rate, percentage of the labor force (official data)
Source: DEP BiH, 2013.

The officially registered unemployment rate has reached 44 percent on more than one occasion, while the Labour Force Survey (which uses a more strict definition of unemployment) reports that in 2012 the unemployment rate stood at around 28 percent (CBBiH 2013). No matter which indicator is viewed as more reliable, it is still clear that unemployment remains one of the biggest macroeconomic challenges for the country. The difference between the two reported unemployment rates is also an indication of the existence of a fairly large informal labor market and significant structural rigidities (EC, 2012), and, hence, the existence of the informal economy.

The Role of the Central Bank

As envisaged by the DPA, the Central Bank has been functioning as a Currency Board since 1998, when the common currency was put in place. The domestic currency (*Konvertibilna marka, BAM*) is covered by foreign exchange reserves, primarily the Euro. This mechanism has supported monetary stability in the economy since its introduction (see Figure 5.5).

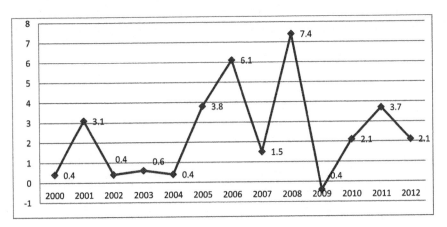

Figure 5.5 Annual inflation rate in percentages
Source: CBBiH, 2013.

The unique positioning of the Central Bank as a Currency Board narrows its function, making it more of a technical-operational mechanism than an institution which creatively acts in the sphere of monetary policy. No crediting of either the government or banks by the Central Bank is allowed; hence, discretionary monetary policy is very limited, while market forces to a large extent determine the monetary base (Gedeon 2010). Still, there is some possibility to use a part of the available foreign exchange reserves in a slightly more flexible way (as "a lender of the last resort"). However, a lack of general political consensus can be identified as the main reason why this possibility has not been used in practice. Still, the holdings of the CBBiH must be fully covered by convertible currency. The Euro (and before it the German Mark) was chosen as a "monetary anchor" for which the foreign exchange rate is firmly pegged, and, because of this, the exchange rate maintains its stability. There are however, consequences. Being pegged to the Euro during the worst points of the economic crisis in the Eurozone put the Currency Board under great strain (Gedeon 2010) caused by several (potential) problems: decreasing exports to the Eurozone; withdrawal of Euro deposits from the banking system to move them to another currency, and potential financial problems with foreign banks in BiH coming from the Eurozone. All these factors could consequently decrease foreign (Euro) reserves in the CBBiH making this arrangement more fragile; something which to date has fortunately not happened. To sum up, a fully fixed relationship between the domestic currency and the Euro brings benefits if the Eurozone is experiencing a desirable economic performance, as well as potential losses if the Eurozone is experiencing economic problems. In spite of this reality, it is hard to imagine what would have happened with the BiH currency if it had not been pegged to the Euro.

The Fiscal Environment

The situation with the fiscal deficits in the past decade has been characterized by significant improvement until the beginning of the economic crisis in BiH (2009), although the share of the public sector in the country's GDP was conspicuously high (close to 50 percent). After immediate post-war fiscal deficits, from 2001 BiH was achieving significant fiscal consolidations resulting in a surplus in 2003; hence, no problems in public sector financing. In addition, the indirect taxation reforms (the state-wide value added tax was introduced in 2006) marked a significant short-term revenue increase (from around 41 percent to 45 percent of GDP) (CBBiH, 2010) providing an additional possibility for an increase in government expenditures, which happened over the next three years (from 42 percent in 2006 to 47.6 percent in 2009) (CBBiH 2013). However, these optimistic expectations together with continued swelling of the public sector, caused fiscal imbalances in 2007 and resulted in deficits from 2008 onwards. As explained earlier, the IMF support was used to overcome these fiscal problems.

External Sector of the BiH economy

An analysis of the balance of payments since 2000 is a subject of specific concern with regard to the sustainability of economic growth. The growing current account deficits (exchange of goods and services) were a key characteristic until the economic crisis (see Figure 5.6), which provoked severe deficits of trade and current accounts. The reflection of the crisis was twofold—through the foreign trade account (trade in goods) and private transfers on one side, and the sudden interruption of inflows of funds on the other.

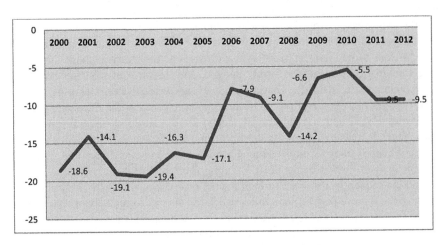

Figure 5.6 Current account balance, percentage of GDP
Source: CBBiH, 2013.

The data presented on the current account deficit implies that during the last 10 years, a more significant *reduction* of the deficit was registered at the time of the global economic downturn (2009–2010). The reason for that is not the result of a significant increase of exports of goods and services from BiH. Simply, the total volume of exchange was reduced over the period of the crisis (in particular in 2009), but a larger decrease was related to BiH import (domestic demand) rather than export (foreign demand). However, a little promising sign is that the current account deficit does not show an increasing trend over the last few years (according to the first estimate for 2013, it has decreased even further). The neighboring countries in the region also registered current account deficits, and in 2012 BiH's current account deficit as a percentage of GDP was higher than in Croatia and Macedonia, similar to Serbia's and smaller than in Montenegro and Albania (Central Bank BiH, 2012).

From 2000 until the beginning of the economic crisis in BiH in 2009, the country achieved significant progress in foreign trade, albeit from a low starting point. Being a small transition economy, the total volume of trade accounted for more than 90 percent of the total GDP, suggesting that BiH is a very open economy. Compared to the years just after the war, exports doubled and imports halved, but the real values of the exports and imports resulted in an overall increase in trade. The five most important trade partners of BiH include Croatia, Germany, Serbia, Italy and Slovenia which together account for more than 50 percent of total trade. The highest level of import comes from Croatia and Serbia, while the highest value of export goes to Germany and Croatia (Spoljnotrgovinska komora BiH, 2013). BiH's biggest trade partner in terms of the total volume of trade (import plus export of goods) is Croatia (17 percent), with Serbia coming in second (10 percent), and Slovenia third (9 percent) (Spoljnotrgovinska komora BiH, 2013a).

The slight shift in foreign trade in favor of regional countries occurred as a result of trade liberalization policies that started in the first years of this century. Consequently, over the last few years the main trading partner of BiH is the EU (over 50 percent of the total volume of trade) and CEFTA countries[8] (over 30 percent) (Spoljnotrgovinska komora BiH, 2013; 2013a). Croatia's membership in the EU since 2013 will therefore have a significant impact on BiH's foreign trade, both in relation to its trade with CEFTA and with the EU.

Remittances

The estimated number of the BiH population settled abroad (in 51 host countries) is about 2 million or 51 percent compared to BiH resident population (MHRRBiH, 2014). This relative size of the BiH diaspora (percentage) is the largest among the former Yugoslavia republics and the highest among developing countries of Europe. The BiH diaspora remains an important source of financial capital for BiH—it sends remittances of more than 10 percent of GDP annually. It is important to understand that foreign remittances to BiH residents from other countries constitute a substantial portion of income, and have a snowball effect on national consumption and broader economic activity. The economic crisis has had a real impact on this source of revenue in BiH, particularly concerning remittances coming from BiH citizens living in Western Europe and the USA. In 2009–2010 there was a significant decline of such inflows (around 30 percent in comparison to 2008), and this went hand in hand with the decline of foreign trade flows. Since 2010 and the slow recovery of the global economy, the negative trend of inflow of remittances ended, although without any significant positive changes in the last three years (2010–2012) (see Figure 5.7).

In 2011 the remittances to BiH were around 13 percent of GDP (WB 2011), which ranks BiH sixth among the 20 leading remittance-receiving countries (as a percentage of GDP) in the world. In comparison with all other countries, BiH had the most significant growth rate of remittances from 1995 until 2004 (IOM 2007). Over $1 billion is mainly sent by money transfer, and the remaining amount is related to other transactions, mostly pensions earned by BiH citizens who had previously worked abroad. The Central Bank of BiH can monitor only the cash flow which comes through bank accounts, so the exact cash flow cannot be known because of direct transfers or cash payments (but might be significantly higher). Having in mind that the Central Bank BiH functions as a Currency Board (and can increase the money supply only if it acquires new Euros or other foreign currency, hence, a net inflow of Euro) and that BiH has a continuously high current account deficit (because of a high import of goods and services, hence, a net Euro outflow), these remittances are an important anchor for the stability and sustainability of the

---

8   Central European Free Trade Agreement, signed in 2006 by a number of non-Schengen and non-EU countries in South East Europe.

domestic currency (foreign currency inflow), and in turn the functioning of the country's economy.

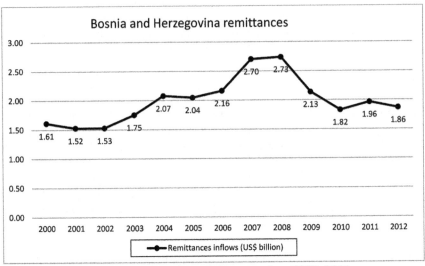

Figure 5.7 Remittances in Bosnia and Herzegovina, 2000–2011
Source: World Bank, 2013.

Foreign Investment

Looking back over the last decade, BiH did not record significant foreign direct investment inflow (see Figure 5.8). However, since 2000 net capital inflows have grown at a higher rate than the current account deficit, which enabled the growth of foreign exchange reserves in the Central Bank. Higher foreign direct investments were recorded in 2007, but primarily as a result of the change of the ownership structure in some existing companies (through privatization) rather than through investment into new capacities. Having no possibility to issue new currency without matching Euro reserves, foreign capital inflow is a mechanism which could increase higher bank reserves, making the Currency Board arrangement more stable.

In 2009, registered net foreign direct investment inflows (1.5 percent of GDP) were substantially smaller than the previous year (5.4 percent of GDP), and there was an additional decrease in investment in 2010 (1.4 percent of GDP). The key reasons for this trend might be related to a slow economic recovery in BiH, and high budget deficits, including the effects of global and Eurozone crises. A slightly better inflow was registered in 2011 (2.1 percent of GDP), which partly explains the slightly higher economic growth recorded in this particular year (in comparison to 2010). In 2012 foreign investment increased by a substantial 86 percent in comparison to the previous year, which is now close to the levels before the crisis, being 3.8 percent of GDP (Central Bank BiH 2013). This increase was registered in the non-financial sectors of the economy, and primarily in the metal and trade industries. Also, the banking sector received close to 30 percent of these investments (Central Bank BiH 2013). However, this was not enough to support positive GDP growth.

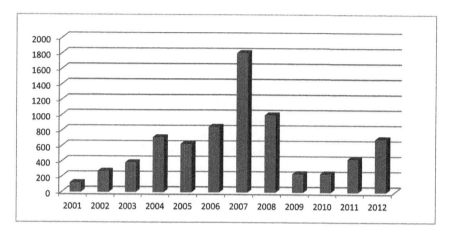

Figure 5.8 Foreign direct investment inflow, million $
Source: World Bank BiH, 2013; CBBiH, 2013.

Integration into the EU

An inseparable part of any analysis of the BiH environment and economy is its "European" path. The relations between the EU and BiH began with the international recognition of BiH by the countries of the Community. After the DPA was signed the EU contributed to the implementation of peace and the development of governing structures. The first post-war challenge—post-war reconstruction—was supported by the Framework Agreement on Usage of Funds for BiH concerning the Country Operational Programme (COP), and BiH thereby officially became a beneficiary of the EU's PHARE program (1996). When in 1998 the program orientation shifted towards preparation of the country for EU accession, there was a need for a new modality of relations with the EU. A Consultative Task Force (CTF) between BiH and the EU was established in 1998 with a basic function—jointly working on adjusting BiH legislation with the EU requirements, which was the first arrangement of this type with a country which was not even a candidate for EU membership (Hadžiahmetović 2011).

The promotion of the Stability Pact for Southeast Europe and the Stabilization and Association Process (SAP) marked the beginning of the next transition phase in BiH. In early 2000 the EU published a "Road Map" noting the conditions to develop a Feasibility Study in line with the Copenhagen criteria. In the same year it announced the continuation of free–trade access to the EU for the majority of BiH products, and adopted a new, specially designed support program for the SAP countries. With the aim of implementing the initiative of the Stability Pact on Regional Cooperation, BiH approached trade liberalization in the region—first through a network of bilateral free trade agreements (until 2002), and then a single multilateral trade agreement—the Central-European Free Trade Agreement (CEFTA) in 2006. As a participant of the Athens Process, BiH also signed the Energy Community Treaty for Southeast Europe (2005), whereby BiH together with other countries in the region assumed an obligation to establish a regional energy market and its integration into the internal market of the EU.

The beginning of activities related to the Feasibility Study in 2003, a precondition for opening negotiations on a Stabilization and Association Agreement (SAA), resulted in the EU's general assessment of economic conditions of BiH, as it confirmed that BiH was not yet firmly on the path towards a self-sustaining economy, and needed to accelerate reforms (EC 2005). It was emphasized that, although BiH managed to maintain macroeconomic stability, slow economic growth, high unemployment, a fragmented internal market, the troublesome situation in the area of public finance and public sector, slow privatization, and other problems, together contributed to the fact that BiH is far from being a self-sustainable system assured of long term stability. In spite of such assessments, the EC concluded negotiations with BiH and signed the SAA in mid-2008. The SAA has been ratified by all EU Member States but has not yet (2013) entered into force. As support to the Stabilization and Association Process generally, the EU approved a specific pre-accession financial instrument—Instrument for Pre-accession (IPA) funding—with five components, of which two are available to BiH (Component I: Transition Assistance and Institution Building, and Component II: Cross-Border Co-operation). From 2007–2009 the IPA (Components I and II) funding available to BiH totaled 266 million Euro, and for the period 2010–2013 it stood at 434 million Euro. By the end of 2011 BiH used around 50 percent of these available funds (Hasanagić et al., 2012). BiH was unable to absorb more, due to political obstruction, poorly functioning institutions and a lack of a strategy to use the funds. Although BiH sees its future in the EU, there is still little domestic consensus on how to achieve the main EU related reform priorities (EC 2011). Primarily due to the political environment the overall pace of reforms remains uneven (EC 2012).

The European Commission in its 2012 annual progress report reminds that the complicated decision-making process in BiH has a negative effect on structural reforms as well as on BiH's capacity to make better progress towards EU membership. Although EU accession should be viewed by BiH policymakers and politicians as a potential source of economic development, BiH's ability to cope with competitive pressures and market forces within the Union will be a clear challenge. Croatia's entrance into the EU will be a test with lessons for the other countries in the region.

Conclusion

BiH's macroeconomic performance in the post-war period cannot be assessed as satisfactory. In spite of massive external financial support, aid, and incentives, the country's economy remains fragile. The global financial crisis certainly affected BiH's growth trajectory; however, the country's political impasse and continuing political bickering illustrates that there is little will among decision-makers to make the difficult decisions needed to ensure a roadmap for growth.

There are many reasons for this non-optimal macroeconomic performance: a complex and inefficient government structure, multiple and at times overlapping levels of authority, a lack of institutional coordination and a limited economic base, together provide a weak framework for the country's economic future, and suggest a need for urgent political and economic restructuring. BiH is a unique example of over-institutionalization that yields to formal institutional inefficiency, higher transaction costs in the market and more reliance on informal institutions. Consequently, informal economic activities are unusually high, limiting the functioning of the official labor market, decreasing public revenues, and making overall macroeconomic performance even worse.

The problem of over-institutionalization also generates unsustainable government expenditures. Consequently, the fragility of the public sector is often identified by the IMF and others as an obstacle to financial stability and growth. Unfortunately, a short-term increase in government debts will lead policy makers to pursue public policies aiming to fulfil liabilities towards international financial institutions, rather than focusing on internal sources of economic growth and development.

BiH's stated intention to become a full member of the EU is recognized as an important domestic strategy that should bring internal benefits, as well as support a number of necessary institutional reforms. However, lip-service to EU membership has not been matched by real policy change or economic development strategies for the state as a whole. Only if conditions for successful reforms are provided (particularly through a politically normalized environment), will the EU integration process work in the medium—to long-term. However, the EU integration and accession process requires political will and functional institutions at all levels. Seeking support and access to external loans without meaningful reforms will provide only short-term solutions and long-term challenges for the country and its people.

Bibliography

Agency for Statistics BiH (2012) *National Accounts*, Sarajevo: Agency for Statistics BiH.

Anđelić, N. (2003) *Bosnia-Herzegovina: The End of Legacy*, London: Frank Cass Publishers.

Central Bank of Bosnia and Herzegovina (CBBiH) (2013) *Annual Report 2012*, Sarajevo: CBBiH.

Directorate for Economic Planning BIH (DEP BiH) (2013) *BiH Annual Report 2012*, Sarajevo: DEP BiH.

Efendić, A. (2003) Specifics of the Transition Process in BiH—Framework of Development Strategy for BiH, *BERG Working Paper Series on Government and Growth*, No. 43, Bamberg: Bamberg University, pp. 111–118.

———. (2010) *Institutions and Economic Performance in Transition Countries—With Special Reference to Bosnia and Herzegovina*, Saarbrücken: Lambert Academic Publishing.

Efendić, A., Babic, B. and Rebmann, A. (2001) *Diaspora and Development – Bosnia and Herzegovina*, Sarajevo: Embassy of Switzerland in Bosnia and Herzegovina.

Efendić, A., Mickiewicz, T. and Rebmann, A. (2014) Growth aspirations and social capital: young firms in a post-conflict environment. *International Small Business Journal*, doi: 10.1177/0266242613516987

Efendić, A. and Pugh, G. (2015) Institutional effects on economic performance in transition: a dynamic panel analysis, *Acta Oeconomica* (forthcoming)

Efendić, A., Pugh, G. and Adnett, N. (2011) Confidence in formal institutions and reliance on informal institutions in BiH: an empirical investigation using survey data *Economics of Transition*, 19(3), pp. 521–540.

European Commission (EC) (2010) *Bosnia and Herzegovina 2010 Progress Report*, Brussels: EC.

———. (2011) *Bosnia and Herzegovina 2011 Progress Report*, Brussels: EC.

———. (2012) *Bosnia and Herzegovina 2012 Progress Report*, Brussels: EC.

European Commission and World Bank (EC/WB) (1999) *Bosnia and Herzegovina, 1996–1998 Lessons and Accomplishments: Review of the Priority Reconstruction and Recovery Program and Looking Ahead Towards Sustainable Economic Development.* A report prepared for the May 1999 donors conference co-hosted by the European Commission and the World Bank.

Gedeon, S.J. (2010) The political economy of currency board: case of Bosnia and Herzegovina, *South-East European Journal*, November 2010, 5-2, pp. 19–32.

Hadžiahmetović, A. (2011) *Ekonomija Evropske Unije*, Sarajevo: University Press.

Hasanagić, E., Mačkić, V., Mujarić, M., Novaković, M., Papac, N., Rapaić, S., Tešić, J., Turuk, M., Zaimović, A. and Zlatković, M. (2012) *Savremeni Institucionalni i Ekonomski Izazovi BiH na Putu EU Integracija: Korišćenje Predpristupnih Fondova EU u Funkciji Generisanja Endogenog Rasta u Kontekstu Iskustava Hrvatske i Srbije*, Sarajevo: Ekonomski fakultet u Sarajevu.

International Monetary Fund BiH (IMF BiH) (2012) *Stand-by Arrangment with Bosnia and Herzegovina*, IMF BiH, Sarajevo.

International Monetary Fund BiIH (MF BiH) (2013) data taken from: http://www.imf.org/external/country/BIH/rr/index.htm [Accessed November 2013].

International Organization for Migration (2007) (IOM 2007) *Bosnia and Herzegovina Migration profile*. Ljubljana: IOM and Republic of Slovenia Ministry of Interior.

Lampe, J.R. (2000) *Yugoslavia as History: Twice There Was a Country*, Cambridge: Cambridge University Press.

Lane, Jan-Erik and Rohner, D. (2004) Institution Building and Spillovers, *Swiss Political Science Review*, Issue 10, No. 1, pp. 77–90.

Mauro, P. (1995) Corruption and growth, *The Quarterly Journal of Economics*, August 1995, pp. 681–712.

Ministry for Human Rights and Refugees of Bosnia and Herzegovina (MHRRBiH) (2014). *Review of the BiH Diaspora (Pregled stanja bosanskohercegovačkog iseljeništva)*, Sarajevo: MHRRBiH.

Mickiewicz, T. (2005) *Economic Transition in Central Europe and the Commonwealth of Independent States*, London and New York: Palgrave Macmillan.

Savezni Zavod Za Statistiku (1991) Statistički *Godišnjak Jugoslavije*, Beograd: Savezni zavod za statistiku,

Spoljnotrgovinska Komora BiH (2013) *Pregled i Analiza Ostvarene Vanjskotrgovinske Razmjene za BiH za Period 01. do 12. Mjeseca 2012/2011*, Sarajevo: Spoljnotrgovinska komora BiH.

——. (2013a) *Pregled i Analiza Ostvarene Vanjskotrgovinske Razmjene za BiH za Period 01. do 06. Mjeseca 2013/2012*, Sarajevo: Spoljnotrgovinska komora BiH.

Tomas, R. (2010) *Crisis and Grey Economy in Bosnia and Herzegovina*, Sarajevo: Friedrich Ebert Stiftung.

World Bank (1996) *Bosnia and Herzegovina Toward Economic Recovery*, Washington, DC: World Bank.

——. (1997) *Bosnia and Herzegovina From Recovery to Sustainable Growth*, Washington, DC: World Bank

——. (2013) Migration and Remittances Factbook 2013, Washington DC: World Bank World Bank (WB BiH) (2006) *Bosnia and Herzegovina, Addressing Fiscal Challenges and Enhancing Growth Prospects—A Public Expenditure and Institutional Review*, WB Report No. 36156-BiH.

——. (2013) Economic indicators downloaded: www.worldbank.org.ba [Accessed November 2013]

World Bank BiH (WB BiH) (1998) *Bosna i Hercegovina—Projekti Prioritetne Rekonstrukcije*, Sarajevo: WB BiH.

World Bank (2014) The World Bank Data. Available on-line at: www.data. worldbank.org. [Accessed January 2014].

Yagar, T.J. (1999) *Institutions, Transition Economies, and Economic Development*, Oxford and Colorado: Westview Press.

Chapter 6

No Exit: The Decline of the International Administration in Bosnia and Herzegovina[1]

Mateja Peter

Introduction

Over the past two decades international actors displayed increased willingness to get involved in diverse areas of governance in post-conflict states. With this comes a specific set of challenges unseen in earlier peace operations. A broad understanding among key international actors is that the continued stability of a (post-) war state is closely linked to adequate standards in other areas, including the rule of law, policing, and developmental and social issues. Peacebuilding has become intertwined with state-building (cf. Paris and Sisk 2009, pp. 1–2). While assisting in the implementation of a plethora of state-building reforms, one of the most pressing questions becomes at what point the international community should leave the state to its own devices. Exit strategies for state-building operations are an immensely complex and challenging task. Leaving too soon could reverse previous achievements and potentially destabilize the country further. This could require another state-building operation to be established in the future. Conversely, staying too long can create conditions resembling neo-imperialist endeavors. Extended international presence can also undermine the entrenchment of a local political culture oriented towards seeking consensus and resolution of conflict through peaceful means (Peter 2013). Exit strategies therefore need to be at the forefront of discussions about the conduct and purposes of state-building in countries emerging from wars.

Consideration of exit strategies is even more pertinent when it comes to international administrations, which are particular forms of state-building missions, through which some or all of the traditionally sovereign powers are temporarily transferred from the hosting state to an institution representing the international community. Established only in exceptional circumstances, these institutions can

1   The author would like to thank Jonathan Agensky, Lili Cole, Lise Morje Howard, Soeren Keil, Valery Perry, Larry Rossin, Brendan Simms and an anonymous reviewer for their invaluable comments on earlier drafts. Information in the empirical sections of this chapter stem from author's extensive interviews in BiH and with interlocutors in the capitals supporting the operation.

have direct legislative, executive and judicial powers over the governed territory.[2] International administrations form a part of larger international efforts to address post-conflict reconstruction. This is unsurprising as they are established in those territories where the international community deemed a heavy footprint operation was needed. Importantly, these institutions are always multilateral and answerable to an international body. It is primarily in negotiation with this oversight body that their policies are conceived and pursued.

This chapter looks at the exit strategies for the international administration in Bosnia and Herzegovina, an operation that has existed since the end of the war in 1995. The negotiations over the closure of the Office of the High Representative (OHR) offer a prime example of a "non-strategy" for exit in many respects. June 2013 marked the eight-year anniversary of the first time that the Peace Implementation Council (PIC) Steering Board—the body overseeing the OHR—announced its intention to abolish the position of the High Representative (HR). In fact three individuals have held this position since—Christian Schwarz-Schilling (January 2006–July 2007), Miroslav Lajčak (July 2007–March 2009) and Valentin Inzko (March 2009–present). In this chapter the changes in the international strategy towards BiH that influenced the hoped-for closure of the OHR are examined. The chapter looks in particular at the disagreements among international actors over closure of the mission and the role the High Representatives played in setting the direction of international policy while attempting to close the mission.

The chapter has four parts. The first section outlines the position of the OHR within local and international politics in BiH. The second section includes a discussion of how the HR was empowered beyond the original intentions at the Dayton peace conference and how that influenced the exit strategy. Section three discusses the increasing divisions in the international community over how and when to terminate the international administration. In section four the role and positions of individual High Representatives that served during this period of increasing division is explored. This chapter concludes with insights that the Bosnian experience holds for planning and closing of international civilian presences elsewhere.

Bosnia and Herzegovina under International Administration

The Dayton Peace Agreement[3] that ended the Bosnian War (1992–1995) was negotiated in the midst of an ongoing violent conflict. It therefore envisaged a highly complex web of domestic institutions, attempting to ensure the participation of all

---

2   For more on international administrations see Caplan (2005) and Chesterman (2005).

3   The General Framework Agreement for Peace (GFAP, or DPA) in Bosnia and Herzegovina, initialled in Dayton, Ohio on 21 November 1995, signed in Paris on 14 December 1995.

three main ethnic groups involved in the conflict—Bosniaks, Croats and Serbs. This kind of a starting point is not unusual in contemporary conflicts that as a rule end in brokered agreements, not military victories. The Dayton Accords detailed a complex multi-level political structure at state, entity and cantonal levels.[4] Linking the sub-national units was a weak state-level structure with a heavily circumscribed list of responsibilities, with most of the powers remaining at the entity and cantonal levels.[5] With the prospect of being faced with implementation of a complex peace agreement in a highly divided society, the international community inserted itself as an intermediary and a guarantor. The implementation of the military side of the peace agreement was organized under a NATO-led Implementation Force (IFOR) mission. In contrast, international civilian efforts were dispersed among a large number of organizations (cf. Kostakos 1998).

The key among the civilian organizations is the OHR, an institution that serves as the international administration of BiH. This ad hoc institution was charged through Annex 10 of the DPA with the dual task of coordinating international civilian peace implementation activities and facilitating local parties' efforts by engaging in the resolution of any difficulties arising in connection with civilian implementation of the agreement.[6] Due to the United States (US) insistence at Dayton, the local role of the High Representative was initially limited to mediation among the previously warring parties. The US wanted a limited involvement and the civilian effort was to be wound down after the elections in September 1996. At the time, there was a broad concern inside the US administration that a more expansive role for the key civilian implementation institution would lead to mission creep (Daalder 2000, p. 157, Holbrooke 1999, p. 207); a prospect US President Bill Clinton particularly wanted to avoid as he faced his own re-election in autumn 1996.

Once the operation was on the ground and as the problems with implementation of the civilian sections of the GFAP were increasing, the Peace Implementation Council (PIC)[7] agreed to increased powers and responsibilities for the OHR. The so-called Bonn powers, accorded to the High Representative in 1997, allowed this institution to pass binding interim legislation and dismiss officials deemed as obstructing the peace process.[8] Over the years the High Representatives have used these powers to enforce decisions relating to state symbols, return of refugees, rule of law, privatization, defense reform and many other key areas. They have also

---

4   For more details on the domestic arrangements see Belloni (2007), Bose (2002) and Keil (2013).

5   Dayton Peace Agreement, Annex 4, Art. III.

6   Dayton Peace Agreement, Annex 10, Art. I and II.

7   The PIC Steering Board serves as the oversight body and offers political guidance to the High Representative. It consists of Canada, France, Germany, Italy, Japan, Russia, United Kingdom, United States, and the Presidency of the European Union, the European Commission and Turkey.

8   PIC Conclusions, Bonn, December 10, 1997, Part XI, Art. 2.

dismissed public officials ranging from mayors, heads of state-run companies, judges, members of parliament, ministers and even a member of the state-level presidency.[9] Some of these decisions proved very controversial with some commentators objecting to the lack of democratic accountability and the absence of an appeals process (for example, Knaus and Martin 2003). With such expansive roles the OHR has become part of the domestic politics in BiH, not only acting as a corrective mechanism for breaches of the peace process but also developing the reform agenda for the country.

The vast roles of the international community in the state-building process in BiH raise considerable concerns about the possibility of installing democracy through undemocratic means. They open questions on whether a state can even be called sovereign under these circumstances and what the implications of this lack of full sovereignty could be. By drawing parallels between contemporary international administrations and imperial experiences of colonial administration more critical authors point out that external imposition stifles domestic political processes and leads to the dependence of the territory on external powers (Chandler 2000; Knaus and Martin 2003). In BiH, some key international actors involved in the oversight of the operation, in particular Russia, have been uncomfortable with the use of enforcement measures from the beginning. Nevertheless, for a long time there existed a broad consensus that Bosnia was better off being under the tutelage of an international institution. The disagreements on what should be the scope of the intervention of the High Representative and what should be the means to achieve the reform started increasing towards the end of Paddy Ashdown's mandate (2002–2006). It is during this time that the international community began seriously discussing the question of exiting the country.

The Changing Exit Strategy

After initial US reluctance had subsided, all key international players supported a strong civilian presence in BiH. This included both a reinforced position of the OHR and considerable powers and financial contributions for other civilian agencies. Because such an expansive mission had not been planned from the beginning, its objectives and goals developed ad hoc, as a response to problems encountered on the ground. This has had implications for the planning of extraction of the mission itself and for the role the OHR has played in this process.

Early on in the process and in response to the resistance of the nationalist parties to cooperate in the state-level institutions, the PIC Steering Board prolonged the mandate of the HR for an additional two-year period.[10] This was intended to consolidate the GFAP by assisting parties in the adoption of a legislative basis for

---

9   For a full list of decisions see http://www.ohr.int/decisions/archive.asp. [Accessed April 11, 2015].

10   PIC Steering Board Conclusions, Paris, November 14, 1996.

the country to operate. The priorities of this consolidation period were phrased as broad objectives with very few firm benchmarks for the measurement of success of the country and the closure of the OHR. They covered everything from refugee return to market economy and education. This was a very ambitious agenda and its implementation in the planned two-year period would have required a full and unconditional cooperation of local parties from the beginning; something unlikely to happen considering tumultuous relations on the ground.

Soon after, the international community acknowledged that the agenda would not be fulfilled during the prescribed time. At a review conference in Bonn in December 1997, the PIC not only awarded the HR enforcement powers to implement this agenda but also granted itself and the HR an indefinite mandate. After the introduction of these extensions the local implementers at the OHR pursued an expansive agenda developed for the consolidation period. This was done by both reacting to clear breaches of the peace agreement and developing proposals local parties were to adopt.[11] When the local parties failed to pass required measures and legislation, the High Representatives could impose them with the Bonn powers.

By the end of the 1990s, international attention had started shifting away from BiH. The "ownership principle" became the guiding strategy for the exit of the international presence. The idea behind this principle was that the people of BiH were becoming the owners of their progress in peace implementation and the eventual entry of BiH into European institutions (Petritsch 2001, pp. 212–213). Local institutions were expected to gradually take over responsibilities under the control of international agencies. In parallel, the rhetoric of exit intensified as a number of responsibilities were reassigned to local actors. For example, the Election Code of 2001 transferred the conduct of elections from the Organization for Security and Co-operation in Europe (OSCE) to a BiH Central Election Commission. However, despite the scaling down of international civilian presence, the OHR remained very hands on, both dismissing obstructionist officials and guiding the direction of reforms.

From 2000 on the termination of the state-building operation has been explicitly tied to progress in negotiations with Euro-Atlantic organizations, in particular, the European Union (EU) and the North Atlantic Treaty Organization (NATO). The PIC and the OHR increasingly referred to EU strategies for engagement with Bosnia as benchmarks for success. This approach has been criticized as detraction from the original goals of the civilian peace implementation as envisaged at Dayton, allowing for mission creep (Chandler 2006). The overlap of the EU accession path and the Dayton state-building endeavors became most visible through the double-hatting of the High Representative as the European Union Special Representative

---

11   Although designed as a reactive mechanism, the international administration in Bosnia mixes both reactive and proactive responses to governance problems. For a distinction between reactive and proactive international administrations see Wilde (2001, pp. 600–602).

(EUSR) in 2002. While primarily in charge of the civilian implementation efforts as the HR, the same person also served as the EU's special envoy to the country. The expectation was that there would be a natural and soft transition from the High Representative with his enforcement powers, to the EUSR, who would then only hold advisory responsibilities.

A particularly problematic aspect of linking the exit strategy for the international administration to progress in Euro-Atlantic integration has been not determining what stage of accession talks would be sufficient for exit. The PIC and EU documents from 2000 refer to conditions required to prepare the EU Feasibility Study.[12] When these conditions were met and the Feasibility Study was published in 2003, the PIC and EU focused on Bosnia meeting the conditions for the next stage, that is, the start of negotiations on the Stabilization and Association Agreement (SAA). In 2005, for the first time, the PIC Steering Board clearly expressed its intention to close down the OHR and issued a recommendation that the position of the HR be replaced by an EU Special Representative. One indicator for BiH's readiness would be the initiation of SAA negotiations with the EU.[13]

After BiH started negotiations with the EU in late 2005, the PIC Steering Board announced its plan to abolish the OHR in June 2007.[14] Local actors were expected to quickly deliver on the remaining EU conditions so that the OHR could close down. By the end of 2006 many planned reforms were still unfinished. Primarily, there had been virtually no progress on police reform, one of the key areas of concern for the EU and the PIC Steering Board.[15] The failure of the April Package of constitutional reforms in mid-2006 was also an area of concern.[16] Due to substantial delays in negotiations on the SAA, the deadline for closure of the OHR was extended for a further year.[17]

By early 2008 the PIC Steering Board abolished its time-driven exit strategy. Instead—in line with the proposals prepared by the OHR— it formulated five objectives and two conditions that would need to be fulfilled prior to the transition (the so-called 5+2 strategy).[18] The five objectives were: apportionment of property between state and other levels of government, resolution of defense property, and completion of the Brčko final award, fiscal sustainability and entrenchment of the rule of law. The two conditions were the signing of the SAA and a positive assessment of the situation in BiH by the PIC Steering Board—based on full compliance with the GFAP. While all the objectives had clearly defined benchmarks and the signing of the SAA could be ascertained, the assessment of compliance or non-compliance with the Dayton Accords remained based on

12   PIC Declaration, Brussels, May 24, 2000.
13   PIC Steering Board Communiqué, Sarajevo, June 24, 2005.
14   PIC Steering Board Communiqué, Sarajevo, June 23, 2006.
15   PIC Steering Board Communiqué, Sarajevo, October 20, 2006.
16   On this issue see Valery Perry's contribution in this volume.
17   PIC Steering Board Communiqué, Sarajevo, February 27, 2007.
18   PIC Steering Board Declaration, Brussels, February 27, 2007.

the Steering Board's judgment of the existence of rhetoric or action that would threaten or violate the Agreement.

In contrast to previous statements, the February 2008 declaration did not contain a clear timeline for the OHR's closure and extended its mandate until the PIC Steering Board was satisfied that the 5+2 plan was met. Seven years later the OHR is still in place. The standards-based closure plan, instead of a time-driven plan, was introduced primarily so that "locals could not sit the international community out," but it also highlighted the indecisiveness of the international community over its policy on BiH.

Some progress has been made towards all five objectives, with the rule of law and economic sustainability criteria completed. On August 31, 2012, the supervision of Brčko was suspended. In March 2012 the leaders of the six political parties in the state-level governing coalition agreed on principles for distribution of both state and defense property. For now, none of the legal acts foreseen by this agreement have been adopted and a subsequent decision by the BiH Constitutional Court further complicated implementation of this agreement. These two objectives therefore remain unfulfilled. The SAA with the EU was signed on June 16, 2008, making that condition achieved.[19] As there has been progress on the rest of the criteria, the key determinant for the closure of the OHR is and will be the PIC Steering Board's assessment of full compliance with the Dayton Accords. This question of compliance of local parties with the peace agreement has been dividing the international community, further complicating the exit of the OHR.

Two Visions of Bosnia and Herzegovina

Since 2008 the disagreements on whether the High Representative was still needed in BiH started increasing. These debates revolve not only around whether the institution should continue operating, but also over whether the states underwriting the operation are affording the institution sufficient support while it is still in existence. Contentions over its purpose have had an effect not only on the working of the institution but also on the overall policy of the international community in BiH.

The states sitting on the PIC Steering Board and the commentators have fallen into two camps, their positions based on their assessment of the situation in BiH. The first group believes that the era of international administration has passed and that the OHR should be closed down immediately. They argue against the use of enforcement powers. This group believes that BiH is stable and needs to negotiate over the EU candidacy as a fully independent state. Any obstructionism and challenges to the Dayton Accords implementation can be addressed through

---

19   Assessments of fulfilment of criteria for the closure of the OHR are prepared by the OHR itself and can be found in regular reports presented to the UN Security Council. For the latest developments, see OHR (2013).

the EU conditionality process. Most EU countries and the EU Commission share this opinion. Over the years this group has gained more supporters. The second group exhibits more concern over the security situation in BiH and sees the HR and his Office as a necessary guarantor for continued peace and territorial integrity of the country. These actors are worried about the continued lack of functioning state institutions and the secessionist tendencies of one of its entities—the Republika Srpska (RS). The United States and Turkey have been the most vocal representatives of this group on the PIC Steering Board. They are joined by many former peacebuilders in BiH and notably also the OHR personnel itself.

Both sides present valid points. The state-building exercise has been in BiH for almost two decades. Many locals, who are overall supportive of the role the international community has played in their country, now believe the international administration has overstayed its welcome. They want the EU to become the only negotiating external actor when it comes to reforms. Similarly, a number of EU officials show increasing frustration over what they have described as the political interventionism of the OHR into the membership negotiation process of an independent state. They are particularly worried that local politicians have been able to "hide themselves behind the High Representative" and not seek compromises with each other. If Bosnia wants to join Euro-Atlantic institutions, then elected politicians should be able to reach an agreement on the most vital issues. Some have even questioned on whether a country under international tutelage can conduct membership negotiations.

In contrast, the US, Turkey and localized peacebuilders at the OHR have been pointing to the potentially volatile security situation and attacks on the territorial integrity of the state. They argue that continued challenges to the Dayton Accords, mostly by the RS, are a cause for concern warranting the presence of the High Representative. They hold that since this institution was created to uphold the Dayton Agreement, its role has not expired. The president of the RS and other high-level Bosnian Serb politicians have on a number of occasions called for secession of this entity from the rest of the country and a creation of a "union of independent states" (BBC 2009), undermining the principles of the Dayton Accords. This group of more worried international actors is concerned that EU conditionality and membership negotiations, which are conceived as a technical process, cannot adequately address these deeply political issues as they arise.

The hollowing out of the military side of the state-building engagement is often raised (in particular by the US) as an additional concern and a major reason for why the position of the HR has been weakened. The reasoning is that unlike in the past the HR cannot rely on military enforcement of his decisions anymore. But as the military and the civilian part of the state-building endeavor in BiH are run completely separately and the military side (EUFOR Althea) is part of the EU Common Security and Defence Policy, any military enforcement of HR's decisions would be highly unlikely in any case given the growing EU opposition to the use of the Bonn powers.[20]

The different positions of international actors stem from the different experiences these actors have had with and in Bosnia. The localized peacebuilders at the OHR, in particular, see patterns in the behavior of local politicians, worrying that any appeasement just encourages an increasingly radical stance. The EU, on the other hand, negotiates with BiH on discrete issue areas, resolving problems one by one and treating them as largely technical and unconnected. These two approaches are fundamentally opposed, leading to continued disagreements.

Since September 2011 the positions of the High Representative and the EUSR have been de-coupled. The Treaty of Lisbon strengthened the foreign and security dimensions of the EU so a creation of a unified EU post was an institutional necessity.[21] Before September 2011 the EU had had a separate Head of the Delegation of the European Union to BiH, an institution that was now to be merged with the EUSR for the country. The separation of the EUSR from the High Representative therefore came as part of that process.[22] But it was also the unsustainability of the double-hatting that led to the decision to detach the OHR from the EUSR. For almost a decade the HR was reporting both to the PIC and the EU High Representative for Foreign Affairs and Security Policy.[23] With different sets of instructions coming from the two overseers, the confusion had to be resolved. Since the decoupling in 2011, the OHR is focused on meeting its existing obligations and upholding the Dayton Accords. While Bosnia is on its way to meeting the 5+2 conditions some key actors, including the US, remain concerned. The fate of the OHR and the end of the state-building operation are therefore unclear.[24] On the other hand, the EUSR is overseeing the broader reform agenda needed for EU candidacy negotiations. It is gradually taking over as the lead international negotiator in BiH.

The disagreement between the two groups in the international community has had two major implications on the state-building exercise in BiH. Firstly, the indecision on whether the OHR was still needed and open opposition to its actions (also from the side of the EU) has undermined the credibility of this institution. This has allowed local parties to successfully defy its positions. Even though the PIC Steering Board has been issuing statements supporting the HR and his powers after every such act, the role of the institution has changed. Secondly, the

---

20   See Kurt Bassuener's contribution in this volume on wider questions of military and security policy in BiH.

21   Treaty of Lisbon amending the Treaty on European Union and the Treaty establishing the European Community, signed at Lisbon, December 13, 2007, entered into force December 1, 2009.

22   For more on double-hatting in the EU see Peter (2012).

23   Before the Lisbon Treaty reform the post was known as the High Representative for Common Foreign and Security Policy.

24   PIC Steering Board Communiqué, Sarajevo, May 23, 2012.

disagreements over the course of state-building in BiH have led to turf disputes among international agencies, disputes that go beyond coordination problems. The lack of a common vision has meant that the efforts of one institution have been undermined by the actions of the other. To an extent, the decoupling and clearer delineation of responsibilities are attempting to mitigate these problems. While the OHR is now concerned with reacting to attempts to undermine the existing commitments of local parties, the active reform agenda is now under the auspices of the EUSR.

Caught in Between

A prevalent narrative is that the departure of Paddy Ashdown from the post of the High Representative at the beginning of 2006 marked the decline of international administration of Bosnia. Writings on his unique personality and leadership abilities support this narrative (for example, Knaus and Martin 2003, The Economist 2005, Toal 2006). However, it was towards the end of his mandate that the international community also started seriously debating the exit of the OHR. His successors were therefore working under starkly different circumstances. They were pursuing their policies while at the same time trying to close the institution they were heading. Under such circumstances, irresolute responses can lead to a stalemate in progress and thus a continuation of the mission; while interventionist policies can make it more difficult to argue that the situation is ripe for the closure of the international administration. Their mandates were therefore caught between the two visions of Bosnia and the resulting power struggles over which vision should be pursued. This section briefly analyses the tenures of the three High Representatives that followed Ashdown—Christian Schwarz-Schilling, Miroslav Lajčak and Valentin Inzko. It points out some of the differences in their approaches to the job.

Ashdown's successor Christian Schwarz-Schilling (January 2006–July 2007) wholly embraced his role as the High Representative that was supposed to facilitate the closure of the OHR and transition its responsibilities to the EUSR. He saw his role as an advisor and mediator, not an enforcer. In one of the interviews before his assumption of office he notably stressed: "… I will listen to the Bosnian politicians. Then I will try to convince them to come to a decision by themselves and then everybody has to follow up that" (Agovic 2005). Schwarz-Schilling's position was likely informed by his previous experience as a mediator in the Federation of BiH. This hands-off approach was seen both by the new HR and the rest of the international community to be in stark contrast with Ashdown's more assertive policies. His appointment suggested that the international community was coming to a consensus that state-building in Bosnia was on the right track and that once police and constitutional reform—two key remaining reforms—were adopted, the EU could take over the Bosnian state-building project.

Schwarz-Schilling followed a two-pronged approach to his job, focusing on the closure of the OHR and on Bosnia's path towards the EU and NATO. He saw these priorities as interconnected, stressing that if Bosnia wanted to join the two international institutions, it would have to be "fully sovereign" (Schwarz-Schilling 2006). As part of the first priority, Schwarz-Schilling quickly adopted measures to address the status of officials removed from their positions by his predecessors.[25] This "limited amnesty"—which did not include cases related to non-compliance with the International Criminal Tribunal for former Yugoslavia (ICTY)—demonstrated the HR's deeply held conviction that Bosnians themselves should and would make responsible choices on whom they entrust public offices. This conviction can be seen also in his expectation that Bosnian parliamentarians would deliver on the remaining reforms and thus "demonstrate to voters and to the International Community that they [were] serious about improving the lives of citizens and taking BiH further along the path of Euro-Atlantic integration" (OHR 2006). When none of the reforms were adopted in the planned timeline, Schwarz-Schilling's worldview came under serious strain from his underwriters sitting on the PIC Steering Board. The US in particular was exerting substantial pressure on the HR to be more proactive and use his enforcement powers to push for the needed reform (cf. Der Spiegel 2007).

Schwarz-Schilling's unwillingness to compromise on the use of enforcement powers on key reform questions contributed to his mandate not being renewed. His tenure is often seen as facilitating a near deadlock in peace implementation and the delivery of reforms required for Bosnia's SAA with the EU. But it was also a realization of one of the visions of Bosnia that was elaborated upon in the previous section. Schwarz-Schilling strongly resisted the notion that Bosnia was unstable to the point that it needed a heavy-handed approach. This is something that differentiates him from his two successors who were attempting (and struggling) to balance both visions. At the same time, Schwarz-Schilling's poor results record also emboldened actors arguing for a more resolute response.

Partly in response to Schwarz-Schilling's inability to push for implementation of a European agenda in Bosnia, the succeeding High Representative Miroslav Lajčak (July 2007–March 2009) had a strong EU background. His rhetoric and priorities for BiH were clearly couched in EU language. Because BiH had made little progress in the Stabilization and Association Process he focused his energies on that. A successful completion of the reform process culminating in the signing of the SAA was seen as one of the conditions for the closure of the OHR.[26] At the same time, early on, Lajčak highlighted that while his primary objective would be supporting and advising local politicians without the use of the Bonn powers, he would not hesitate to resort to them if deadlock continued (Lajčak 2007).

---

25 In April 2006 he issued a decision that limited the scope of the ban from public office, and in July the same year a similar one that limited the scope of the ban from office within political parties (The High Representative 2006a, The High Representative 2006b).

26 In February 2008 it also became one of the formal conditions of the 5+2 strategy for the closure of the OHR. See above.

The main roadblock for Bosnia to sign the SAA was police reform. Comprehensive police reform had been on the (international) state-building agenda for Bosnia for a long time before Lajčak's arrival.[27] In 2004 the European Commission (EC) declared three principles that should guide the reform process; they represented fundamental conditions necessary for the reform to be sufficient to allow Bosnia to sign the SAA.[28] Several rounds of negotiations were unsuccessful and the international community was increasingly impatient with Bosnian leaders. In a compromise decision in October 2007—known as the Mostar Declaration[29]— representatives of the three ethnic groups endorsed the three principles but postponed full reform. In a tense political climate, Lajčak embraced this compromise. Soon after, the EU initialed Bosnia's SAA (OHR 2007). Although the compromise had not been exactly to the standard of the original conditions set out by the EC, the EU and the High Representative deemed it satisfactory. The HR (and the EU) received criticism over this course of action from actors concerned about the severity of the situation in Bosnia. The primary worry was that the EU rewarded local politicians too soon.[30] The clash of the two visions was again visible, with the HR siding with the "European" one.

At the same time, Lajčak acted more decisively to speed up the reform process in another way, living up to his initial promise that he would not shy away from using his enforcement powers if need be. An important reason why the reform process in Bosnia was (and still is) lagging behind are the ineffective decision-making procedures in the state-level bodies. These are a legacy of Dayton, where the international community needed to ensure buy-in from all previously warring parties. Guarantees were therefore built into the procedures ensuring that no ethnic group could be outvoted.[31] In practice, this meant that each of the three ethnic groups could take a stance and not have to compromise with the other two over the solution, including by boycotting sessions so that these would not reach a quorum. The international community had long been pushing for reforms that would ensure protection of all three constituent peoples—that is, Bosniaks, Serbs and Croats—but also streamline the decision-making process of these institutions. In October 2007 Lajčak enforced a decision intended to break the stalemate in the Council of Ministers (the state-level government) and instructed local parties to negotiate new voting rules for the Parliamentary Assembly (The

---

27   On this issue see Kurt Bassuener's contribution in this volume.

28   Letter of Christopher Patten, EU Commissioner for External Relations to the Chairman of the Council of Ministers, November 16, 2004.

29   Declaration on honoring the commitments for implementation of the police reform with aim to initial and sign the Stabilisation and Association Agreement, October 29, 2007.

30   For a good overview of police negotiations in Bosnia see Lindvall (2009).

31   Bosnia and Herzegovina has a consociational political system. For more on how this type of system functions see Lijphart (1977). On consociationalism in Bosnia, see also Soeren Keil's chapter in this volume.

High Representative 2007a). If they failed to do so themselves, he as the High Representative, would impose them.

The HR's resolute action was welcomed by his staff at the OHR and the US. On the other hand, the use of enforcement powers was strongly resisted by Bosnian Serbs. Importantly, Bosnian Serb opposition to the HR's use of Bonn powers received unequivocal support from Russia, which deemed that it was Lajčak's actions, and not the local politicians' that incited a political crisis (RIA Novosti 2007). Caught between the two poles were most European actors, who, although openly supporting the HR's decision, would have preferred a negotiated outcome.

In November 2007 local parties agreed to changes to the rules of procedure for the Bosnian parliament. These were weaker than those requested by the OHR. Most importantly, local parties did not resolve whether the rules of procedure, when mentioning the need for a one-third quorum of votes from the RS, were referring to those present and voting or all elected representatives from the entity. Instead, they included a compromise that, if differing interpretations arose, the matter would be referred to the Constitutional Court. Although this was a detraction from the OHR's original proposal, the HR deemed the compromise acceptable. Similarly, under pressure from local parties and the EU to find a compromise solution, Lajčak issued an Authentic Interpretation of his earlier decision on the Council of Ministers. While most of the original measures were unaffected, the Authentic Interpretation required that, "best efforts be made in order to ensure that the vote of at least one member of each constituent people referred to in the said provision be cast by the Chair of the Council of Ministers and the Deputy Chairs of the Council of Ministers" (The High Representative 2007b). In the original decision, the required votes could be cast by any member of the Council of Ministers belonging to the concerned ethnic group. These changes were not seen as of immense significance by the HR, but what is important for the discussion here is that this was the first time in the history of the institution that the HR partially retracted a decision after pressure from local parties.

Lajčak's mandate shows that he was trying to balance between the two visions of Bosnia and thus also the two types of responses required from the international community. While acting resolutely, his willingness to amend the earlier decision shows that his personal preference was likely for negotiated solutions, even if these were suboptimal. He was often seen as the High Representative that was the most aligned with the EU Commission preferences.

Lajčak's successor had to be found extremely quickly, after Lajčak suddenly resigned the post to take up a position as foreign minister of Slovakia. The choice of his successor itself was again a battle between the two visions of Bosnia. On the one hand, Russia opposed the appointment of strong candidates willing to use enforcement powers while in office. On the other, the US did not want a weak candidate that would be unable to implement a clear policy and counter local challenges to the GFAP (cf. Sopinska 2009). Again, European members of the PIC Steering Board, who were in charge of nominating the candidate, were caught in-between. Although with considerable experience from the Western Balkans, the new HR Valentin Inzko (March 2009–present) was not seen as a particularly strong candidate for the post. His limited experience in leading large institutions combined with his diplomatic background made him seem more receptive for negotiations and compromises instead of action. But instead of adopting the more "European" conciliatory vision of Bosnia, the new HR has been relying on advice from his staff more than any of his predecessors. Since they are particularly worried about the security situation in Bosnia and challenges to the Dayton Accords, this has resulted in the HR being seemingly at least initially less reluctant to use enforcement powers.

Inzko quite quickly experienced first-hand the increasing marginalization of the HR from international state-building processes. In October 2009 the EU and the US convened emergency constitutional talks in Butmir. Although the HR is still the highest international authority in the country and also acts as a protector of the BiH Constitution, which forms a part of the Dayton Peace Agreement, the newly arrived High Representative was nearly excluded from the Butmir process. He was ultimately invited to the meeting itself but his Office was not involved in its preparation. Although the process eventually failed, the visible exclusion of the HR was remarkable. In response three former HRs (Petritsch, Ashdown and Schwarz-Schilling) sent an extremely critical joint letter, warning against the exclusion of the HR from the constitutional negotiations (Ashdown et al. 2009). This marginalization of the HR meant that in order for any of his actions to make a substantial mark, they would need to be decisive.

Inzko's attempts to exert the powers of the HR and act as a protector of the Dayton Agreement have been most clearly seen during the RS's repeated challenges of state-level powers. In the last several years the RS National Assembly (RSNA) started twice (May 2009 and April 2011) legal procedures against state-level competencies. Both times, the problem was resolved through international intervention. In the 2009 confrontation, the High Representative, after protracted negotiations, repealed the conclusions of the RSNA parliament (The High Representative 2009). The European Commission was not particularly happy with his use of the Bonn powers and would have preferred a negotiated solution. In the 2011 instance, the OHR wanted to act decisively, but the immediate problem was instead resolved by the EU High Representative for Foreign Affairs and Security Policy Catherine Ashton, without engaging the HR. After meeting with the RS president, Ashton gave the entity assurances that their concerns about the state-level judiciary would be addressed through a new "structured dialogue." This time the OHR had a cause for concern. The Office was alarmed that the RSNA revoked its previous position with a statement that the referendum was "not necessary for now" (Republika Srpska National Assembly 2011). In response the High Representative submitted a special report to the United Nations Security Council (UNSC), arguing that BiH faced the worse crisis since Dayton. He warned against viewing the deteriorating situation as only a short term negative trend and continued: "the need for an international presence, both civilian and military, with an executive mandate is still evident" (OHR 2011).

Such resolute action by the HR was an attempt to send a message that enforcement powers were still needed. At the time when this crisis was unfolding, the EU was preparing to decouple the EUSR from the post of the HR. This process was completed on July 18, 2011, when the EU Council officially appointed Peter Sørensen as the EUSR in Bosnia from September 1, 2011 (Council of the European Union 2011). Inzko's special report to the UNSC therefore sent an additional message. It indicated that the OHR and the HR were carving out their post-decoupling presence in the international state-building efforts in Bosnia. As stated above, with the EU assuming the role of primary negotiator with local parties, the remaining role was that of the protector of the peace agreement and integrity of BiH. And this is how the OHR defines its own identity also at the time of writing.

Conclusion: Beyond Bosnia and Herzegovina

The international administration of BiH represents a particular case of state-building, one that often exhibits little resemblance to other post-conflict situations. The BiH operation is taking place in a region with close proximity and strategic importance to the key actors in the (liberal) peacebuilding community, that is, Western democracies. Not only is BiH aspiring to become an EU and NATO member, but more importantly, the current members see it as a potential future addition to the clubs. This has had important implications on the contours of the intervention, notably the time and resource commitments of states underwriting the operation. It has also shaped the types of incentives that have been offered as a reward for reform. The best examples of this kind of an incentive have been continued progress in EU and NATO accession negotiations in return for reforms, as well as financial incentives associated with the progress.

While similar engagements and such a vast use of enforcement powers might not be replicated in the near future, the operation in BiH holds important lessons for planning transitions from international to local ownership elsewhere. The Bosnian mission was one of the first to take on a complex peace implementation and state-building mandate. It offers a unique insight into long-term perspectives in the implementation of key institutional reforms. Additionally, BiH local institutions were, as in a number of other sites of engagement, designed through external intervention and without a clear victory of one side or another. They similarly include and reify ethnic tensions in their formal composition, for example, through group representation in legislative bodies. BiH offers some pertinent insight when it comes to planning and extraction of international civilian presence. Three such lessons are highlighted below: (1) the termination of state-building missions should be objective and benchmark driven; (2) time defined mandates should be avoided as they encourage obstructionist behavior; and (3) state-building exercises should have a clearly defined lead agency.

First, the civilian state-building operation in Bosnia has been driven by several different exit strategies, switching between objective and time-defined mandates.

Initially designed as an addition to the very specific and precisely enforced military component, the civilian efforts were to draw down quickly after the security situation was deemed as stabilized. This meant that while the GFAP included a long list of civilian goals that the local parties were supposed to deliver on, the concrete objectives of the international administration as well as its priorities were not pre-planned. Instead they developed on the ground. Such an arrangement is not unusual with contemporary conflicts but can lead to continued complications over the mission's closure. In BiH the lack of pre-defined, specific benchmarks led to mission creep, with new areas of concern to the OHR added as they arose. Although some flexibility is advisable in the planning at the onset of a mission, each broad objective should include mission priorities and minimum conditions for exit. This allows for key implementation efforts to be addressed while a mission still has the attention and the support of the international community. When a thorough overhaul of objectives and strategy is needed—as is often the case with complex peace operations—there should be a broader buy-in from the international community for any extension of the original objectives and benchmarks.

Second, time-defined mandates should be avoided as they are not sensitive to the local context and encourage obstructionist behavior. Setting a deadline for exit provides an incentive to the more radical parties to delay on cooperation with other elected politicians in an attempt to "sit the international community out." This has been most clearly witnessed in BiH between 2006 and 2008, when the OHR closure was time-defined. The mere presence of a state-building operation strengthens the positions of more moderate parties. Radical parties assess that the balance of power is going to change to their advantage as soon as the international community departs. They have an incentive to delay any discussion on reform for after the announced date of closure. Setting a clear date for exit therefore not only does not benefit the reform negotiations, but actually impedes them.

Third, the problem of an institutional overlap is difficult to completely eliminate in complex peace and state-building operations. Different state-building areas are intertwined and agencies implementing them contribute to their different aspects. In order to remedy the duplication of efforts the international community should appoint a lead agency for the overall mission. This addresses the question of duplication of efforts and discourages agencies from trying to take the lead on the ground, as has often been the case in BiH. These efforts inevitably result in turf wars between various agencies with each of them having their work undermined by others. When such turf disputes occur throughout a transition period, this complicates the extraction of the international state-building efforts.

Bibliography

Agovic, M. (2005) Bosnia-Herzegovina: High Commissioner Candidate Interview. *RFE/RL, Radio Free Europe/Radio Liberty*, November 18.

Ashdown, P., Petritsch, W. and Schwarz-Schilling, C. (2009) Assuring Peace and a European Future in Bosnia and Herzegovina. *IP Journal—DGAP*, October 18.

BBC (2009) Bosnian Serbs Denied Right to Referendum, *BBC*, March 4.

Belloni, R. (2007) *State Building and International Intervention in Bosnia*. Abingdon: Routledge.

Bose, S. (2002) *Bosnia after Dayton: Nationalist Partition and International Intervention*. Oxford: Oxford University Press.

Caplan, R.D. (2005) *International Governance of War-Torn Territories: Rule and Reconstruction*. Oxford: Oxford University Press.

Chandler, D. (2000) *Faking Democracy after Dayton*. London: Pluto Press.

——. (2006) State-building in Bosnia: The Limits of Informal Trusteeship. *International Journal of Peace Studies*, 11(1), pp. 17–38.

Chesterman, S. (2005) *You, the People: The United Nations, Transitional Administration, and State-building*. Oxford: Oxford University Press.

Council of the European Union (2011) *Council Decision appointing the European Union Special Representative in Bosnia and Herzegovina*, July 11.

Daalder, I.H. (2000) *Getting to Dayton: The Making of America's Bosnia Policy.* Washington: Brookings Institute Press.

Declaration On Honouring the Commitments for Implementation of the Police Reform with Aim to Initial and Sign the Stabilisation and Association Agreement, October 29, 2007.

Der Spiegel (2007) Zunehmend Ungeduldig, *Der Spiegel*, Vol. 93, January 29.

The Economist (2005) Blame it on Paddy: Bosnia's Political Culture, *The Economist*, November 24. Holbrooke, R. (1999) *To End a War: Sarajevo to Dayton: An Inside Story*. New York: Random House.

The General Framework Agreement for Peace in Bosnia and Herzegovina (1995) Initialled in Dayton, Ohio on November 21, 1995, signed in Paris on December 14, 1995.

The High Representative (2006a) Decision Further Limiting the Scope of the Ban from Public Office in the Removal Decisions. *The High Representative*, April 4.

——. (2006b) Decision Lifting the Ban from Office Within Political Parties in the Removal Decisions. *The High Representative*, July 7.

——. (2007) Decision Enacting the Law on Changes and Amendments to the Law on the Council of Ministers of Bosnia and Herzegovina. October 19.

——. (2007b) Decision Enacting the Authentic Interpretation of the Law on Changes and Amendments to the Law on the Council of Ministers of Bosnia and Herzegovina. *The Decision of the High Representative*, October 19 and December 3, 2007.

——. (2009) Decision Repealing the Conclusions of the Republika Srpska National Assembly. Vol. 01-787/09 and 01-788/09 [Accessed May 14, 2009 and June 20, 2009].

Keil, S. (2013) *Multinational Federalism in Bosnia and Herzegovina*. Farnham: Ashgate.

Knaus, G. and Martin, F. (2003) Travails of the European Raj. *Journal of Democracy*, 14(3), pp. 60–74.

Kostakos, G. (1998) Division of Labor among International Organizations: The Bosnian Experience. *Global* Governance, 4, pp. 461–484.

Lajčak, M. (2007) TV Address to Citizens of BiH, Sarajevo, July 2, 2007.

Lijphart, A. (1977) *Democracy in Plural Societies: A Comparative Exploration.* New Haven, CT: Yale University Press.

Lindvall, D. (2009) *The Limits of the European Vision in Bosnia and Herzegovina: An Analysis of the Police Reform Negotiations.* Stockholm: Stockholm Studies in Sociology.

Mateja, P. (2012) Double-hatting in EU external engagements: EU Special Representatives and the question of coherence post-Lisbon. *SWP Comments*, 46, December 2012.

———. (2013) Whither Sovereignty? The Limits of Building States Through International Administrations. In: Rudolph, J.R. et al. (eds), *Mediation to nation-building: Third parties and the management of communal conflict.* Lanham, MD:Lexington Books, pp. 419–438.

Office of the High Representative (OHR) (2006) Press Release: 100 Days to Make History, OHR, May 24.

———. (2007) Press Release: BiH back on the European Road, OHR, December 3.

———. (2011) Press Release: HR Inzko at United Nations: BiH Faces Worst Crisis Since Dayton, OHR, May 9.

———. (2013) 43rd Report of the High Representative for Implementation of the Peace Agreement on Bosnia and Herzegovina to the Secretary-General of the United Nations, OHR, May 8.

Paris, R. and Sisk, T.D. (2009) Introduction: Understanding the Contradictions of Postwar Statebuilding. In: Paris, R. et al. (eds), *The Dilemmas of Statebuilding: Confronting the Contradictions of Postwar Peace Operations.* New York: Routledge, pp. 1–20

Patten, C. (2004) EU Commissioner for External Relations to the Chairman of the Council of Ministers, November 16, 2004.

Petritsch, W. (2001) Bosnien und Herzegowina: Fuenf Jahre nach Dayton: Hat der Frieden eine Chance? Klagenfurt: Wieser Verlag, pp. 212–213.

PIC Conclusions (1997) Bonn, December 10. Part XI, Art. 2.

PIC Declaration (2000) Brussels, May 24.

PIC Steering Board Communiqué (2006) Sarajevo, June 23.

———. (2012) Sarajevo, May 23.

———. (2005) Sarajevo, June 24.

PIC Steering Board Conclusions (1996) Paris, November 14.

Republika Srpska National Assembly (2011) Odluka broj 01-867/11, Sluzbeni glasnik Republike Srpske 58 [Accessed June 2, 2011].

Ria Novosti (2007) Russlands Aussenminister Kritisiert UN-Beauftragten in Bosnien-Herzegowina, November 14, 2007.

Schwarz-Schilling, C. (2006) High Representative's TV Address to Citizens of BiH. Sarajevo, January 31.

Sopinska, J. (2009) Question Mark Hangs over Inzko's Candidacy. *Europolitics*, March 4.

Toal, G. (2006) Geopolitical Discourses: Paddy Ashdown and the Tenth Anniversary of the Dayton Peace Accords. *Geopolitics*, 11, pp. 141–158.

Wilde, R. (2001) From Danzig to East Timor and Beyond: The Role of International Territorial Administration. *American Journal of International Law*, 95(3), pp. 583–605.

Chapter 7

Successes and Failures of Transitional Justice in BiH: The Case of the ICTY

Iva Vukušić

Introduction

More than 20 years have passed since the first shots were fired in Bosnia and Herzegovina (BiH) in what would become the bloodiest conflict in the breakup of Yugoslavia. The war lasted nearly four years (1992–1995) and destroyed both lives and infrastructure. Thousands perished and the economy was destroyed. Numerous crimes were committed and many of the survivors still suffer the consequences. There are two sources for the number of dead and missing from the war in BiH that are widely recognized as credible: the demographic reports produced for the trials at the International Criminal Tribunal for the former Yugoslavia (ICTY) (ICTY 2011) and the database of the Sarajevo-based Research and Documentation Center. Both put the total number of dead and missing at around one hundred thousand. Today, there are about ten thousand people still missing in BiH (Dzidic 2012a).

This chapter assesses the ICTY's role in BiH's transitional justice process, to determine whether it has contributed to state-building in the country, and to determine whether lessons may be learned from this significant war crimes tribunal. To discuss the full impact of the Tribunal, this chapter will address war crimes trials being held in the country now. It is, after all, impossible to assess the impact the Tribunal has had without analyzing prosecutions in local institutions.

Some Theoretical Considerations

Before reviewing the successes and shortcomings of the ICTY in relation to BiH, discussing some theoretical concepts will provide grounding for this complex issue. In an article on transitional justice in BiH, Olga Martin-Ortega (Aggestam and Björkdahl 2012, p. 184, UN 2010) summarizes it as follows, "the term transitional justice encompasses the broad range of tools and mechanisms by which societies—including the international community—deal with the violent and/or repressive past. These mechanisms include criminal prosecutions, truth-telling initiatives, documentation and enquiry commissions, reparation programs, reconciliation and memorialization ceremonies and monuments, and vetting and institutional reform." Criminal justice has been the chosen option for BiH. Martin-

Ortega further explains that international criminal justice was "prioritized even before achieving a peace agreement, and since then justice has been approached mainly through retributive means, emphasizing the prosecution and punishment of perpetrators of international crimes. Other approaches to dealing with the past in the country have until recently been largely neglected, and even rejected, by both international community and national authorities" (Martin-Ortega 2012a, p. 187).

In "Beyond justice versus peace," the authors discuss the rationale underlying support for criminal prosecutions. Those promoting justice and accountability in the wake of violent conflict mainly focus on the retributive aspects of this approach: "those that do wrong ought to be punished" (Herman et al. 2012, p. 52). Other reasons include potential deterrence, though empirical evidence has yet to prove the deterrent potential of international trials in any conclusive manner. Further, the failure to prosecute could undermine the trust of citizens in the government and the rule of law—a potential disability in a country struggling to establish a modern and independent justice sector based on the rule of law (Ibid.).

The ICTY: From a Slow Start to the Controversial Last Days

The Security Council of the United Nations established the ICTY in 1993, when bloodshed was being aired on televisions across the globe, leading to growing pressure to react.[1] It was an historic decision, and one that transcended the former Yugoslavia and opened the doors for other institutions such as the International Criminal Tribunal for Rwanda in 1994, and the International Criminal Court established by the Rome Statute in 1998. This paradigm shift—the move from almost complete impunity for political elites and military leaders suspected of committing war crimes towards a system that could provide some justice for victims—developed largely as a result of the work of the ICTY. The decision to establish the ICTY ended up influencing the world of international criminal law significantly, and has made an emerging consensus for war crimes prosecution possible, both as a principle and in practice (Sikkink 2011). Arguably, the system is far from perfect, dependent on government cooperation and selective, but a system is in place (and can be improved).[2] That was not the case 20 years ago.

In total, the Tribunal has indicted 161 individuals and sentenced 69. After many years of difficulties in arresting some of the suspects, it finally has all those

---

1   UN Security Council (1993) *Resolution 827*. Available from: http://daccess-dds-ny. un.org/ [Accessed April 11, 2015].

2   The International Criminal Court, for example, has 122 member states (May 2013). More information available here: http://icc-cpi.int/en_menus/icc/about%20the%20court/ icc%20at%20a%20glance/Pages/icc%20at%20a%20glance.aspx [Accessed March 15, 2013].

it indicted in the dock.[3] Many individuals have already served their sentences and have been free for years. Not all trials ended with a final verdict; the trial of former Serbian President Slobodan Milošević being the most notable example (ICTY 2006). Nevertheless, having all indicted suspects arrested was something even optimists would not have dared to dream a few years ago.

Currently, the Tribunal has ongoing proceedings for 25 accused.[4] The last trial to start, that of Goran Hadžić, is underway (ICTY 2013a). The case of long-term fugitive Ratko Mladić is also unfolding (ICTY 2013b). Radovan Karadžić, the Bosnian-Serb wartime leader is presenting his defense (ICTY 2009, 2011).

The expectations from the Tribunal have been exceptionally high, with both victims and the international public welcoming it as an instrument to fight impunity. Among the goals, the most ambitious—and problematic—was reconciling the people in the region (mentioned specifically in two UN Security Council resolutions: 1329 (November 2000) and 1534 (March 2004)). Such a lofty goal was likely always out of reach for either a Tribunal or any other remedies, and experience to date suggests that the ICTY will be condemned a failure at least in that one respect (Tolbert 2002). Diane Orentlicher concluded that many Bosnians are disappointed in the ICTY's performance but feel it was important that it was created (Orentlichter 2010, p. 40).

However, after the acquittals in the cases of Gotovina et al., Haradinaj et al. and Perišić, as well as the Stanišić and Simatović first instance verdicts, the standing of the Tribunal among victims in BiH is likely to be less favorable, judging by the reactions of victim associations and discussions in the media. Clearly, not everyone that is brought before a court is guilty, and acquittals form a part of the process and can be understood to demonstrate the impartiality and fairness of a system (Jordash and Martin 2013). If the prosecution does not provide sufficient evidence that the individuals are guilty beyond a reasonable doubt, and if the judges are not convinced, the defendants will be acquitted. The necessary standard of proof is being re-examined as observers question whether judges' standards could make convictions of key figures effectively impossible (Judah 2013, Economist 2013). In sum, these acquittals have resulted in victims voicing frustration, not understanding why and how these leadership cases collapsed.

Resentment was heightened when a controversial e-mail came to light in 2013. Sitting ICTY judge Frederik Harhoff, from Denmark, sent a message to 56 contacts that was then leaked to the press. The e-mail alleges possible political motivations of the ICTY president and appeals Judge Theodor Meron and casts doubt on the integrity of the decision-making process. Harhoff accused the ICTY president of pressuring other judges into making decisions in a way that would be more favorable for the accused and that could also indirectly benefit some governments

---

3   ICTY (2013) *Key Figures*. Available from: http://www.icty.org/sid/24 [Accessed June 28, 2013].

4   This paper was finished in mid-2014.

engaged in conflicts. The controversial case is still unfolding, possibly having long-term consequences in the case of Vojislav Šešelj where Harhoff sits as a judge.

Challenges Faced by the ICTY

Operational Challenges

The ICTY faced a myriad of operational challenges, seven of which are discussed below.

First, and perhaps most critically, the Tribunal has had no capacity to make arrests on its own and remained entirely dependent on government cooperation. Pressure has been regularly applied on countries in the region to arrest suspects and transfer them to the Tribunal but they were often reluctant to arrest "their own" and had trouble containing the nationalism of their populations (Subotic 2009). The dependence on government cooperation is clearly a weakness: the Tribunal has always been very vulnerable to political will or the lack of it.

Along with the involvement of the United States (US), the European Union (EU) was heavily involved in the region through the "conditionality" principle which demands cooperation with the ICTY in order to make progress towards EU membership, a stated goal for all former Yugoslav countries (Aybet and Bieber 2011). The conditionality principle impacted Croatia and Serbia most. Supporting the rule of law, as vague as that might seem, was high on the agenda for the US and the EU as they became involved in rebuilding post-war Bosnia.

Second, as the first international war crimes court after Nuremberg, the ICTY had little to lean on in terms of best practices. It had to learn as it went along, because war crimes prosecution practice and institutional design for tribunals at the time were, in many ways, a "tabula rasa" (Schaffer 2012). Rules, policies and working procedures were devised as the Tribunal grew and as it handled more and more cases. The ICTY learned on the job.

The length of trials is a third challenge often mentioned, as well as the length of detention. One factor to keep in mind is that due to the complexity of these cases (both in terms of facts and in terms of law); they cannot simply be compared with cases in other criminal courts. At the international courts, cases are typically more complex, and are against individuals with a high(er) level of responsibility. They often include hundreds if not thousands of deaths, deportations, detention, torture, sexual abuse and other crimes. Establishing facts, applying the law and determining responsibility requires meticulous effort, dealing with thousands of documents, and dozens or even hundreds of witnesses and experts.

The Office of the Prosecutor (OTP) has learned important lessons and the cases are now more streamlined. Trials can be shorter by using witnesses and evidence that already proved reliable and by cutting charges in very complex, long indictments. This is frustrating for victims or families of those who perished in crimes that are *not* included in the indictments, but this is a discretionary right of the prosecutor (Nettlefield 2010). That is not an unusual practice and is often seen as a necessary measure to cut the length of trial and secure a judgment. Usually, organizations of victims are consulted.

A fourth widely known challenge concerns the cost of this endeavor. The budget for 2012 and 2013 is around 250 million US dollars, though the budget is decreasing as a consequence of the lower number of investigations and trials (ICTY Annual Report 2012).

Another challenge is the physical distance from the affected populations, and the potential that such distance lessens the impact of the procedures and weakens the connection with the victims. It is easier to access witnesses and collect evidence when in the country, but when the ICTY was established that was not possible, and even later there remained issues of security. Some years after the war the State Court of BiH was established, it complements and supplements the work of the ICTY.

Witness protection remains a major challenge, as it is costly and difficult to implement in a country where many witnesses live in small communities and where word about neighbors testifying travels quickly. The ICTY had difficulties with witness intimidation in certain cases (it was alleged in Šešelj and Haradinaj), but overall it managed to provide protection to those that testified. Relocation to third countries and assignment of new identities were rare and only for those facing serious threats to their lives. In certain cases, the number of protected witnesses was very high (just over a quarter of the total number of witnesses testified with some type of protective measure) (ICTY Witnesses, n.d.).

Finally, another operational challenge worth noting is communicating effectively with the populations in the region. The Tribunal's Outreach section was established several years after the ICTY became operational, and it took some time for the Court to begin to produce materials in the local languages (Hellman 2012). Nevertheless, the ICTY learned its lesson, and today the Outreach Section is active, hosting journalists and students, organizing presentations and producing films about its work (ICTY Outreach, n.d.). However, that section faces frequent funding issues as it is not included in the core budget for the institution.

Prosecution Challenges

In addition to these operational challenges, the prosecution faced a number of challenges of its own. Establishing a clear and transparent prosecution strategy was among the most challenging aspects of the Tribunal's work. Obviously, the Prosecutor's Office could not have known what the long-term prosecution strategy would be, as the first investigations started while the war was still ongoing. Only when some initial work had been done was there a sense of the number of crimes that required investigation. Moreover, the ICTY initially had no political power and the arrests of the most high-ranking officials were to follow years later. The first cases were lower-ranking suspects that the ICTY targeted because it needed to start the trials and these suspects were, frankly, the only ones they could indict and bring to The Hague. However, the cases of the lower ranking perpetrators later contributed to "building" cases against their commanders and superiors. Fighting accusations of ethnic bias in case selection and prosecution was always a struggle for the ICTY, mainly concerning Bosnian Serbs and Serbians who often thought that they were treated unfairly (Vesti 2012).

The list of suspects tried by the ICTY cannot be seen to follow a consistent policy. International courts are supposed to prosecute only the "most responsible" individuals (ICTY 1993); national institutions should address other cases. The ICTY investigated many more suspects along with the individuals it indicted. Some suspects died before trial, some investigations were handed over to national courts and some trials were transferred after the investigations were completed (11*bis* cases) (ICTY 2013c). Other cases have been investigated and then abandoned. The list of defendants was never properly explained to the public, which might have been beneficial in fighting some misperceptions.

Another challenge to the prosecution is the mere number of suspects (Sadović 2007). Thousands are mentioned only in relation to BiH. No judicial system can successfully prosecute that number of suspects in a reasonable time frame; there are simply not enough resources, personnel, courtrooms, etc. Even if this number is too high and includes overlap of files among several prosecutors' offices, suspects that have died or are unwell and unfit to stand trial, or cases where there is not enough evidence, this is still too significant of a challenge for *any* system, international or national, to overcome. Here, again, selection comes into play: how prosecutorial strategies are developed, which cases are and are not pursued and how these choices are explained to the public and, especially, to the victims.

With the imminent closure of the ICTY it is up to the national institutions to prosecute as many remaining cases as possible, to the highest standards, in the shortest period of time. Even if there are no statutory limitations in war crimes cases, there is biology at work as many suspects and witnesses die or are unable to give evidence, and, therefore, some cases cannot go forward. It is vital that as much as possible is accomplished in the next few years. This is made much more difficult by the fact that there is no shared perception of the past among the political representatives in BiH and there is no consensus on the importance of war crimes prosecution. On the contrary, several politicians are doing their best to sabotage the process and destroy the institutions (Jukić 2012).

An effort to ensure more progress in prosecuting at the national level in BiH was made with the National War Crimes Strategy, adopted in December 2008 (Bosnia and Herzegovina War Crimes Strategy 2008).[5] This was the result of a difficult political battle with the High Representative intervening at the last minute with support. However, in the end the document was more of a declaration of ambitions than a real plan, and today the country is lagging behind on implementing even these broad goals (Husejnović 2010). The Strategy put some deadlines in place for prosecuting cases, but as David Schwendiman argues, these might not be useful in guiding the country towards a more effective war crimes prosecution system

---

5   See also the contribution by Meagan Smith-Hrle in this volume.

(Schwendiman 2011). There are several more challenges such as the lack of evidence in many cases, which influences the possibility of successful prosecution. For many crimes, there is not sufficient evidence, or the available evidence is not of high enough quality to ensure a confirmation of indictment, let alone a conviction. There are also cases of sexual abuse and rape that are particularly difficult to prosecute (Amnesty International 2012).

Finally, regional cooperation is clearly a big challenge in working through the case load, as there are certain limitations to extraditing suspects that are nationals of one country to another in order to face trial. This is important as many of those suspected for committing crimes in Bosnia reside in Serbia, Croatia and Montenegro. Some progress has been made through the years (Dzidic 2012b),[6] but claims of political manipulation are frequent.

Accomplishments and Positive Impact on Prosecuting War Crimes Cases in BiH

Even with all the challenges, the ICTY has had immense success in achieving certain goals. As ICTY President Judge Meron points out, "most fundamentally, in case after case, the ICTY demonstrated that trials of the gravest crimes are possible and that those alleged to be most responsible for such crimes, including top political and military leaders, can be brought to justice and tried in accordance with internationally recognized fair trial rights" (Meron 2012).

The arrest of all indicted fugitives was a success no one believed would ever be achieved (Albright 2012). In BiH, the political situation might not be ideal but it would probably be much worse if Radovan Karadžić was the president of Republika Srpska. Removing certain individuals from the political scene was crucial. However, this does not really apply to defendants who were convicted and served their sentences. Some of these individuals came back and ran in local elections in October 2012 (Jahić 2012), as BiH laws allow it.

Secondly, the process of finding and identifying missing persons is a major accomplishment, and one that had an undoubtedly positive effect on people across the country.[7] Thousands disappeared during the war in BiH and many remains have been found as a direct result of the investigations of the ICTY and local courts.

Further, there has been a rise in domestic prosecutions. Advocating for national trials, capacity building and transfer of evidence have all led to national prosecutions which are now one of the most important parts of the ICTY's long-term legacy

---

6   A Protocol between BiH and Serbia was finally signed in early 2013. International Center for Transitional Justice notes on the subject: http://ictj.org/news/serbia-and-bosnia-sign-war-crimes-protocol [Accessed March 20, 2013].

7   The International Commission for Missing Persons has done groundbreaking work in locating, recovering and identifying remains. More information available at: www.ic-mp.org [Accessed January 15, 2013].

(ICTY 2010). The State Court in Sarajevo has been judged as rather successful by international observers such as the representatives of the Organization for Security and Cooperation in Europe (OSCE) and United Nations Development Program (UNDP) (OSCE 2010, UNDP 2010). Various academics have expressed support for the work of the court (Martin-Ortega 2012b), as well as representatives of international NGOs such as Human Rights Watch (BIRN, n.d.).[8]

Trials at local courts, in the cantons and districts, are still challenging, as there is a lack of resources allocated exclusively to war crimes related investigations (UNDP 2011), and sometimes a lack of expertise. Nevertheless, much effort and time have been invested into capacity building and, even with all the problems stemming from applying different criminal codes (BIRN 2008) and clashing jurisdictions, the trials continue and there is a window of opportunity to learn from the past and improve (HRW 2012). Caseload management now seems clearer, and the transfer of cases from the State Court to lower level courts should soon be complete. These local bodies are expected to complete the investigations and indict suspects (BIRN 2012).

The development of substantive and procedural law is another success of the Tribunal and one that cannot be explored in detail in this chapter as there were so many decisions that advanced law and are influencing other jurisdictions (Boas and Schabas 2012). The ICTY also developed investigative practices as well as procedures to deal with protected or vulnerable witnesses (ICTY 2009).

Furthermore, establishing facts has been critical in determining responsibility of a particular individual for a particular crime. The facts come from millions of pages of documents, expert reports, witness testimonies, guilty pleas, photographs, video footage, journalistic reports and forensic examinations, and this plethora of material provides unlimited possibilities for future exploration by historians, political scientists and human rights activists. Nevertheless, the Tribunal does not and cannot paint a complete picture of all the relevant historic facts, causes of the war or other important information. In addition, the ICTY through its Press and Outreach sections has played a role in building the capacity of local journalists to cover these important trials both in The Hague and around BiH. The impact various courts will have largely depends on how they communicate with the public and for that, journalists and editors are crucial. After lacking an outreach program, the Tribunal established outreach offices and eventually hired a Bosnian/Croatian/Serbian-speaking spokesperson. Material in the local languages is provided; films are produced and social media used to reach out to young people; journalists and researchers are hosted and lectures are organized in the region.

Plea-bargaining is another very controversial topic (Clark 2009), though as a policy and practice of prosecutors, plea-bargaining has had only limited success, both in The Hague as well as in Sarajevo. In the legal tradition of post-Yugoslav countries, this practice was unfamiliar to the local legal community as well as the

---

8 The chapter by Meagan Smith Hrle in this volume provides more detail on the judiciary and the reform of the justice sector more broadly.

general public, and this unfamiliarity has resulted in significant misunderstandings and tensions. With this practice being applied in more and more cases, the tensions have lessened. Nevertheless this accomplishment of solving cases more expeditiously than through trials, is still viewed critically, especially by the victims. The positive aspects of plea-bargaining are perhaps most clear in terms of deals made to get information and find mass graves and recovering missing persons.

Several observers have argued, mostly off the record, that the ICTY is likely regarded as more successful in international law circles than among victims and, sadly, this is probably true. Today, it appears that activists, researchers and international law professors in Leiden, New York, London, and Geneva mostly stress the overall successes of the Tribunal and its contribution to the development of international criminal law (and they do that while often arguing about the substance of various controversial decisions). Widows and survivors in Sarajevo, Vogošća, Mostar or Sanski Most in BiH are often less enthusiastic. The Tribunal itself focuses on the accomplishments and when principals or other representatives speak publicly, not a lot of attention is given to exploring all the ways in which the institution could have done better in the eyes of the victims, arguably its primary constituents.

In sum, given the difficult political and social circumstances in this post-war setting, the Tribunal has been fairly successful in some important aspects of its work in Bosnia and Herzegovina. However, some opportunities were missed. The following section will discuss why.

Shortcomings in Prosecuting War Crimes Cases

Some of the shortcomings in war crimes prosecution will echo the challenges, as they are a direct consequence of difficulties the ICTY has faced and has yet been unable to fully solve.

First, the lack of a clear prosecution strategy both in case selection as well as case-management has been one of the biggest problems as it was not always clear why decisions were made to focus on certain accused while leaving others (sometimes high-ranking officials and commanders) aside. Similarly, there has been a lack of clarity in strategies for the presentation of evidence in court (for example, the case of Slobodan Milošević, who died in detention before a judgment was delivered). The gravity of the crime, the suspects' position of responsibility, the harm done to the community, the availability and quality of evidence, the particular gruesomeness of the crime and the availability of suspects for arrest are, presumably, some of the standards considered, but this was never fully explained to the public. It would be useful to know why the ICTY took some cases, but not others.

Second, sentencing has been an issue of much contention, causing tensions with victims but also among the broader public. It would have been useful for the Tribunal to discuss more thoroughly sentencing rationale and options and to explain how the judges reached their conclusions.

A third shortcoming of the Tribunal is the public support it enjoyed throughout the years. The data paints a grim picture in this context showing that among certain groups, the ICTY was never very popular. For example, a 2004 IDEA survey reported that only 4 percent of Bosnian Serbs support the Tribunal (IDEA 2004). The support is highest among Bosnian Muslims (Bosniaks), while the Bosnian Croats supported it less after the Gotovina first instance judgment in 2011 (Ronen 2011). Predictably, the citizens of Croatia supported it more after the final ruling in the Gotovina case (Pavelic 2013). The support of various groups depends largely on the judgments that the ICTY delivers in relation to "their" defendants and, as such, changes over time. Verdicts in high-profile leadership cases also affect how the public perceives the Tribunal, as illustrated by the judgments in the cases of Gotovina, Haradinaj and Perišić that all had a strong impact on the Tribunal's standing in the region. These controversial decisions, together with the 2013 acquittal by majority of Stanišić and Simatović (in the first instance), might have even permanently damaged the ICTY's standing. However, the support for the Tribunal and its work might be most accurately measured only years after the trials have been completed as then, perhaps, it will be less influenced by ongoing trials and the political manipulations that occur in each of the countries of the region.

It is clear that the Tribunal cannot and should not require absolute support in the region to prove efficiency or to have legitimacy. Some groups do not accept rational arguments and remain convinced that the Tribunal is one-sided and built to persecute one group as opposed to another. That does not, however, mean that the ICTY should not engage in an honest debate with local populations about what it achieved and where it failed. The Tribunal should continue working on strengthening its legacy, providing accurate information about its work and finding ways in which to maximize its achievements. Complementary mechanisms such as victims' funds can be useful in that regard. Judge Robinson, the former ICTY president, has presented one such initiative of establishing a fund that would provide resources for communities that have suffered mass human rights violations (Robinson 2011a, 2011b). This initiative has so far produced no visible results, but it is a valuable issue to raise and one that emphasizes that justice could be conceptualized in broader terms and that restorative measures should work hand in hand with retributive ones.

Finally, it is critical to address a common criticism of the ICTY: that it did not contribute to reconciliation though it was stressed, especially in the early years, that this was one of its goals.[9] Perhaps that should not have been the case. Maybe

---

9   When established, the Tribunal was effectively the only "tool" available to deal with the conflict in the former Yugoslavia. As there was nothing else, those looking for actors to contribute to reconciliation decided they had to look to the ICTY. As time passed and the situation on the ground showed reconciliation was not happening (not happening at all or not to the desired extent, depending on who you ask) and because reconciliation is so difficult to define and measure, the concept and the word were used less and less. Today, ICTY principals do not refer to reconciliation very often, probably realizing that it

"reconciliation" should not be a task of a tribunal—maybe it can be regarded as a desired outcome, but not a set goal. If impossible goals such as "reconciliation" are set, then such institutions could be condemned to failure. The best possible outcome one might expect is that the Tribunal can assist the processes of normalization of relations between former enemy groups and perhaps contribute to the ultimate verdict of history.

Complementary Mechanisms: Other Tools to Address the Legacy of War Crimes

In order to maximize the effects of war crimes prosecution, the system needs to be supported by complementary mechanisms. This is especially important in communities that suffered human rights abuses on a massive scale, as for example in Prijedor or in Srebrenica. Prosecution then remains significant but cannot be the sole response to the legacy of violence.

First, the establishment of fact-finding missions, the location and identification of missing persons, the organization of frequent public discussions about the past, the open provision of evidence from the trials to the public (whenever possible), the commemoration of the loss of life of all innocent victims,[10] reparations for victims of gross human rights violations and property return, all represent the complex and multi-faceted needs of a country recovering from war. These are all policy measures that can be employed to maximize the effects of trials and contribute to rebuilding a society after war (Martin-Ortega 2012b). Some of these policy measures were applied with greater success than others, but only in concert can they potentially remove some of the burdens facing victims and the broader society in a post-war era.

Other mechanisms have been few and far between, but have been gaining ground recently. Associations of victims have been very active in this regard. There have been two public investigative bodies, similar in character, but very different in their produced results. One was the so-called Srebrenica Commission and its subsequent report (The Srebrenica Report). The other planned commission was on the events that took place in Sarajevo during the war. That commission never started its inquiry, blocked and stalled by political bickering and a lack of any consensus, and it was eventually forgotten.[11]

---

is too ambitious of a goal for a court to reach. What they speak of today is *contributing to* reconciliation, which is significantly different than achieving reconciliation.

10   Memorials are a separate, highly complex topic, but an interesting example to explore are all the problems regarding commemorating the victims of the camps around Prijedor, primarily Omarska, Keraterm and Trnopolje. For a valuable insight see Hodžić (2012).

11   Author observation based on discussions with individuals that followed the process closely in Sarajevo. More generally, see a Radio Netherlands Worldwide article

One important development in this context is the regional fact-finding body called RECOM (Regional Commission Tasked with Establishing the Facts about All Victims of War Crimes and Other Serious Human Rights Violations Committed on the Territory of the Former Yugoslavia in the period from 1991–2001). After several years of debate among civil society groups in the region, the idea of a network that now includes more than 1800 NGOs was born. The process has been everything but simple and was often damaged by personal competitiveness among some NGO leaders as well as legitimate differences concerning the desired form RECOM would take, but the initiative still stands, and many work on establishing what they see as the only "solution" to transitional justice in the former Yugoslavia, which is regional cooperation and promoting mutual understanding and empathy for victims. The progress however has been slow, and the outcome remains uncertain. Establishing facts about the past, RECOM advocates believe, is essential in building a stable democratic environment and long lasting peace. Even if the final result is not as it was planned—the establishment of a commission with the full support and cooperation of governments—this initiative is valuable as it promotes collaboration across the borders and fosters deeper connections among victim organizations, even those that were on opposing sides during the war.

Another potentially helpful initiative is the Transitional Justice Strategy for BiH. The proposed strategy was developed by the Ministry of Justice of BiH in close collaboration with civil society organizations, assisted heavily by UNDP. It is a detailed document including many elements and goals that were identified through consultation with various stakeholders.[12] Victims had an active role in developing the Strategy. Criminal justice plays an important part of the envisioned approach to transitional justice issues, but the document goes further, addressing many of the issues important to victims' families and survivors of war crimes (Karabegović 2012). However, it remains to be seen if the document will be adapted and implemented in light of the difficult political environment.

Conclusion

For several years a "completion strategy" has been discussed and there has been pressure to complete the trials and close the Tribunal as soon as possible (ICTY, n.d.). The initial deadlines were extended several times but trials will be most likely completed by 2015, with only the trial of Mladić and, possibly, Hadžić running past that date. A Residual Mechanism was established to "inherit" some of the work of the ICTY (ICTY, n.d.), mainly assisting trials in local institutions in the region, dealing with the individuals serving sentences and managing the vast archives of the Court (ICTY Residual Mechanism, n.d.). The archives are

---

from June 11, 2006: http://www.rnw.nl/international-justice/article/sarajevo-commission-creates-political-trouble [Accessed March 15, 2013].

12   Copy of the draft version of the Transitional Justice Strategy on file with author.

an important element of the legacy of the Tribunal and should be made available, as widely as possible while not compromising the safety of witnesses in order to promote an honest fact-based debate about the past. The archives are an invaluable source for research and this material needs to be used in the future. Over four thousand witnesses testified in court—their statements remain in The Hague, along with millions of pages of documents, reports, transcripts, thousands of still images, video footage, *artifacts* and records of DNA identifications (ICTY, n.d., Huskamp 2008).

The justice the ICTY delivers is by no means flawless or perfect—far from it—but some positive outcomes can be observed from the work of this experiment of international law. Given the circumstances, it has had an overwhelmingly positive impact on BiH.

Many of the defendants have already served their sentences and went home. It might be that when they come out, the perpetrators are still regarded as heroes—that happened with Mitar Vasiljević[13] and more prominently Momčilo Krajišnik.[14] Arguably, one might then wonder what the point of the ICTY's efforts was. This leads to the fundamental question of what is the purpose of war crimes prosecution: convicting (some of) those who are guilty and establishing facts, or re-educating an entire population on what to think about these individuals and their acts. The latter might not be an assignment for a tribunal at all.

What any war crimes tribunal might hope to achieve is by all means imperfect justice, because how does one provide adequate justice for thousands of victims, wounded women and men, children and the elderly; all the detainees and victims of sexual abuse; whole families whose lives have been so deeply affected by violence and injustice? What is an adequate punishment for systematic torture, humiliation, starvation and a campaign of expulsion and deportation, for the destruction of schools, mosques, churches and libraries? This chapter argues that the situation in Bosnia might be bleak today,[15] but if it had not been for the Tribunal, it would have most certainly been worse. War crimes prosecutions were, and continue to be, a necessity (Schwendiman 2010).

Furthermore, in order to maximize the positive effect of the trials, complementary mechanisms are needed, all working in concert in order to achieve peace, security, stability and respect for human rights in a post-conflict environment. Supporting local prosecutions (with resources, expertise and staff), finding missing persons,

---

13 ICTY Momčilo Krajišnik case information: http://www.icty.org/case/krajisnik/4. Krajišnik recently returned to Republika Srpska after serving his sentence and was celebrated as a hero by numerous citizens at a party organized in Pale [Accessed September 8, 2013].

14 ICTY Mitar Vasiljević case information: http://www.icty.org/cases/party/793/4. Vasiljević was convicted of aiding and abetting persecutions and murder and sentenced to 15 years imprisonment for crimes in Višegrad [Accessed January 14, 2013].

15 For more on the political stalemate in Bosnia and Herzegovina, refer to the chapter by Valery Perry in this volume.

designing adequate reparation programs, providing assistance to survivors and witnesses, establishing fact-finding projects and commemorating victims forms a cluster of measures that can be applied to post-conflict situations. Given the fact, that all societies in a post-war period are different, the measures need to be designed with specific requirements in mind. This requires ongoing research. Resources will be a challenge and budgets need to be planned carefully and decision-makers must be aware which policy measures bring the best results and what the population of a post-conflict society needs. It is crucial that victims' voices are heard.

Bibliography

Aggestam, K. and Björkdahl, A. (eds) (2013) *Rethinking Peacebuilding: The Quest for Just Peace in the Middle East and the Western Balkan.* London: Routledge, pp. 48–63.

Akhavan, P. (2001) Beyond Impunity: Can International Criminal Justice Prevent Future Atrocities? *American Journal of International Law,* 95, p. 12.

Albright, M. (2003) In: Against All Odds. Documentary Film. *Sense News Agency.* Available from: http://www.sense-agency.com/documentaries.42.html [Accessed January 15, 2013].

Amnesty International (2012) Bosnia and Herzegovina: Submission for European Commission Progress Report, on file with author.

Aybet, G. and Bieber, F. (2011) From Dayton to Brussels: The Impact of EU and NATO Conditionality on State-Building in Bosnia and Herzegovina. *Europe-Asia Studies,* 63(10).

Balkan Investigative Reporting Network (n.d.) HRW: International Presence Encouraged Public Faith. *Balkan Investigative Reporting Network.* Available from: www.bim.ba (http://www.bim.ba/en/313/10/34683/?tpl=30) [Accessed January 15, 2013].

——. (2008) *OSCE: Harmonized Application of Criminal Code.* Available from: www.bim.ba/en/1/80/ [Accessed January 15, 2013] and http://www.oscebih. org/documents/osce_bih_doc_20101223115043693eng.pdf [Accessed March 15, 2013].

——. (2012) Court of Bosnia and Herzegovina Finishes Transfer of Cases. *Balkan Investigative Reporting Network,* March 8. Available from: http://www.bim. ba/en/312/10/34642/ [Accessed January 15, 2013].

Bassuener, K. and Weber, B. (2012) Democratization Policy Council (DPC) Policy Study: Croatian and Serbian Policy in BiH: Help or Hindrance? How to effectively employ Western Leverage. Available from: http://ceas-sebia. org/root/prilozi/Croatian-and-Serbian-Policy-in-Bosnia-Herzegovina.pdf [Accessed April 11, 2015].

Bieber, F. (2013) Die Grenzen des ICTY: Nach den Freisprüchen von Gotovina, Markac und Haradinaj (In English: The boundaries of the ICTY: After the

acquittals of Gotovina, Markac and Haradinaj). Available from: http://www.
suedosteuropa-gesellschaft.com/mitteilungen/2013/heft_02_2013.pdf.
[Accessed July 1, 2013].

BiH State Court (n.d.) Summary of the budget of the State Court. In: FAQ, 2009.
Available from: http://www.sudbih.gov.ba/?opcija=sadrzaj&kat=7&id=15&je
zik=e [Accessed January 15, 2013].

———. (n.d.) Jurisdiction, Organization, and Structure of the Court of Bosnia and
Herzegovina. Available from: http://www.sudbih.gov.ba/?opcija=sadrzaj&kat
=3&id=3&jezik=e [Accessed January 15, 2013].

Boas, G. and Schabas, W. (2003) *International Criminal Law Developments in the
Caselaw of the ICTY*. Leiden: Martinus Nijhoff.

Bosnia and Herzegovina (2008) National War Crimes Strategy. Available
from: http://www.adh-geneva.ch/RULAC/pdf_state/War-Crimes-
Strategy-f-18-12-08.pdf [Accessed January 15, 2013].

Brammertz, S. (2012) Presentation by Serge Brammertz, Chief Prosecutor at the
ICTY. A lecture at Asser Institute. The Hague, notes on file with author.

Case of *Sejdic and Finci* v. *Bosnia and Herzegovina* (2009) Applications nos.
27996/06 and 34836/06. Available from: http://hudoc.echr.coe.int/sites/eng/
pages/search.aspx?i=001-96491. See also: and http://www.coe.org.rs/eng/
news_sr_eng/?conid=1545 [Accessed January 15, 2013].

Central Intelligence Agency (2013) *Factbook*. Available from: https://www.cia.
gov/library/publications/the-world-factbook/geos/bk.html [Accessed January
15, 2013].

Clark, J.N. (2009) Plea Bargaining at the ICTY: Guilty Pleas and Reconciliation.
The European Journal of International Law, 20(2), pp. 415–436.

Coalition for Recom (n.d.) Available from: http://www.zarekom.org/The-
Coalition-for-RECOM.en.html [Accessed January 15, 2013].

Dayton Accords—The General Framework Agreement (1995) Available from:
http://www.ohr.int/dpa/default.asp?content_id=380 [Accessed April 11, 2015].

Dzidic, D. (2012a) ICMP Seeks to Help Families of the Missing, *Balkan Insight*,
March 14. Available from: http://www.balkaninsight.com/en/article/icmp-
seeks-to-help-families-of-missing-persons [Accessed April 11, 2015].

———. (2012b) Improvement of Court's Relation to Victims Needed, *Balkan
Insight*, September 21. Available from: http://www.balkaninsight.com/en/
article/improvement-of-courts-relation-to-victims-needed [Accessed January
15, 2013].

The Economist (2013) Winding Down with a Whimper, *The Economist*, June
8.   Available   from: http://www.economist.com/news/europe/21579049-
controversial-recent-judgments-tribunal-hague-winding-down-whimper
[Accessed July 1, 2013].

Gordy, E. (2013) What happened to the Hague Tribunal? *The New York Times*, June
2. Available from: http://www.nytimes.com/2013/06/03/opinion/global/what-
happened-to-the-hague-tribunal.html?pagewanted=all&_r=1& [Accessed July
1, 2013].

Harhoff, F. (2013) Personal E-mail leaked to the Danish Press. Available from: http://www.bt.dk/sites/default/files-dk/node-files/511/6/6511917-letter-english.pdf [Accessed July 1, 2013].

Haynes, D.F. (2008) *Deconstructing the Reconstruction: Human Rights and the Rule of Law in Postwar Bosnia and Herzegovina*. London: Ashgate.

Hellman, M. (2012) Challenges and limitations of outreach in international justice interventions. *Forthcoming, draft version on file with author.*

Herman, J., Martin-Ortega, O. and Sriram, C.L. (2012) Beyond Justice Versus Peace: Transitional Justice and Peace Building Strategies. In: Aggestam, K. and Björkdahl, A. (eds), *Rethinking Peacebuilding: The Quest for Just Peace in the Middle East and the Western Balkan*. London: Routledge.

Hodžić, R. (2012) Shadow of London "Orbit" in Bosnia: Steel, Blood, and the Suppression of Memory. Available from: http://ictj.org/news/shadow-london-%E2%80%9Corbit%E2%80%9D-bosnia-steel-blood-and-suppression-memory [Accessed January 15, 2013].

Human Rights Watch (2012) *World Report 2012*. Available from: http://www.hrw.org/world-report-2011/bosnia-and-herzegovina [Accessed January 15, 2013].

——. (2013) *Human Rights in Bosnia*. Available from: www.hrw.org http://www.hrw.org/europecentral-asia/bosnia-and-herzegovina [Accessed January 15, 2013].

Husejnović, M. (2010) Deadlines Slip by for Bosnia's War Crimes Strategy, *Balkan insight*, December 30. Available from: http://www.balkaninsight.com/en/article/deadlines-slip-by-for-bosnia-war-crimes-strategy/btj-latest-headlines-all/127 [Accessed January 15, 2013].

Huskamp Peterson, T. (2008) Temporary Courts, Permanent Records. Available from: http://www.wilsoncenter.org/sites/default/files/TCPR_Peterson_HAPPOP02.pdf [Accessed Accessed March 20, 2013].

International Center for Transitional Justice (2013) Note on the Protocol for cooperation. Available from: http://ictj.org/news/serbia-and-bosnia-sign-war-crimes-protocol [Accessed March 20, 2013].

International Commission for Missing Persons (ICMP) (n.d.) More Information about the Organization. Available at: http://www.ic-mp.org/about-icmp/ [Accessed January 15, 2013].

International Criminal Tribunal for the former Yugoslavia (ICTY) (n.d.) Budget reports. Available from: http://www.icty.org/sid/325 [Accessed April 11, 2015].

——. (n.d.) Completion Strategy. Available from: http://www.icty.org/sid/10016 [Accessed April 11, 2015].

——. (n.d.) Establishment. Available from: http://www.icty.org/sid/319 [Accessed April 11, 2015].

——. (n.d.) Outreach. Available from: http://icty.org/sections/Outreach/OutreachProgramme [Accessed April 11, 2015].

——. (n.d.) Residual Mechanism—Archives. Available from: http://www.icty.org/sid/10874 [Accessed April 11, 2015].

———. (n.d.) Witnesses at the ICTY. Available from: http://www.icty.org/sid/10175 [Accessed April 11, 2015].

———. (1993, last updated in 2009) Statute. Available from: http://www.icty. org/x/file/Legal%20Library/Statute/statute_sept09_en.pdf [Accessed April 11, 2015].

———. (2001) Esad Landzo case information. Available from: http://icty.org/case/ mucic/4 [Accessed April 11, 2015].

———. (2001) Goran Jelišić Case Information. Available from: http://icty.org/case/ jelisic/4 [Accessed April 11, 2015].

———. (2004) Mitar Vasiljević Case Information. Available from: http://icty.org/ case/vasiljevic/4 [Accessed April 11, 2015].

———. (2006) Ivica Rajic Case Information. Available from: http://icty.org/case/ rajic/4 [Accessed April 11, 2015].

———. (2006) Slobodan Milošević Case Information. Available from: http://www. icty.org/cases/party/738/4 [Accessed April 11, 2015].

———. (2009) Indictment against Radovan Karadžić. Available from: http://icty. org/case/karadzic/4#ind [Accessed April 11, 2015].

———. (2009) Press Release: On the Manual of Developed Practices. Available from: www.icty.org (http://www.icty.org/sid/10145) [Accessed January 15, 2013].

———. (2010) Report of the President on the Conference: Assessing the Legacy of the ICTY. Available from: http://www.icty.org/x/file/Press/Events/100427_ legacyconference_pdt_report.pdf [Accessed January 15, 2013].

———. (2011) Indictment against Ratko Mladić. Available from: http://icty.org/ case/mladic/4#ind [Accessed April 11, 2015].

———. (2011) War Demographics. Available from: http://www.icty.org/sid/10622 [Accessed January 15, 2013].

———. (2012) *Annual Report 2012*. Available from: http://www.icty.org/x/file/ About/Reports%20and%20Publications/AnnualReports/annual_report_2012_ en.pdf [Accessed September 8, 2013].

———. (2013) Goran Hadžić Case Information. Available from: http://www.icty. org/cases/party/694/4 [Accessed April 11, 2015].

———. (2012) Gotovina et al. Case Information. Available from: http://icty.org/ case/gotovina/4 [Accessed April 11, 2015].

———. (2012) Haradinaj et al. Case Information. Available from: http://icty.org/ case/haradinaj/4 [Accessed April 11, 2015].

———. (2012) Milan Lukić Case Information. Available from: http://icty.org/case/ milan_lukic_sredoje_lukic/4 [Accessed April 11, 2015].

———. (2013) Key Figures. Available from: http://www.icty.org/sections/TheCases/ KeyFigures [Accessed April 11, 2015].

———. (2013) Momčilo Krajišnik case information. Available from: http://www. icty.org/case/krajisnik/4 [Accessed April 11, 2015].

———. (2013) Perišić Case Information. Available from: http://icty.org/case/ perisic/4 [Accessed April 11, 2015].

———. (2013) Ratko Mladić Case Information. Available from: http://www.icty. org/cases/party/704/4 [Accessed April 11, 2015].

———. (2013) Stanisic and Simatovic Case Information. Available from: http://icty. org/case/stanisic_simatovic/4 [Accessed April 11, 2015].

Institute for Democracy and Electoral Assistance (IDEA) (2004) Summary of Survey Results. Survey previously available from: http://www.idea.int/ europe_cis/balkans/see_survey.cfm [Accessed April 11, 2015].

Ivanisević, B. (2013) Falling Out of Love with the Hague Tribunal. *Balkan Insight*, June 11. Available from: http://www.balkaninsight.com/en/article/falling-out-of-love-with-the-hague-tribunal [Accessed July 1, 2013].

Jahić, A. (2012) Convicted War Criminals Run for Office, *Balkan Investigative Reporting Network*, October 5. Available from: www.bim.ba (http://www.bim. ba/en/342/10/35888/) [Accessed January 15, 2013].

Jordash, W. and Martin, S. (2013) Acquittals at the ICTY: Shows Health of the System. *ILawyer blog*, June 10. Available from: http://ilawyerblog.com/ acquittals-at-the-icty-it-shows-the-health-of-the-system/ [Accessed   July 2, 2013].

Judah, T. (2013) Two Puzzling Judgments in the Hague, *The Economist*, June 1. Available from: http://www.economist.com/blogs/easternapproaches/2013/06/ war-crimes-former-yugoslavia [Accessed July 1, 2013].

Jukić, E. (2012) Bosnian Serbs Will Ask End of State Level Court and Prosecutor, *Balkan Insight*, January 23. Available from: http://www.balkaninsight.com/ en/article/bosnian-serbs-will-ask-end-of-state-level-court-and-prosecutor [Accessed January 15, 2013].

———. (2013) Bosnian Serbs Welcome Home Freed Wartime Politician. *Balkan Insight*, September 2. Available from: http://www.balkaninsight.com/en/ article/pale-prepares-to-welcome-momcilo-krajisnik [Accessed September 8, 2013].

Karabegović, Dz. (2012) Strategija tranzicijske pravde korak ka istini iz devedesetih (In English: The Strategy for transitional justice a step towards the truth about the 1990es). Pred Licem Pravde (In English: Facing Justice). Available from: www.slobodnaevropa.org (http://www.slobodnaevropa.org/content/strategija-tranzicijske-pravde-korak-ka-istini-iz-devedesetih/24702273.html) [Accessed January 15, 2013].

Letter to the UN Secretary General Mr. Ban Ki-Moon (2013) June 25. Available from: http://www.hlc-rdc.org/wp-content/uploads/2013/06/Letter-to-His-Excellency-Secretary-General-of-the-United-Nations-25-June-2013.pdf [Accessed July 1, 2013].

Martin-Ortega, O. (2012a) Transitional Justice in the Quest for Just and Durable Peace in Bosnia and Herzegovina. In: Aggestam, K. and Björkdahl, A. (eds), *Rethinking Peacebuilding: The Quest for Just Peace in the Middle East and the Western Balkans*. London: Routledge, pp. 183–196.

———. (2012b) Prosecuting War Crimes At Home: Lessons from the War Crimes Chamber in the State Court of Bosnia and Herzegovina. *International Criminal Law Review*, 12, pp. 589–628.

Meron, T. (2011) Press Release about the ICTY President—Addressing the UN Security Council. Available from: http://www.icty.org/sid/10873 [Accessed January 15, 2013].

———. (2012) Comments by Judge Theodor Meron, ICTY President in September 2012—On International Day in The Hague, Welcome Address. Notes on file with author.

Milutinović, R. (2012) ICTY Trials Come to Light. International Justice, Radio Netherlands Worldwide, February 29. Available from: http://www.rnw.nl/international-justice/article/icty-trials-come-light [Accessed January 15, 2013].

Nettlefield, L. (2010) *Courting Democracy in Bosnia and Herzegovina. The Hague Tribunal's Impact in a Postwar State.* Cambridge: Cambridge University Press.

Nielsen, C.A. (2013) A Freedom of Information Act is Needed for International Criminal Courts and Tribunals. *ILawyer*, June 2. Available from: http://ilawyerblog.com/a-freedom-of-information-act-is-needed-for-international-criminal-courts-and-tribunals/ [Accessed June 11, 2013].

Orentlicher, D. (2010) That Someone Guilty Be Punished: The Impact of the ICTY in Bosnia. Available from: http://www.soros.org/publications/someone-guilty-be-punished-impact-icty-bosnia [Accessed January 15, 2013].

OSCE (n.d.) OSCE's War Crimes Justice Project. Available from: http://www.osce.org/odihr/74803 [Accessed July 2, 2013].

———. (2009) *Reasoning in War Crimes Judgments in Bosnia and Herzegovina. A report of the Capacity Building and Legacy Implementation Project.* Available from: http://www.oscebih.org/documents/osce_bih_doc_2010122314244699eng.pdf [Accessed January 15, 2013].

———. (2010) *Delivering Justice in BiH: An Overview of War Crimes Processing from 2005 to 2010.* Available from: http://www.oscebih.org/Download.aspx?id=602&lang=EN [Accessed January 15, 2013].

Oslobodjenje (2013) Stop cenzuri o ratnim zlocinima (In English: Stop censorship about war crimes) June 25. Available from: http://www.oslobodjenje.ba/vijesti/bih/birn-stop-cenzuri-o-ratnim-zlocinima [Accessed July 1, 2013].

Pavelić, B. (2013) Croatian Support for the Tribunal Triples After Generals Freed, *Balkan Insight*. Available from: http://www.balkaninsight.com/en/article/support-to-icty-tripled-in-croatia [Accessed March 16, 2013].

Raab, D. (2005) Evaluating the ICTY and its Completion Strategy. Efforts to Achieve Accountability for War Crimes and Their Tribunals. *Journal of International Criminal Justice*, 3.

Radio Netherlands Worldwide (2006) Sarajevo Commission Creates Political Trouble, Radio Netherlands Worldwide. Available from: http://www.rnw.nl/international-justice/article/sarajevo-commission-creates-political-trouble [Accessed January 15, 2013].

Research and Documentation Center (n.d.) Bosnian War Crimes Atlas. Available from: http://www.idc.org.ba/index.php?option=com_content&view=category &layout=blog&id=112&Itemid=144&lang=bs [Accessed January 15, 2013].

Ristić, M. (2012) Serbs Still Support War Crime Defendants. *Balkan Insight*, February 28. Available from: http://www.balkaninsight.com/en/article/serbs-still-supports-war-crime-defendants [Accessed January 15, 2013].

Robinson, P. (2011a) Press Release about President Robinson's address at the UN Security Council. Available from: www.icty.org (http://www.icty.org/ sid/10690) [Accessed January 15, 2013].

——. (2011b) The Way Forward. In: Steinberg, R. (ed.), *Assessing the Legacy of the ICTY*. The Hague: Nijhoff.

Ronen, Y. (2011) DOMAC Report: Bosnia and Herzegovina: The Interaction Between the ICTY and Domestic Courts in Adjudicating International Crimes. Available from: http://www.domac.is/reports/ [Accessed January 15, 2013].

Sadović, M. (2007) Thousands Suspected of Crimes in Bosnia. *Institute of War and Peace Reporting*, September 14. Available from: http://iwpr.net/report-news/thousands-suspected-crimes-bosnia [Accessed January 15, 2013].

Schaffer, D. (2012) *All the Missing Soul*, Lecture at the American Book Center, March 14. Notes on file with the author. Available from: http://www.treehut. abc.nl/index.php?page=details&itemid=831.

Schwendiman, D. (2010) Prosecuting Atrocity Crimes in National Courts: Looking Back On 2009 in Bosnia and Herzegovina. *Northwestern Journal of International Human Rights*, 8(3).

——. (2011) Capacity Building: The Institutional War Crimes Prosecution Legacy of the ICTY and the International Donor Community in Bosnia and Herzegovina. In: Steinberg, R. (ed.), *Assessing the Legacy of the ICTY*. The Hague, Nijhoff.

Sikkink, K. (2011) *The Justice Cascade. How Human Rights Prosecutions are changing the World*. New York: W.W. Norton and Company.

Simons, M (2013) Hague Judge Faults Acquittals of Serb and Croat Commanders. *The New York Times*, June 14. Available from: http://www.nytimes. com/2013/06/14/world/europe/hague-judge-faults-acquittals-of-serb-and-croat-commanders.html?ref=marlisesimons&_r=0 [Accessed July 2, 2013].

The Srebrenica Report—Bosnia and Herzegovina. Republika Srpska. Republika Srpska Government. the Commission for Investigations of the Events in and Around Srebrenica Between the 10th and 19th July 1995 (2004) Available from: http://trial-ch.org/fileadmin/user_upload/documents/trialwatch/ Srebrenica_Report2004.pdf [Accessed April 11, 2015].

Stover, E. (2005) *The Witness. War Crimes and the Promise of Justice in The Hague*. Pennsylvania: University of Pennsylvania Press.

Subotic, J. (2009) *Hijacked Justice. Dealing with the Past in the Balkans*. Ithaca: Cornell University Press.

Teitel, R. (2000) *Transitional Justice*. Oxford: Oxford University Press.

Tolbert, D. (2002) The International Criminal Tribunal for the Former Yugoslavia. *Fletcher Forum of World Affairs*, 26(2), pp. 7–19.

TV Justice Magazine (2013) Episode 41: 20 Years of the Hague Tribunal, *TV Justice Magazine*, June 5. Available from: http://www.youtube.com/watch?feature=player_embedded&v=9CthH0X1fEQ#at=77 [Accessed July 1, 2013].

Ucanbarlic, S. (2011) State Court Hands Down More than 400 Years for War Crimes. *Balkan Investigative Reporting Network*, December 30. Available from: http://www.bim.ba/en/302/10/34162/ [Accessed July 1, 2013].

——. (2013) Anonymisation has caused chaos. *Justice Report*, May 30. Available from: http://www.justice-report.com/en/articles/anonymisation-has-caused-chaos [Accessed July 1, 2013].

United Nations (2004) Press Release: Secretary-General, Welcoming Republika Srpska Apology for Srebrenica Tragedy, Says Authorities Have Set Example of Confronting Painful Past. Available from: http://www.unis.unvienna.org/unis/pressrels/2004/sgsm9591.html [Accessed April 11, 2015].

——. (2010) Guidance Note of the Secretary General: United Nations Approach to Transitional Justice. Available from: http://www.unrol.org/doc.aspx?d=2957 [Accessed April 11, 2015].

United Nations Development Program (UNDP) (n.d.) Procjena potrebe na polju podrske svjedoka i zrtava (In English: Assessment of the needs in protecting witnesses and victims). Available from: http://www.undp.ba/upload/publications/Procjena%20potrebe%20na%20polju%20podrske%20svjedoka-zrtava.pdf [Accessed January 15, 2013].

——. (2011) Press Release: Witness Support Office Opens in Banja Luka and Sarajevo. Available from: http://www.undp.ba/index.aspx?PID=7&RID=658 [Accessed January 15, 2013].

UN Security Council (1993) *Resolution 827*. Available from: http://daccess-dds-ny.un.org/doc/UNDOC/GEN/N93/306/28/IMG/N9330628.pdf?OpenElement [Accessed April 11, 2015].

Vesti (2012) Nikolic: Hag postoji da bi sudio Srbima (In English: Nikolic: The Hague exists in order to prosecute Serbs), November 29. Available from: www.vesti.rs http://www.vesti.rs/Tomislav-Nikoli%C4%87/Nikolic-Hag-postoji-da-bi-sudio-Srbima-2.html.

Vinjamuri, L. (2010) Deterrence, Democracy, and the Pursuit of International Justice. *Ethics and International* Affairs, 24(2), pp. 191–211.

Chapter 8

Leader-dominated Ethnic Parties and Dysfunctional Institutional Design in Bosnia-Herzegovina and Kosovo

Tina Mavrikos-Adamou

Introduction

While Bosnia and Herzegovina (BiH) dominated the news in the early 1990s, and Kosovo did so in 1999, in the twenty-first century international focus and attention has moved beyond the Balkans. However, 20 years after the dissolution of Yugoslavia lessons may be learned from both of these peace and state-building projects. Both examples raise questions about the international community's efforts to help consolidate functioning states, especially since billions of dollars in aid have poured into BiH (the US alone provided a little over $2 billion in peacekeeping support and aid to BiH from the time of its independence to 2011) (Woehrel 2013a), and Kosovo has likewise received substantial assistance (Woehrel 2013b, p. 8). With international attention now turned to the Middle East, Afghanistan, Pakistan and other regions, an assessment of the political challenges that BiH and Kosovo have faced in creating functional democratic systems is relevant.

The Balkan cases show that constructing functional democratic systems in the aftermath of conflict is much harder, and takes much longer, than policy-makers, leaders, or academics might like. The multifaceted project faced by post-communist, post-war societies includes building democratic institutions where they did not exist, and at the same time facilitating reconciliation in the aftermath of war. One of the hurdles in undertaking the establishment of a democratic system in such states is the consolidation of institutions that can sustain democratic consolidation, prevent future violence, and are seen as legitimate. The design and function of such structures must be locally contextualized within the existing political culture, just as the institutionalization of power-sharing arrangements should balance local interests and international norms.

Consociationalism, according to Lijphart and other adherents of that approach, focuses on decentralization and power-sharing as the main elements of the political system. Advocates of this approach argue it is best suited for societies that have high levels of heterogeneity and whose composition is not conducive to majoritarian style policy-making decisions (Lijphart 1997). Lijphart outlined the four key principles of a consociational model: "grand coalition, mutual veto, proportionality, and segmental autonomy" (Lijphart 1979, p. 500). He also presumes an interest among the elites in making the consociational model work. The biggest problem BiH has had in adopting this framework—grafted onto the country at Dayton—has been this assumption that the participating groups will develop a level of trust and elite cooperation to allow the system to function. This has not happened in BiH.

Further, the absence of a sense of "demos" can create formidable obstacles for both statehood and legitimacy. Hayden poses the critical question: "What happens, however, when there is no demos, no single political community that accepts a state (a territory with a government) as its own, because the population divides itself into different ethnic groups, no one of which comprises a majority of the population, and most of the members of each seeing their worst danger as subordination to the others?" (Hayden 2005, p. 227). By creating a state where a sizeable percentage of the population does not have an allegiance to the country and where respective nationalist leaders possess power over decision-making—the question as to how the state and government can effectively operate often remains unanswered.

There is an extensive body of literature concerned with democracy promotion and democracy construction (Diamond 1999, 2005, Burnell 2000, Carothers 2004, 2009, De Zeeuw 2006, Crawford 2011). Opinions diverge over timeframes, and there is no universally accepted agreement as to whether democracy promotion should be seen as a process leading to a specific end product, a primarily political or administrative task, or both; or most recently, whether it is possible and/or even desirable to export the western democratic model. Debates continue over whether the focus should be on *type* of government (for example, is it better to adopt a presidential or parliamentary system or some combination); or *degree* of government—when and how to empower citizens, and how to assist these fragile states to become economically viable. Both BiH and Kosovo are states where the international community has left a heavy footprint. If not for international actors and organizations, these two states would likely not exist in their present form. Much has been written about internationally designed states as a form of conflict resolution (Chandler 2000, McMahon 2005, Hayden 2005, Zahar 2008, Perry 2009, Chong 2009, Bhuta 2010). Often due to either the nature of the conflict and its outcome, or the local political elites, the type of institutional design is complex, characterized by a decentralized system and weak central authority. Governance structures that are designed so that no single ethnic group can make decisions opposed by any other group often result in dysfunction, and do not facilitate compromise among ethnic groups. This dysfunction is compounded by nationalist leaders who constantly reinforce ethnic difference. These institutional designs are often the only viable outcome given the immediate post-war environment in these deeply divided societies (Keil 2013). If one agrees that integration is preferable over partition as the only viable and realistic path for maintaining long-term peace (and there are many who do not agree), some form of democratic design has to be hammered out that includes some schema of power-sharing (Tzifakis 2007, Bieber and Keil 2009). The difficulty is how to build such institutional designs with minimally complicated governance structures, avoiding decision-making gridlock.

Many of the specific political challenges that these states face include dysfunctional political institutional designs that continue to accentuate ethnic politics, weak central institutions that lack power, public trust and legitimacy, and leader-dominated ethnic parties that have not drawn support across ethnic lines. This chapter will explore two of these difficulties, mainly the dysfunctional legislative bodies in BiH and Kosovo and the role played by leader-dominated ethnic parties. Both of these post-communist, post-war states face mounting challenges in maintaining stable and functioning democratic systems. The dysfunctional legislatures in the two countries and the predominance of nationalist political leaders are two intertwined variables that feed off each other, and that together account for much of the stalemate that both BiH and Kosovo have experienced in establishing democratic systems. While each of these issues and challenges could form a study in their own right, taken together with the other contributions in this volume the significant political and structural barriers to reform and democratization in fragile, post-war states, and the critical role of elites in these processes, become abundantly clear.

Institutional Design and Legislative Bodies in BiH and Kosovo

This section will examine the institutional choices made in BiH and Kosovo that shed light on the apparent disjunction between political structures and practical governmental functionality. BiH's ongoing political crisis can in part be explained by institutional choices that were made during Dayton by leaders of the warring parties and the USA, which institutionalized ethnic divisions.[1] The recent Kosovo crises lasted for 20 years, and although Kosovo declared independence in February 2008, uncertainty remains, as revealed by continuing northern border skirmishes between Kosovar Serbs and Kosovo state authorities from 2011 through 2014—testament to how existing tensions between ethnic groups can escalate into violence.

The Example of BiH

BiH's *triple transition*, that of "transition from war to peace, the transition from the self-management system to a market economy and from Yugoslavia to independence" has posed immense challenges for the country (Bieber 2006, p. 35). NATO's engagement in ending the war and enforcing peace along with many other international actors has made BiH a country where external intervention has dominated the state-building project. The Dayton Agreement set

---

1   See the chapter by Soeren Keil in this volume which focuses on power-sharing arrangements in BiH, Kosovo, and Macedonia.

up a consociational model of governance, where it was hoped that ethnic tensions could be managed in a post-war environment (Lijphart 1996, Lijphart and Waisman 1999). The boundaries of the entities were legitimized: the Republika Srpska (RS), and the Federation of Bosnia and Herzegovina (FBiH). The Federation was further divided into 10 cantons, with the status of the disputed city of Brčko in the northeast put on hold to await arbitration (ultimately being established as a District). The Parliamentary Assembly at the state level is bi-cameral, with a House of Peoples and a House of Representatives. Decisions in both chambers are taken by majority of those present and voting but there is a stipulation that a veto can be utilized such that: "A proposed decision of the Parliamentary Assembly may be declared to be destructive of a vital interest of the Bosniak, Croat, or Serb people by a majority of, as appropriate, the Bosniak, Croat, or Serb Delegates." (General Framework Agreement, Annex 4 BiH Constitution, Article IV 3(e)). Studies have noted that this veto power has thwarted the legislative process, and that, in addition, the "entity veto" has prevented important legislation being passed (Bahtic-Kunrath 2011). Likewise, power-sharing is enshrined in the executive, as the Chairmanship of the Presidency in BiH rotates every eight months among three Presidency members (Bosniak, Croat, Serb), each elected for a four-year term. The three members are directly elected (the Federation votes for the Bosniak and Croat member, and the RS for the Serb member). The Presidency theoretically was created to carry out many of the responsibilities of the central government including conducting foreign affairs, appointing ambassadors, and representing BiH in international organizations and institutions (General Framework Agreement, Annex 4 BiH Constitution, Article V (3)). However, as it turns out, the provisions set out in the Dayton Agreement make effective government extremely difficult (Venice Commission 2005). In 2006 a reform package led by the US to rationalize the constitutional system was narrowly rejected.[2] Much rests on how to reconcile the need for a functioning state and to provide a space for multiple and overlapping identities to be formed among the three constituent groups. Other reform efforts have also resulted in a lack of agreement and consensus amongst the political elites.

The institutional framework of the country has thus left BiH with a weak, complex and convoluted system. Power-sharing theoretically takes place at all four levels of government; however, the multiple layers of governance lack clear competences and parallel institutions create redundancies that reinforce weak public legitimacy (Marko 2006). Some of the unintended consequences of the Dayton Accords and its broad-brush approach include a lack of legitimacy of the institutional structures of the country. Compromise and common policy-making is nearly impossible within the existing framework since, as will be discussed below, nationalist leaders dominate the main political parties in power and continue to support policies that favor their group. There is little space for "collective responsibility" or a "community of interests" to grow within the

---

2   The chapter by Valery Perry in this volume provides more details on this initiative.

existing institutional framework that would cut across institutional divisions and ethnonationalist cleavages. The impact of the lack of functioning central authorities on state consolidation and peacebuilding is clearly evident in two issues (though there are many more): culture and education. For example, at present there is no state Ministry of Culture, and as a result some of BiH's most important museums, such as the National Museum, have closed due to political wrangling over which government body should finance them. The three constituent peoples are unable to reach consensus as to how to manage cultural sites. Bosnian Serbs oppose giving the central government any role in cultural sites, arguing that each of the country's ethnic groups should be responsible for their own management of sites and in effect their own cultural heritage. Since there is no central/state Ministry of Culture to fund and oversee cultural sites, several cultural institutions located in Sarajevo have received virtually no funding from authorities, resulting in these centers having to shut their doors in 2012, since they were no longer able to pay their employees or even cover their utility bills.

Other concrete functional dilemmas arising from such a loose federal system are evident through BiH's 13 separate ministries of education, which create logistical and political barriers to the coordination of a harmonized educational system. As a result, there is no consensus on a common educational curriculum. The educational system in BiH is regulated by the respective Ministries of Education of the Federation and the RS (Perry 2003). Additionally, each of the 10 cantons also has its own Ministry of Education as does the Brčko District. Giving responsibility for education to small, ethnically exclusive units whose commitment is to the children of their "own" ethnic group has created enormous obstacles to social reconciliation. A lack of a coordinated system of educational laws and little or no centralized regulations create dilemmas for democracy-building where nationalist parties dominate the political landscape, further hindering the acceptance of pluralism and delaying the process of reconciliation. There have been numerous bilateral and multilateral international agencies that have supported the educational sector in BiH in the post-conflict era, including UNDP, the World Bank, the EC, USAID, and the OSCE. Despite the assistance of these organizations, the public education system in BiH continues to exacerbate difference and intolerance.

These two examples show the clear results of fragmentation. However, institutional integration in the conventional sense of the term is not viewed as an option for BiH at present due to domestic elite political resistance—particularly among forces in the RS.[3] A focused approach to reform that can simultaneously accommodate national identities and promote cross-ethnic cooperation appears to be the best way to balance a multitude of variables in BiH. There are those that claim that institutional arrangements need to be accompanied by the creation of a shared public identity that transcends ethnic divisions (Nagle and Clancy 2012).

---

3   Meagan Hrle's chapter in this volume explores RS opposition to justice sector reforms; this is indicative of trends in every sector.

In practical terms, the question remains as to how to get voters to put their support behind parties that advocate non-ethnic issues.

The Case of Kosovo

As in BiH, Kosovo has been shaped by a decisive international role via UNMIK (the United Nations Interim Administration Mission in Kosovo). In 1999, the UN took over full administration of Kosovo, and the effects of this "heavy" footprint have had long-lasting ramifications for the country and its people. The *Ahtisaari Comprehensive Proposal for the Kosovo Status Settlement* set out to provide a set of general principles and included 12 annexes. Constitutional provisions, decentralization, community (that is, minority) rights and a justice system are covered in the first four annexes. One of the underlying premises of the Ahtisaari proposal was to ensure that a multi-ethnic, democratic state would be secured to ensure lasting peace. An additional objective of the proposal was to address how the communities would be represented in the institutions of the state. Provisions were also made for an internationalized constitutional court. The construction of state institutions and government structures in Kosovo reflected choices brokered by a multitude of actors. The first annex of the proposal outlined the obligations that Kosovo was to follow concerning important international human rights conventions and protocols, including the European Convention for the Protection of Human Rights and Fundamental Freedoms and its Protocol, and the International Covenant on Civil and Political Rights (Ahtisaari Comprehensive Proposal for the Kosovo Status Settlement 2007, Annex 1, Article 2(1)).

The 2008 Constitution of Kosovo provided for a unicameral assembly made up of 120 members: 100 members to be elected through a preference voting (PR) system to serve 4-year terms, and 20 members reserved to represent Kosovo's national minorities—10 for Kosovar Serbs and 10 for non-Serb minorities which could include Bosniaks, Ashkali, Roma, Turks, and Balkan Egyptians (Constitution of Kosovo 2008, Article 64(1)). Power-sharing takes place in the assembly as outlined by Article 67 of the Constitution which provides that the Assembly of Kosovo elects the president of the Assembly along with five deputies, three of which are proposed by the three largest parliamentary groups, and two of which represent non-majority communities in the Assembly. Further, Article 78 of the Kosovo Constitution provides for the creation of a Committee on Rights and Interests of Communities, which requires that 1/3 of members represent the group of deputies of the Assembly holding seats reserved or guaranteed for the Serbian Community, 1/3 who represent the group of deputies that are not in the majority, while the remaining 1/3 are from the majority community represented in the Assembly. Hence from a *de jure* perspective, there are several safeguards for non-majority communities built into the institutional structure of Kosovo. Both the Ahtisaari Proposal and the Kosovo Constitution of 2008 provide for several layers of protection for the communities residing in Kosovo including a Law on the Promotion and Protection of the Rights of Communities and Persons

Belonging to Communities in Kosovo, which specifically outlines use of language, educational provisions and decentralization (Ahtisaari Comprehensive Proposal for the Kosovo Status Settlement 2007, Annex 1, Article 2). These are found in Chapter III of the Kosovo Constitution of 2008, which addresses the rights of communities and their members.

The president of Kosovo is elected by parliament to serve a five-year term. Recent discussions about constitutional reform have included the recommendation that the president should be popularly elected rather than by parliament which is currently the case. In April of 2011 a Parliamentary Commission was established to review how the president of Kosovo would be elected by a popular vote. The *de facto* reality, however, is that a sizeable percentage of the ethnic Serb community refuses to recognize the legitimacy of the Kosovo government and continues to boycott its elections and institutions. In many ways, as with the case of BiH, the institutional framework reifies ethnic difference in its incorporation of the communities in the decision-making process. As with BiH, unless purposeful efforts are made to reduce the significance of ethnicity in Kosovo, and create a common state-building endeavor, "cooperation by coercion" will have limited success (Simonsen 2004).

As in the case of BiH, cultural geography in Kosovo plays a decisive role in local politics. Due to the physical segregation of the country with ethnic Serbs in enclaves in central and southeastern Kosovo and the largest group in the north of Mitrovica, a high level of mistrust has developed between the two main ethnic groups and there are few arenas where shared interests can be pursued. Even linguistic communication has been stymied. Before 1981 the University of Pristina was bilingual, and up until 1987 primary-aged school students in Kosovo were introduced to the "other language"—the one that they were not speaking at home—in first grade (Kostovicova 2005, p. 43). That has changed, and today there is little encouragement for Kosovo Serbs to learn the Albanian language fluently. Likewise, the young Albanian population sees little reason to learn Serbian, especially since independence. Discrimination against the other ethnic minorities in the country continues to occur despite moves to incorporate them into the decision-making processes of government via a minimum number of seats allotted for minority groups.

UNMIK and EULEX continue to play important roles in assisting Kosovo to further consolidate its political institutions, maintain stability, and promote democracy-building in the country, although UNMIK's 13-year tenure in the country has prompted many, both Kosovar Serb and ethnic Albanian, to resent their continued presence. A recent report by the European Court of Auditors has found that the strengthening of the rule of law in Kosovo has been painfully slow and that both the continued control by ethnic Serbs in the north and the lack of real commitment by the government in Kosovo has been major obstacles for EULEX (European Court of Auditors 2012). NATO troops continue to monitor northern borders, which has been particularly important after a series of violent skirmishes occurred in July 2011 between Kosovar Serbs and Kosovo state authorities near the town of Zubin Potok, where Serbs were protesting NATO's attempts to remove a barricade that was blocking a main road in the region. Additionally, the ethnic Serb minority conducted a non-binding referendum in northern Kosovo in February of 2012 asking ethnic Serbs whether they accept Kosovo's institutions. The referendum had no legal effect but it further strained relations between Kosovar Serbs and ethnic Albanians and aggravated ethnic tensions that already existed in the northern region of the country (Euronews, February 14, 2012).

Kosovo suffered a political institutional crisis in September 2010, demonstrating the continuing impact of domestic party politics even in a country with a significant international presence. The Constitutional Court found that Fatmir Sejdiu, then president, could not be simultaneously leader of the Democratic League of Kosovo party (LDK) and head of state. Sejdiu resigned and the president of the Assembly took over as acting president. This triggered a vote of no confidence that was submitted by the AKR—Alliance for New Kosovo Party—to pull out of the existing coalition that was led by the PDK (Democratic Party of Kosovo) headed by Prime Minister Thaçi. The December 2010 elections saw new political parties and social movements taking part in the elections, and various party coalitions were formed. The elections, however, were marred by a series of irregularities in voting procedures that were detected by independent monitoring agencies and resulted in re-run elections in several municipalities (European Parliament 2010). The re-run election results were likewise disputed, leading to prosecutors in Kosovo to file charges for election fraud and other election related crimes in some 200 individual cases.[4] The role of political parties and electoral systems will be further discussed below, including the April 2013 15-Point Agreement between Serbia and Kosovo.

Political Parties and Party Elites: BiH and Kosovo

The previous section sought to illustrate the broad consequences of the institutional choices decided at Dayton for BiH, as well as the importance of the Ahtisaari proposal and ensuing 2008 Constitutional design for Kosovo. This section builds upon those arguments and focuses on the role of political parties and party elites. In a consolidated democratic system political parties are mechanisms that act as a vehicle for citizens' interests to be articulated into policy alternatives. Political parties play a decisive role in channeling and aggregating demands from citizens, and they are one of the main actors for political expression in a democratic society. Parties are also seen as promoting political stability, and facilitating the staffing of government institutions. Much of the literature on the role of political parties in ethnically divided societies over the past decade suggests, however, that in

---

4   See OSCE Mission in Kosovo report of October 2012, Fair Trial Rights in Election Related Cases. Available from: http://www.osce.org/kosovo/96447 [Accessed April 12, 2015].

these cases, ethnically based parties' narrow appeals and views have thwarted the process of democratic expression and have acted as obstacles to good governance (Palermo and Woelk 2003, Norris 2005, Reilly 2006, Nenadović 2010, Hulsey 2010). In ethnically based party systems such as those in BiH and Kosovo, political parties appeal to ethnic allegiances rather than ideology or issue-based platforms. Identity issues are paramount, and there is little incentive to develop platforms that might attract the votes of "others."

In *Democracy in Plural Societies* Lijphart enumerates those factors that are most important in assuring the success of the consociational model and which are conducive to elite cooperation: "… a multiple balance of power, small size of the country involved, overarching loyalties, segmental isolation, prior conditions of elite accommodation, and … the presence of crosscutting cleavages" (Lijphart 1977, p. 54). Lijphart perceived elite cooperation as the principal feature of consociationalism. In the two country cases here under examination, the role of political elites, the inability to create broad-based, multi-ethnic parties with all-encompassing allegiances, and all this in a post-conflict political environment, have created unfavorable conditions and major obstacles impeding the success of consociational democracy. There appear to be few political, structural or popular incentives to encourage elites to pursue accommodation and coordination. Elections have failed to result in elites with this Lijphart-inspired consociational mindset.

Free and fair elections are one of the cornerstones of democratic political systems, and international actors involved in post-war reconstruction are keen to have elections take place soon after a new system has been put in place. In post-conflict environments this impetus to hold elections as soon as possible is, however, often not matched by logistical readiness on the ground, nor the requisite political and media culture. Although not intended, what often occurs in these first post-war elections is that the elections help consolidate ethnic exclusivism to the detriment of the peacebuilding process (Belloni 2004). Many agree that the post-war elections in BiH were organized and conducted prematurely. In a detailed report prior to the first post-war general elections, the International Crisis Group (ICG) recommended to the OSCE that elections be postponed until minimal prerequisite conditions be met that included that indicted war criminals have no influence on the elections (ICG 1996). The ICG documented how the return of those displaced during the conflict was limited, as was freedom of movement, that free media and press had not been established, and that "the political environment was anything but neutral" (International Crisis Group 1996, p. 9). In Kosovo, there was a bit less haste in rushing to hold elections, and the experiences in BiH helped to shape the electoral, approach in Kosovo. For example, the decision was made to stagger elections and sequence local and national elections. Local elections in Kosovo were held first (October 2000), followed by national elections for parliament in November 2001. The theory was that local elections would have a greater likelihood to focus on non-ethnic issues than would general elections, perhaps preparing the ground for issue-based politics. Ultimately, however, this was not the case.

In both countries, these first post-war elections did not result in a clean break from pre-war party politics. In BiH elections were held in September 1996, and the results confirmed the roles of the three nationalist parties who had brought the country to war (Belloni 2004). In Kosovo, political party leadership in part emerged from the Kosovo Liberation Army (KLA) which split with the non-violent LDK. In both countries, political parties formed along ethnic/national lines rather than around a party ideology or a clearly articulated issue-based party platform. The party elite established their support based on members of their own ethnic group and espoused nationalist rhetoric to get elected. In the absence of election laws that might have required attracting "cross group support," it was rational to simply consolidate support among one's own ethnic base. Creating a post-war political environment of "us" versus "them" after the war was not difficult for the political elite who took office in the first post-war elections. Drawing on the human atrocities that had been committed by all sides in the war and the fact that all groups perceived their role in the war as having been defensive, a zero-sum relationship was adopted by politicians (Sejfija 2013). Although the specific leaders representing the three constituent peoples have changed since the initial elections in BiH, the rhetoric by nationalist politicians has not: vote for us so that we can protect the interests of "our" ethnic group, since any gain made by the "other" ethnic group will come at our expense (Mujkić and Hulsey 2010). The situation is the same in Kosovo. There is no need for the development of cross-national parties, political moderation or cooperation with other ethnic groups.[5] Voters feel that they are obliged to vote for the candidate representing their ethnic group, otherwise no one will safeguard their ethnic interests (Van Willigen 2010).

Subsequent election cycles in BiH have seen international agencies react to ethnic party dominance by attempting to influence the election processes and outcomes. Most directly, in BiH the High Representatives have used their powers to remove democratically elected officials from office.[6] Further, there were some limited attempts at electoral engineering to promote the development of multi-ethnic, cross-national parties. For example, in the 2000 elections, open lists and multi-member constituencies were adopted, replacing the previous PR closed party lists that were used in legislative elections in the hope that such reforms would break the dominance of the nationalist parties.[7] A preferential voting system was adopted for the elections of the RS Presidency. Additionally, new rules were implemented for the election of members of the House of Peoples in the Federation. The intention behind these changes was to assist in the development of inclusive parties that would facilitate integration and undermine support for mono-ethnic parties (Palermo and Woelk 2003). However, these minimal structural changes were

---

5   See John Hulsey's chapter in this volume that focuses on electoral rules in BiH.

6   See Mateja Peter's chapter in this volume which discusses the role of the international community in BiH.

7   Even this minimal reform now appears to be in jeopardy, as discussions are on-going to return to a system of closed lists.

not more successful due to the continued influence of an election law structured around the fragmented constitutional state framework, and the lack of any cross-group voting incentive. In addition to this structural challenge, developing party platforms that are inclusive and moderate rather than exclusive is much more difficult and complex than the international community had hoped (Reilly 2006). The BiH election law, and the constitution itself, continue to practically inhibit the emergence of multi-ethnic constituencies, and discourage moderation.

Leader-dominated ethnic parties in BiH have been led by individuals who emerged within a political culture fraught with ethnic fears and intolerance made political via national leadership which ignited ethnic intolerance for political purposes. Compromise in such an environment is seen as a sign of weakness and of selling out group interests. BiH suffers from a *prisoner's dilemma* in which political elites have little incentive to collaborate with the leaders of other groups, since they cannot ensure what the other leaders will do (Hayden 2011), and since they rarely need to do so. Appealing to nationalist concerns allows leaders to win elections and safeguard their groups' interests, while party leaders emphasize personal over legal authority. This demonstrates the practical reality that trumps Lijphart's hoped for "prudent leadership" that should serve as an alternative or counterweight to cross-cutting cleavages (Lijphart 1977).

A glance at the leadership of the main political parties in BiH attests to the predominance of ethnic party leaders impacting party politics. Milorad Dodik's SNSD (Party of Independent Social Democrats) party has significantly influenced party politics in the RS, and Dodik has aroused nationalist sentiments among the Serb populations in the RS via provocative public statements which are undeniably ethno-centric (Toal 2013). Before 2006, however, the SDS (Serb Democratic Party), which was established by Radovan Karadžić, now on trial at the ICTY (International Criminal Tribunal for the former Yugoslavia), was the predominant Serb party in BiH. Biljana Plavšić, a leading member of the SDS, convicted of war crimes by the ICTY in 2001, was the epitome of an ethnocentric leader. Dragan Čović, head of the Croatian Democratic Union (HDZ) who was charged with abuse of power, has championed the interests of the ethnic Croat population in BiH and continues to claim to preserve Croat interests from being expropriated by Bosniaks. The Social Democratic Party (SDP), dominated by Zlatko Lagumdžija for many years, nominally advocates strengthening political institutions at the state level to ensure its group's interests from within the structures of government; however, deal-making with SNSD in 2012 and 2013 has actually led to the SDP playing a role in the weakening of BiH institutions. The SDA (Party of Democratic Action), led by Alija Izbetbegović, is primarily a Bosniak party. Once Izbetbegović, stepped down as party leader in 2001, Sulejman Tihić was elected to lead the party, before Izetbegović's son Bakir took over. Under his leadership, the party has moved somewhat towards the political center, favoring a decentralized but unitary BiH state with ethnically mixed cantons. Across all of the main parties it is clear that the political stance taken by the nationalist political elite in BiH has led to uncompromising party politics based on distrust, which has left little room for the development of non-nationalist parties (UNSC 2013).

In Kosovo, state-building was to be facilitated through the electoral system which also provided for representation of Kosovo's national minorities through reserved seats in the unicameral assembly. The case of party formation in the post-conflict era in Kosovo differs from that of BiH since there were no officially organized political parties before the conflict. A peaceful resistance movement led by Ibrahim Rugova, an ethnic Albanian, who held the leadership role until his death in 2006, organized the Democratic League of Kosovo (LDK) (Nenadović 2010). A military group known as the Kosovo Liberation Army (KLA) soon boasted its own party, with the PDK (Democratic Party of Kosovo) winning the most votes in the 2007 elections. Hashim Thaçi, a former KLA leader, took up the post of party leader and became prime minister the same year. Besides clearly representing only the Kosovar Albanian population, there have been allegations that Thaçi has been at the head of an international organ donor smuggling ring and other forms of organized crime, including arms and narcotics smuggling. In a Council of Europe report submitted by Dick Marty, human rights rapporteur, Thaçi was directly involved in the "Drenica Group" that was directing organized criminal activities (Marty 2010). Other members of the "Drenica Group" who are being investigated for war crimes or organized crime include Xhavit Haliti, Kadri Veseli, Azem Syla, and Fatmir Limaj (former minister of Telecommunications). On the other side of the ethnic spectrum, Kosovar Serb minority parties have periodically boycotted elections in Kosovo as they do not recognize Kosovo institutions and electoral processes, and refuse to recognize an independent Kosovo. The largest Kosovar Serb party is the SLS—Independent Liberal Party—which was formed in 2006, whose main stated aim is to protect the interests of the Serb communities in Kosovo-Metohija. Slobodan Petrović heads the party and represents the ethnic Serb population in Kosovo, becoming one of five deputy prime ministers in 2011. There remains a sizeable population of Serbs in central Kosovo who, due to their location, tend to cooperate more with Kosovo state authorities than those in the north, and they tend to vote. A new coalition known as the "Serb Movement of Kosovo" emerged, claiming to have cultivated relations and support from various parties in Pristina including the ethnic Albanian population (SE Times, February 13, 2012). This movement includes the Serb Movement of Resistance, the Serb Social-Democratic Party, the leaders of the municipalities of Ropotova and Klokot, and several NGOs.

Kosovo conducts elections according to the Electoral Laws of 2007 and 2009. The first elections in the post-independence era of 2010 saw a few changes; the PR system is now entirely an open-list system, with voters able to select up to five preferred candidates from a list of up to 110 names. Kosovo remains a single electoral district, which many believe should be changed: "Delimiting districts would serve a number of commendable purposes: it would democratize the election process by decentralizing power within the political parties; it would provide geographic representation for many currently neglected areas of Kosovo; it would improve the accountability of representatives to their constituency voters; and it may decrease voter apathy and increase voter participation in Kosovo" (Electoral Knowledge Network 2012). Another advantage noted is that districts would assist in securing geographic diversity in the assembly, which given the cultural geography of Kosovo at present, could be very influential. Geographic diversity can likewise be required in a closed list PR system by establishing geographical distribution requirements on the candidate list, but this can result in an even more confusing electoral process, especially if there are already requirements for gender or other forms of diversity placed. Since there are already a variety of administrative units, including the 5 UNMIK regions, the 7 regions delineated by the Statistical Institute, and the existing 30 municipalities within Kosovo, these could be converted into electoral constituencies quite easily. In April of 2011 an Ad-Hoc Commission for Amending the Law on General Elections in the Republic of Kosovo was established, charged with reconsidering the method of election of the 100 deputies in a direct manner, whether lists should remain open or be closed, creating electoral zones, and whether the distribution of seats in these zones should be by a majoritarian system or mixed. However, such changes need a 2/3 majority in parliament to get passed. At the present time, this has yet to occur. Largely due to leader dominated parties that are uncompromising, political stalemate thwarts necessary reforms. Under international pressure, political leaders have re-entered electoral reform talks since the country is set for a parliamentary election in 2014.

The 2010 elections saw the inclusion of two new parties, a left-wing nationalist party Vetëvendosje! (VV), and the centrist FER—New Air Party. These elections were marred by irregularities in the municipalities of Skenderaj/Srbica, Gllogoc/Glogavac, and Decan/Decane which were cited by monitors from the European Parliament and the ENEMO (European Parliament 2010, ENEMO 2011). Although it was remarked that the 2010 elections generally did take place in an atmosphere of calm, technical problems were observed and the Kosovo Serb municipalities in the north of the country continued to boycott the elections. The Central Election Commission ordered a recount of the ballots, and this led to five municipalities conducting repeat elections. A further re-run of elections was ordered by the Kosovo Central Election Commission in Mitrovica on January 23 (International Civilian Office Kosovo 2011). In the end a great deal of skepticism remained among the general population and losing parties alike as to the legitimacy of the elections.

In April 2013, a 15-point agreement was mediated by the EU between then-Serbian Prime Minister Ivica Dačić and Kosovo Prime Minister Hashim Thaçi over the administration of Serbian municipalities in northern Kosovo. Although both countries' parliaments backed the agreement, the ultra-nationalist Democratic Party of Serbia and the Serbian Orthodox Church have protested its implementation. The local elections of November 5, 2013, in Kosovo were a tangible result of the Belgrade-Pristina Agreement. Although generally deemed successful, violence in three polling stations in northern Mitrovica required a repeat election to be organized two weeks later in selected electoral districts, under the tight control of international police officers and NATO-led peacekeepers from KFOR. The major problem in both rounds was low turnout by the Serb minority, who despite being urged by Serbian politicians to vote, often opted out. These elections were considered an important test of whether the Serb minority in the north could perceive the Pristina government as legitimate in return for a certain degree of autonomy.

One of the greatest challenges in democracy promotion is how to support the development of systems in which political party leaders might address pressing concerns of citizens irrespective of ethnic affiliation, transcending ethnic identity to instead tackle issues such as unemployment, educational reform, more efficient social services, and the like. As long as political elites continue to benefit from the current system where patron-clientelist practices operate; where elites wield much influence over public-sector jobs, privatization projects, the media, and many other economic activities; and where constitutional or electoral structures allow for candidates to seek votes from a narrowly-defined ethnic area, then ethno-centric electoral outcomes will continue. The dysfunction of the system fuels patron-client practices. A vicious cycle is created: political elites use their position to dispense favors to members of their own ethnic group further entrenching ethnic competition and divisiveness, and citizens come to rely on these patrons who they become obliged to support when elections come around. Constantly changing electoral rules is likewise disorienting for a population that may suffer from election fatigue, frequently tasked to go to the polls while having to continually learn new rules (Coles 2007).

Returning to Lijphart's assumption that a certain level of elite cooperation and trust is needed for consociationalism to work, in both BiH and Kosovo no such cooperation or trust has evolved. At present the BiH and Kosovo constitutions do not include any provisions that explicitly promote cross-ethnic cooperation. Lipjhart contends that for the consociational model to operate effectively, "elites have to accommodate the divergent interests and demands of the subcultures" (Lijphart 1969, p. 216). This in turn depends upon "a relatively low total load on the decision-making apparatus" which, in another words, depends upon a productive economy and a political apparatus that is manageable (Lijphart 1969, p. 218). Arguably, none of these prerequisites can be found in either BiH or Kosovo.

Part of the problem in both countries is the dilemma of elite recruitment. Political elites are selected by a small elite group within the political parties in power rather than by the voters (a particular problem in electoral systems characterized by closed lists and indirect elections), reinforcing cronyism and excluding potential moderate newcomers. Moderate candidates in both countries have a hard time getting endorsements from existing political parties since they need to toe the nationalist line in these leader-dominated parties. The question is how to get voters more involved in the selection of party leaders *before* elections (van Biezen 2008). The other dilemma is how to get party leaders more interested in the bread-and-butter issues that trouble all citizens, and to move away from ethnic politics and towards more accountability based on practical governance results. An additional concern is that citizens often vote for nationalist parties during times of economic crisis because they believe that these parties will provide them with what state mechanisms otherwise cannot or delay in providing a permit or license, a job, personal security, and other necessities.

A Way Forward

The main political dilemmas that both BiH and Kosovo have faced are that their institutional arrangements create substantial handicaps for consensus and effective government. Ethnic identity over civic identity has been cemented into the institutional foundation of these countries, and this has been further exasperated by the continued monopoly of nationalist political leadership. Party leaders have been unable to meet the challenges of reform to overcome or to mitigate the dysfunction of their respective political systems; in fact it is unclear if they even *want* to seek such improvements. The list of failed reform efforts in BiH is extensive. As noted by Valentin Inzko, High Representative for BiH, "the ongoing failure of local institutions to implement a November 2010 Bosnia and Herzegovina Constitutional Court decision on Mostar's electoral system resulted in Mostarians not being able to vote in the 2012 local elections with the rest of the country. The two largest parties in Mostar, the SDA and the HDZ in BiH, bore the most responsibility for the failure to reach an agreement" (UNSC 2013). The political party leaders in BiH have likewise been unable to reach agreement on how to implement the ruling by the European Court of Human Rights on the Sejdić-Finci case which involves changes to the constitution, in spite of the suspension of BiH's EU accession talks.[8] Similarly, in Kosovo political leaders have not yet come up with a final solution concerning electoral reform purportedly sought for more than a year. In 2013, the speaker of the parliament, Jakup Krasniqi, blamed political leaders for this delay in passing reforms. Differences remain among the party leaders over whether to retain open lists, whether to divide Kosovo into electoral zones, and the potential legal basis for the direct election of the president. Under heavy US pressure, the Kosovo Parliament elected Atifete Jahjaga as president in April 2011 as a compromise candidate following a dispute between Prime Minister Thaçi, Behgjet Pacolli, and the head of the opposition party, the Democratic League of Kosovo, Isa Mustafa. Political leaders again were identified as the main culprits responsible for this political crisis.

As emphasized throughout this chapter, the role of nationalist political leadership has had a debilitating effect on the political systems of both countries, and party politics has continuously reflected nationalist rhetoric. The larger question remains how to promote party change from within these countries. There is little consensus as to how to encourage voters to vote for parties based on accountability and results rather than just ethnic identity. The dilemma remains how to get voters

---

8   See Valery Perry's chapter in this volume.

to hold their leaders accountable for their actions and address the needs of citizens. While systems and structures can play a strong role in shaping the choices and opportunities available to a voter, in the end, de-ethnicizing politics must also come from a genuine domestic political will with representatives from all ethnic groups, supported by education, civil society, and the media.

Bibliography

Alić, A. (2012) Closing of Cultural Institutions Undermine Bosnian Multiethnic Heritage. *Southeast European Times*, January 17.

Ahtisaari Comprehensive Proposal for the Kosovo Status Settlement (2007) Available from: http://www.unosek.org/docref/Comprehensive_proposal-english.pdf [Accessed May 4, 2012].

Bahtic-Kunrath, B. (2011) Of Veto Players and Entity-Voting: Institutional Gridlock in the Bosnian Reform Process. *Nationalities Papers*, 39(6), pp. 899–923.

Belloni, R. (2004) Peacebuilding and Consociational Electoral Engineering in Bosnia and Herzegovina. *International Peacekeeping*, 11(2), pp. 334–353.

Bhuta, N. (2010) New Modes and Orders: The Difficulties of a Jus Post Bellum of Constitutional Reform. *University of Toronto Law Journal*, 60(3), pp. 799–854.

Bieber, F. (2004) Institutionalizing Ethnicity in the Western Balkans: Managing Change in Deeply Divided Societies. *ECMI Working Paper*, No. 19.

———. (2006) *Post-War Bosnia*. Hampshire and New York: Palgrave.

Bieber, F. and Keil, S. (2009) Power-Sharing Revisited: Lessons Learned in the Balkans? *Review of Central and East European Law*, 34, pp. 337–360.

Black, R. (2001) Return and Recognition in Bosnia-Herzegovina: Missing Link, or Mistaken Priority? *SAIS Review*, 21(2), pp. 177–199.

Bormann, N.C. (2011) *Conditional Consociationalism: Electoral Systems and Grand Coalitions*. Inequality, Grievances and Civil War Workshop, Zurich. Available from: http://www.cis.ethz.ch/workshops/Workshop5/Paper_Bormann [Accessed April 1, 2012].

Bose, S. (2002) *Bosnia after Dayton*. New York: Oxford University Press.

Burnell, P. (ed.) (2000) *Democracy Assistance: International Cooperation for Democratization*. London: Frank Cass.

Burnell, P. (2007) From Evaluating Democracy Assistance to Appraising Democracy Promotion. *Political Studies*, 56(2), pp. 414–434.

Carothers, T. (2004) *Critical Mission: Essays on Democracy Promotion*. Washington, DC: Carnegie Endowment for International Peace.

———. (2009) Democracy Assistance: Political vs. Developmental. *Journal of Democracy*, 20(1), pp. 5–19.

Central Election Commission of Bosnia and Herzegovina. Available from: http://www.izbori.ba/eng/default.asp?COL=columne&ID=478 [Accessed April 12, 2015].

Chandler, D. (2000) *Bosnia: Faking Democracy after Dayton*. London: Pluto Press.

Chong, J.I. (2009) Making States from the Outside: External Intervention and State-Building in Weak Polities. *International Studies Association Conference Papers*, Annual Meeting.

Clinton, W.J. (1995) Bosnia Peace Settlement: President Clinton's Address to the Nation on the Bosnia Peace Agreement. Address to the Nation, November 27. Available from: http://www.youtube.com/watch?v=Bau6aw9VqDw [Accessed May 2, 2013].

Coles, K. (2007) *Democratic Designs: International Intervention and Electoral Practices in Postwar Bosnia-Herzegovina.* Ann Arbor: The University of Michigan Press.

Constitution of Kosovo (2008) Available in English from: http://www. kushtetutakosoves.info/?cid=2,246 [Accessed February 17, 2012].

Council of Europe (2010) *Resolution 1701, Functioning of Democratic Institutions in Bosnia and Herzegovina.* Parliamentary Assembly. Available from: http:// assembly.coe.int/Mainf.asp?link=/Documents/AdoptedText/ta10/ERES1701. htm [Accessed May 10, 2012].

Crawford, G. and Abdulai, A. (2011) The Conceptual Politics of Democracy Promotion. In: Hobson, C. and Kurki, M. (eds) *The Conceptual Politics of Democracy Promotion.* London and NY: Routledge, pp. 131–150.

Crisis Group Europe Briefing (2009) Bosnia's Dual Crisis. Briefing No. 57, November 12. Available from: http://www.crisisgroup.org/~/media/Files/ europe/B57%20Bosnias%20Dual%20Crisis.pdf [Accessed June 20, 2012].

de Zeeuw, J. and Kumar, K. (2006) *Democracy Promotion in Postconflict Societies.* London: Lynne Rienner Publishers.

Diamond, L. (1999) *Developing Democracy: Towards Consolidation.* Maryland: John Hopkins University Press.

——. (2005) Promoting Democracy in Post-Conflict and Failed States Lessons and Challenges. *Taiwan Journal of* Democracy, 2(2), pp. 93–116.

Dryzek, J.S. and Holmes, L. (2002) *Post-Communist Democratization.* Cambridge: Cambridge University Press.

Electoral Knowledge Network (2012*) Kosovo: Delimiting Electoral Districts for a Proportional Representation System.* Available from: http://aceproject.org/ ace-en/topics/bd/bdy/bdy_kos [Accessed February 1, 2012].

ENEMO (European Network of Election Monitoring Organizations) (2010) Election Observation Mission Kosovo Assembly Elections 2010. Final Report, April 2011. Available from: http://www.enemo.eu/kosovo2010.htm [Accessed July 12, 2012].

Euronews (2012) Serb Vote Defiant. *Euronews*, February 14. Available from: http://www.euronews.com/2012/02/14/kosovo-serb-vote-defiant/ [Accessed April 12, 2015].

European Court of Auditors (2012) Press Release ECA/12/41, October 30. Available from: http://eca.europa.eu/portal/pls/portal/docs/1/17830743.PDF [Accessed July 10, 2013].

European Court of Human Rights (2009) Case of *Sejdić and Finci* v. *Bosnia and Herzegovina*. Applications nos. 27996/06 and 34836/06. Available from: http://cmiskp.echr.coe.int/tkp197/view.asp?action=html&documentId=86026 8&portal=hbkm&source=externalbydocnumber&table=F69A27FD8FB8614 2BF01C1166DEA398649 [Accessed February 12, 2012].

European Parliament (2010) Election Observation Delegation to the General Election in Kosovo. December 12. Available from: http://www.europarl.europa. eu/intcoop/election_observation/missions/2009-2014/kosovo_gene_2010.pdf [Accessed August 10, 2012].

Friedman, F. (2006) *Bosnia and Herzegovina: Polity on the Brink*. London and New York: Routledge.

General Framework Agreement for Peace in Bosnia and Herzegovina [Dayton Agreement] (1995), Available from: http://www.ohr.int/dpa/default. asp?content_id=380 [Accessed April 12, 2015].

Gromes, T. (2009) The Vicious Cycle of State-Building during the Democratization of Ethnically Divided Post-Civil War Societies. *International Studies Association Paper*, Annual Meeting.

Hayden, R.M. (2005) Democracy Without a Demos? The Bosnian Constitutional Experiment and the International Construction of Nonfunctioning States. *East European Politics and Society*, 19(2), pp. 226–259.

——. (2011) The Continuing Reinvention of the Square Wheel. *Problems of Post-Communism*, 58(2), pp. 3–16.

Hays, D. and Crosby, J. (2006) *Special Report: From Dayton to Brussels—Constitutional Preparations for Bosnia's EU Accession*. United States Institute of Peace.

Hromadzić, A. (2013) Discourses of Trans-ethnic Narod in Postwar Bosnia and Herzegovina. *Nationalities Papers*, 41(2), pp. 259–275.

Hulsey, J.W. (2010) Why Did They Vote for Those Guys Again? Challenges and Contradictions in the Promotion of Political Moderation in Post-war Bosnia and Herzegovina. *Democratization*, 17(6), pp. 1,132–1,152.

International Civilian Office Kosovo (2011) Available from: http://www.ico-kos. org/data/Image/110111_RTK_interview_with_Andy_-_Elections_in_Kosovo. pdf [Accessed May 4, 2012].

International Crisis Group (1996) *Why the Bosnian Elections Must Be Postponed*. ICJ Bosnia Report No. 14, August 14. Available from: http://www.crisisgroup.org/en/ regions/europe/balkans/bosnia-herzegovina.aspx [Accessed February 14, 2013].

International Monetary Fund (2010) *IMF Executive Board Concludes 2010 Article IV Consultation with Bosnia and Herzegovina*. Public Information Notice (PIN), No. 10/154. Available from: http://www.imf.org/external/np/ sec/pn/2010/pn10154.htm [Accessed February 14, 2013].

Karabaku, L. and Safet, K. (2012) Kosovo Serbs Get a New Political Group. *SE Times*. February 13.

Keil, S. (2013) *Multinational Federalism in Bosnia and Herzegovina*. Farnham: Ashgate Publishing.

Kim, J. (2008) *Bosnia: Overview of Current Issues*. Congressional Research Service—Report for Congress, June 16. Available from: http://www.usembassy.it/pdf/other/RS22324.pdf [Accessed May 12, 2012].

Knudsen, T.B. and Laustsen, B. (2006) *Kosovo between War and Peace: Nationalism, Peacebuilding and International Trusteeship*. London and New York: Routledge.

Kostovicova, D. (2005) *Kosovo: The Politics of Identity and Space*. London and New York: Routledge.

Lijphart, A. (1969) Consociational Democracy. *World Politics*, 21(2), pp. 207–225.

——. (1977) *Democracy in Plural Societies*. New Haven and London: Yale University Press.

——. (1979) Consociation and Federation: Conceptual and Empirical Links. *Canadian Journal of Political Science*, 12(3), pp. 499–515.

Lijphart, A. and Waisma, C.H. (1996) *Institutional Design in New Democracies*. Boulder, CO: Westview Press.

Manning, C. (2006) Political Elites and Democratic State-building Efforts in Bosnia and Iraq. *Democratization*, 13(5), pp. 724–738.

Marko, J. (2006) International Law "Unified in Diversity"? Problems of State and Nation-Building in Post-Conflict Situations: The Case of Bosnia-Herzegovina. *Vermont Law Review*, 503(30), Spring.

Marty, D. (2010) *Committee on Legal Affairs and Human Rights. Inhuman Treatment of People and Illicit Trafficking in Human Organs in Kosovo*. Council of Europe Report, AS/Jur 46, December 12. Available from: http://www.assembly.coe.int/CommitteeDocs/2010/ajdoc462010prov.pdf [Accessed December 19, 2012].

Mcmahon, P. (2004) Rebuilding Bosnia: A Model to Emulate or Avoid? *Political Science Quarterly*, 119(4), pp. 569–593.

Mujkić, A. and Hulsey, J. (2010) Explaining the Success of Nationalist Parties in Bosnia and Hezergovina. *Političa Misao*, 47(2), pp. 1,143–1,158.

Nagle, J. and Clancy, M.C. (2012) Constructing a Shared Public Identity in Ethno Nationally Divided Societies: Comparing Consociational and Transformationist Perspectives. *Nations and* Nationalism, 18(1), pp. 78–97.

Nenadović, M. (2010) An Uneasy Symbiosis: The Impact of International Administrations on Political Parties in Post-Conflict Countries. *Democratization*, 17(6), pp. 1,153–1,175.

Norris, P. (2005) *Ethnic Pluralism and Consensus Democracy Revisited*. American Political Science Association, Annual Meeting, Washington, DC.

Palermo, F. and Woelk, J. (2003) No Representation without Recognition: The Right to Political Participation of (National) Minorities. *European Integration*, 25(3), pp. 225–248.

Perritt, H.H., Jr. (2010) *The Road to Independence for Kosovo*. New York: Cambridge University Press.

Perry, V. (2003) *Reading, Writing and Reconciliation: Education Reform in Bosnia and Herzegovina*. ECMI Working Paper, No. 18.

——. (2009) At Cross Purposes? Democratization and Peace Implementation Strategies in Bosnia and Herzegovina's Frozen Conflict. *Human Rights Review*, 10, pp. 35–54.

Reilly, B. (2006) Political Engineering and Party Politics in Conflict-Prone Societies. *Democratization*, 13(5), pp. 811–827.

Sebastian, S. (2009) *The Role of Domestic Elites in External State Building: Lessons from the Case of Bosnia-Herzegovina.* Midwestern Political Science Association Conference Paper, Annual Meeting.

Sejfija, I. (2013) *Analysis of Interviews with Representatives of Political Parties in Bosnia-Herzegovina.* Berlin: Berghof Foundation, Report No. 18. Available from: http://www.berghof-conflictresearch.org/documents/publications/book_sections/Chapter7a.pdf [Accessed January 6, 2013].

Simonsen, S.G. (2004) Nationbuilding as Peacebuilding: Racing to Define the Kosovar. *International Peacekeeping*, 0(0), pp. 289–311.

Toal, G. (2013) "Republika Srpska Will Have a Referendum": The Rhetorical Politics of Milorad Dodik. *Nationalities Papers: The Journal of Nationalism and Ethnicity*, 41(1), pp. 166–204.

Tsifakis, N. (2007) The Bosnian Peace Process: The Power-Sharing Approach Revisited. *Perspectives*, 28, pp. 85–101.

United Nations Security Council (2013) Bosnia and Herzegovina Faces Stark Choice—Fail Together or Succeed Together. *Department of Public Information, News and Media Division.* Available from: http://www.un.org/News/Press/docs/2013/sc11009.doc.htm [Assessed April 6, 2013].

van Biezen, I. (2008) Party Regulation and Constitutionalism: A Comparative Overview. In: Reilly, B. and Nordlunds, P. (eds), *Political Parties in Conflict-Prone Societies: Regulation, Engineering and Democratic Development.* Tokyo and New York: United Nations University Press, pp. 25–46.

van Willigen, N. (2010) From Nation-building to Desecuritization in Bosnia and Hezergovina. *Security and Human Rights*, 21(2), pp. 127–138.

Venice Commission (2005) *European Commission for Democracy Through Law: Opinion on the Constitutional Situation in Bosnia and Herzegovina and the Powers of the High Representative.* CDL-AD, March 11.

Weller, M. (2009) *Contested Statehood: Kosovo's Struggle for Independence.* Oxford: Oxford University Press.

Woehrel, S. (2013a) *Bosnia and Herzegovina: Current Issues and U.S. Policy.* RS21721, January 24. Washington, DC: Congressional Research Service. Available from: http://www.fas.org/sgp/crs/row/RS21721.pdf [Accessed August 13, 2013].

——. (2013b) *Kosovo: Current Issues and U.S. Policy.* R40479, May 7. Washington, DC: Congressional Research Service. Available from: http://www.fas.org/sgp/crs/row/RS21721.pdfhttp://www.fas.org/sgp/crs/row/RS21721.pdf [Accessed April 6, 2013].

Zahar, S. (ed.) (2008) *Constitutional Design for Divided Societies: Integration or Accommodation?* Oxford: Oxford University Press.

Chapter 9

Power-Sharing Success and Failures in the Western Balkans[1]

Soeren Keil

Introduction

Peace agreement implementation and state-building initiatives have led to the introduction of new forms of power-sharing in the post-Yugoslav states. International actors have been heavily involved in the design, implementation and continued application of these mechanisms. What is striking when analyzing the different mechanisms of power-sharing is the fact that despite their variety, they are very similar in many ways. They all focus on ethnic power-sharing among different national groups. Further, they are all the result of violence in the societies under examination. Finally, they were all implemented with direct involvement of international actors.

This paper will compare power-sharing arrangements in Bosnia and Herzegovina,[2] Kosovo and Macedonia.[3] The different forms of power-sharing applied in the Dayton Peace Agreement, that ended the war in Bosnia and introduced a new constitutional architecture, the Ohrid Framework Agreement (OFA) for Macedonia in 2000 and Kosovo's constitutional framework (2001) and its Constitution of 2008 will be used to demonstrate some of the successes and failures of power-sharing. The argument is particularly focused on three areas of successes and failures, namely peacebuilding (ending violent conflict and encouraging peaceful conflict-resolution), state-building (building efficient state institutions), and democratization (ensuring democratic governance and democratization of previously non-democratic practices). All three arrangements refer to democratic principles of government, and they were used by international

---

1 The author would like to thank Dr. Valery Perry and Trish Moore for helpful comments on the draft of this paper.

2 Following the general use of term, Bosnia and Herzegovina will be shortened to Bosnia or BiH.

3 The constitutional name of the country is Republic of Macedonia. However, the UN and the European Union (EU) refer to it as the former Yugoslav Republic of Macedonia, because Greece does not accept the constitutional name of the country. In this paper I will refer to it as "Macedonia."

actors to act as conflict-resolution and state-(re)building mechanisms (Chesterman 2005, Daskalovski 2006, Keil 2013a, Krasniqi 2011).

The chapter will progress as follows: first, there is a discussion on power-sharing in theory and practice, followed by a comparison of the power-sharing arrangements in the three countries; in the third section the successes and failures of these arrangements are compared; finally, the conclusion will discuss possible consequences of the successes and failures of these different arrangements.

Power-Sharing in Theory and Practice

According to Rothchild and Roeder (2005, p. 5) in recent years, "power sharing has become the international community's preferred remedy for building peace and democracy after civil wars." Indeed since the end of the Cold War, the rise of power-sharing arrangements as part of peace agreements all over the world is evident (Hartzell and Hoddie 2003).

There is a distinction between two forms of power-sharing in the academic literature. On one side, Arend Lijphart (1969) provided as early as 1969 a description of what he called consociational democracy. According to Lijphart, the best way to ensure peaceful cooperation through legitimate means in a divided society is by ensuring as much autonomy as possible for the different ethnic groups, while at the same time focusing on elite cooperation in central decisions to ensure cooperation and compromise. Lijphart (1977, p. 25) defined the theory as follows:

> Consociational democracy can be defined in terms of four characteristics. The first and most important element is government by a grand coalition of the political leaders of all significant segments of the plural society ... The other three basic elements of consociational democracy are (1) the mutual veto or "concurrent majority" rule, which serves as an additional protection of vital minority interests, (2) proportionality as the principle standard of political representation, civil service appointments, and allocation of public funds, and (3) a high degree of autonomy for each segment to run its own internal affairs.

The core of consociational theory therefore is the focus on group autonomy on the one side and elite cooperation on the other. This according to Lijphart ensures consensus in those decisions that will affect all ethnic groups while at the same time allowing for self-government in those policy fields that are of key importance for identity issues and the survival of each ethnic group (Lijphart 1985).

On the other side of power-sharing arrangements, Donald Horowitz and his integrative approach can be positioned. Horowitz (1993, 2000) argues that close cooperation and moderation between different ethnic groups is of key importance for political progress in these states. He suggests the creation of multi-ethnic regions in decentralized and federal states and promotes alternative voting, in which political elites will be required to get support from voters of different ethnic groups. This according to Horowitz will promote moderate political elites who will be able to seek compromise and represent all citizens. However, his approach lacks empirical evidence and while consociationalism has been used in a number of Western states including Switzerland, the Netherlands and Belgium as well as in the Western Balkans, Horowitz's ideas have found little consideration worldwide, including in the Western Balkans.[4]

More recently the academic focus has shifted to new forms of power-sharing. Roeder (2005), for example, suggests a power-dividing approach that focuses on civil liberties and the separation of powers as an alternative to power-sharing. McGarry (2005) and O'Leary (2005) meanwhile focus on a readjustment of consociationalism towards a more "liberal" direction. According to them, new power-sharing agreements should not generally specify the groups involved in the power-sharing but leave it open for groups to opt in and opt out of power-sharing arrangements. This allows for different forms of coalition-building and more political options. However, vital minority rights and veto rights ensure nevertheless that no decisions are taken against a specific ethnic group. Finally, Timothy Sisk (1996) and Stefan Wolff (2009) point out that power-sharing arrangements need to include a mixture of measures from different power-sharing theories. This will ensure that different institutional options exist that can be applied to the specific conflict and its unique circumstances.

As the following discussion of power-sharing institutions in the Western Balkans will demonstrate, consociationalism remains of key importance as the most commonly used power-sharing arrangement.[5] However, power-sharing has indeed been adjusted and specified for the unique circumstances in BiH, Kosovo and Macedonia.

Comparing Power-Sharing in BiH, Kosovo and Macedonia

This section will discuss the institutional power-sharing arrangements in these three countries by focusing on the four core elements of consociationalism,

---

4   His focus on cross-community voting has however been used by the Organization for Security and Cooperation (OSCE) for the elections of the President of the Republika Srpska in Bosnia in 2000.

5   There are a number of reasons for the use of consociationalism as the main form of power-sharing. First, its success in Western democracies (such as Switzerland) demonstrates that it can indeed accommodate diversity. Second, it has proven to be the most acceptable form of post-war institutional arrangement for warring parties all over the world, because it ensures their participation in central government, while at the same time protecting their autonomy. Third, international negotiators have favored consociationalism as an institutional provision which is easier to understand and implement than most of the alternatives. Its success record, however, remains mixed.

namely, grand coalition, proportionality, veto rights and autonomy. Before starting the discussion on formal and non-formal arrangements of ethnic power-sharing in BiH, Kosovo and Macedonia, it is important to point out why a comparison between these three cases is fruitful and will help to assess the successes and failures of these new models of power-sharing.

BiH, Kosovo and Macedonia were all federal units in socialist Yugoslavia. While BiH and Macedonia had the status of republics in Yugoslavia, Kosovo was an autonomous province, but part of the republic of Serbia. Consequently, while it was generally recognized that the republics had a right to independent statehood as a result of the dissolution of Yugoslavia, this principle was not extended to Kosovo and its unilateral declaration of independence remains highly contested by Serbia.[6] The common Yugoslav heritage and the experiences with ethnic power-sharing matter. Further, Bosnia, Kosovo and Macedonia can be described as post-war societies. All three countries faced violent conflicts among the major ethnic groups. In Bosnia, the war erupted in April 1992 when the Bosniak and Croat members of the Bosnian parliament declared the independence of the Republic based on a referendum that was largely boycotted by Serbs. Consequently, the Bosnian Serb elites declare their independence from Bosnia and attempted to conquer as much territory as possible for the newly created Republika Srpska (the RS, established in January 1992).[7] The war in Bosnia ended in late 1995 when BiH, Croatia and Yugoslavia signed the General Framework Agreement for Peace in Bosnia and Herzegovina (GFAP) in Dayton (Ohio, USA), which also included a constitution for a united but highly decentralized Bosnian state.[8]

In Kosovo, there has been a long history of difficult relations between Kosovo Albanians and the Serbs (including Serbian state authorities). When the Dayton Peace Agreement failed to address the political situation in Kosovo as some had hoped, and in response to escalating violence, an armed resistance—the Kosovo Liberation Army UCK formed. In 1998 and 1999 the conflict developed into a full-scale war as NATO intervened once Serbian forces started the mass expulsion of Kosovo Albanians from the province. At the end of the violence a UN Mission (UNMIK) took control over Kosovo and all Serbian forces left (Bieber and Daskalovski 2003).

---

6   As of November 18, 2013, 105 countries had recognized the Republic of Kosovo. These include important international actors like the United States of America (USA) and the vast majority of EU Member States, including Germany, France and the United Kingdom. However, other important countries have not recognized Kosovo. These include Russia and China, as permanent members of the UN Security Council, as well as Greece, Romania, Slovakia, Spain and Cyprus, as member states of the European Union. For a list of countries that have recognized Kosovo's independence, see: http://www.kosovothanksyou. com/ [Accessed April 12, 2015].

7   On the war in Bosnia and Herzegovina, see specifically Burg and Shoup (1999) and Calic (1996).

8   The GFAP, which includes the Bosnian Constitution in Annex IV is available at: http://www.ohr.int/.

The violent conflict in Macedonia was a result of the continued political and societal discrimination of Macedonian Albanians. The events in Kosovo encouraged Macedonian Albanians to fight for their rights as well, and consequently violent clashes between Albanian fighters and Macedonian security forces resulted in a number of people being killed[9] and widespread fears that a civil war would break out in Macedonia that would destabilize the entire region. The Ohrid Agreement[10] re-established relations between Macedonians, Albanians and other minorities and established a power-sharing framework (Daftary 2001).

What can be witnessed in all three cases are different forms of ethnic power-sharing. Certainly, the Dayton Peace Agreement for Bosnia established the most complex, comprehensive and some would say convoluted framework for the institutional power-sharing in the post-war Bosnian state.[11] However, the Ohrid Agreement in Macedonia[12] and the 2001 Constitutional Framework for Provisional Self-Government in Kosovo,[13] which was introduced by UNMIK, also included elements of elite cooperation and decentralization as well as important veto rights to certain groups. Finally, it has to be pointed out that international actors played a key role in ending the violent conflicts in the three countries as well as in the negotiation and implementation of the agreements that re-organized these countries and included the power-sharing mechanisms. The importance of the role of international actors cannot be overstated.

While the conflicts in Bosnia, Kosovo and Macedonia differed in their intensity, scope and political motivation, their nature as ethnic conflicts as well as the high involvement of international actors in conflict-resolution and post-conflict reconstruction provides an appropriate framework to compare the different forms of power-sharing (Bieber 2004a, Bieber and Keil 2009, Gromes 2011). The following section will analyze the power-sharing arrangements in BiH, Kosovo and Macedonia by focusing on the four key elements of consociationalism (grand coalition, proportionality, veto rights, autonomy).

---

9   Official statistics on the number of deaths have not been released. It is assumed that between 100 and 250 people died in the conflict. See on this problem Partos (2001).

10   The Framework Agreement was signed in August 2001 in Ohrid. It is generally known as the Ohrid Agreement. The full text of the Agreement is available at: http://faq.macedonia.org/politics/framework_agreement.pdf [Accessed April 12, 2015].

11   On this issue see Valery Perry's chapter in this volume.

12   The Ohrid Agreement was the basis of wider constitutional changes in Macedonia.

13   The framework is available at: http://www.unmikonline.org/constframework.htm. [Accessed April 12, 2015]. It was succeeded by the Constitution of the Republic of Kosovo in 2008, which is available at: http://www.kushtetutakosoves.info/repository/docs/Constitution.of.the.Republic.of.Kosovo.pdf [Accessed April 12, 2015].

Grand Coalition

Grand coalitions are at the heart of consociationalism. As Lijphart (1997, pp. 28, 30) argues, "in a political system with clearly separate and potentially hostile population segments, virtually all decisions are perceived as entailing high stakes, and strict majority rule places a strain on the unity and peace of the system." Consequently, he concludes that "the grand coalition is a vital instrument for the attainment of political stability in plural societies."

In BiH, Kosovo and Macedonia grand coalitions have been established in a number of different ways. Formal requirements for the participation of selected different communities exist in Bosnia and Kosovo. In Macedonia there is no legal requirement for grand coalitions but these have been applied informally between Macedonian and Albanian parties since the first multi-party elections in 1990. In Bosnia, there is a legal requirement for the government to consist of representatives from the two entities, the Federation of Bosnia and Herzegovina (FBiH) and the Republika Srpska (RS). Article V.4, which describes the composition and role of the Council of Ministers, Bosnia's central government, does, however, not stipulate from which ethnic group these representatives have to come. Strict ethnic power-sharing is, however, applied in the Presidency, which is responsible for foreign policy and the appointment of the Council of Ministers and important diplomatic staff. The Bosnian Presidency consists of three members, one Bosniak, one Croat (both elected in the Federation of BiH) and one Serb (elected in the RS). Article V of the Constitution further requires the Serb candidate for the Presidency to reside in the RS and the Bosniak and Croat representative to reside in the FBiH.[14] In the Bosnian entities, power-sharing has been required as a result of important constitutional changes in 2002, following a significant decision of the Constitutional Court in 2000 (Bieber 2004b). In practice, grand coalitions between Bosniak, Serb and Croat parties have been applied in the central government since the first free elections in 1990 and in the entities since 2002.[15]

Bosnia's very formalized requirements for grand coalitions and its strict application in practice have to be distinguished from the political practice in Macedonia and Kosovo. While grand coalitions have been established since the first free elections in Macedonia, this has taken place on a voluntary basis and as part of an informal power-sharing arrangement between parties representing ethnic Macedonians and Albanians (Bieber 2008). Kosovo can be characterized as a mixture of grand coalition practices in Bosnia and Macedonia. While there are

---

14   This has been criticized by a number of international organizations including the Venice Commission of the Council of Europe. The European Court of Human Rights (2009) has also pointed out in an important judgment that these constitutional provisions have to be changed as they are discriminating on the basis of ethnicity.

15   In the FBiH power-sharing between Bosniaks and Croats was established in 1994 when the Federation was created as part of the Washington Agreement of 1994 that ended the war between Bosniaks and Croats.

formal requirements for the composition of the government, these are less strict and detailed than in Bosnia. Article 96.3 of the Kosovan Constitution (2008) states:

> There shall be at least one (1) Minister from the Kosovo Serb Community and one (1) Minister from another Kosovo non-majority Community. If there are more than twelve (12) Ministers, the Government shall have a third Minister representing a Kosovo non-majority Community.

Furthermore, Article 96.4 points out two deputy ministers have to be appointed from the Kosovo Serb Community and two others from other non-majority communities. This inclusion of Serbs and other minority communities was also part of the Constitutional Framework, which UNMIK implemented in 2001. Further, the Ahtisaari Plan,[16] which was first developed as a solution to Kosovo's status and has since been implemented unilaterally by the Kosovo authorities also foresaw the active participation of the Kosovo Serb community and other minority representatives in the government.

Proportionality

Proportionality serves two important functions in divided societies. "First, it is a method of allocating civil service appointments and scarce financial resources in the form of government subsidies among the different segments" (Lijphart 1977, p. 38). This is particularly important, because very often minorities find it hard to get employment in public institutions and promote their cultural, linguistic and religious autonomy without adequate financial support. Proportionality serves however another major purpose. As an electoral principle, it ensures the representation of all major ethnic groups in the legislature of a diverse society.

In BiH, proportional representation is ensured through territorial and ethnic proportionality. As already discussed above, the government represents proportionally the two entities, while the Presidency is comprised of representatives from the three constituent peoples. In practice the parties have also ensured equal representation of the three constituent peoples in the Council of Ministers. The lower chamber of the Bosnian parliament, the House of Representatives, is elected by proportional representation and the Constitution states that no more than two-thirds of the members can be elected from the FBiH and no less than one-third of its members has to come from the RS. There are no ethnic criteria for the members of the House of Representatives, similarly to the provisions for the Council of Ministers. However, the upper chamber connects territorial and ethnic representation. Article IV.1 of the Bosnian Constitution reads: "The House

---

16   The Ahtisaari Plan's (named after former Finish President Martti Ahrisaari) official name is The Comprehensive Proposal for Kosovo Status Settlement by the Special Envoy of the General Secretary of the UN and it is available at: http://www.unosek.org/unosek/en/statusproposal.html [Accessed April 12, 2015].

of Peoples shall comprise 15 Delegates, two-thirds from the Federation (including five Croats and five Bosniaks) and one-third from the Republika Srpska (five Serbs)." Further, the Constitutional Court consists of nine judges, two from the RS and four from the FBiH. There are no ethnic criteria attached to the appointment of judges but in reality these have always been two Bosniaks, two Serbs and two Croats. There are also three international judges in the Constitutional Court, who are appointed by the President of the European Court of Human Rights. Further, the entities have also applied proportional representation after the decision on the "constituent peoples" case of the Constitutional Court in 2000.[17] In the two mixed cantons in the FBiH as well as in the entity institutions and administration, strict proportionality between Bosniaks and Croats has been applied since the creation of the entity in 1994. This strict focus on proportionality in state and entity institutions has a number of remarkable features. First, the system is a mix of proportional representation according to territorial criteria and according to ethnic criteria. Sometimes, as is the case in the Presidency, the House of Peoples and the Central Bank, these two overlap. Second, as a result of this mixture, representation focuses solely on Bosniaks, Serbs and Croats. While there are provisions for the participation of "Others" in the entity constitutions, those who do not identify with one of the constituent peoples continue to face political and legal discrimination. Third, there is also discrimination of those Serbs that live in the FBiH and those Bosniaks and Croats that live in the RS. They cannot stand as candidates for the Presidency and while their access to civil service posts has been made easier by the changes to the entity Constitutions in 2002, they often remain politically weak.[18]

In comparison to BiH, Macedonia and Kosovo have applied less strict and less formal forms of proportional representation. Article 1.3 of the Ohrid Framework Agreement states that "[t]he multi-ethnic character of Macedonia's society must be preserved and reflected in public life." Because the conflict in Macedonia was much more about the equal treatment of Albanians and their fair inclusion in the Macedonian state, the Ohrid Agreement puts strong emphasis on equal treatment and representation. Articles 4.1 read as follows:

> 4.1. The principle of non-discrimination and equal treatment of all under the law will be respected completely. This principle will be applied in particular with respect to employment in public administration and public enterprises, and access to public financing for business development.

In terms of political representation, Macedonia does not apply a system of strict proportionality in the form of reserved seats for the different ethnic groups, as is the case in the BiH House of Peoples. Instead, an electoral system of proportional

---

17   See Constitutional Court of Bosnia and Herzegovina: Judgment U 5/98, in particular part III.

18   There are ongoing court cases to remedy this (such as the Pilav case) and it remains to be seen how the census in October 2013 will affect such practices.

representation and the readjustment of the electoral districts in the aftermath of the Ohrid Agreement ensure minority participation. This, however favors mainly Macedonian and Albanian parties, therefore, and as Bieber and Keil (2009, p. 347) have observed, "smaller minorities have often struggled to enter parliament through minority parties." Indeed, Jenny Engström (2002) explained that Macedonia was more and more moving towards a bi-national state because of the dominance of Macedonian and Albanian parties in parliament.

Kosovo applies a more formal proportional system, as there are reserved seats for Kosovo Serbs and representatives of other minorities in the Parliamentary Assembly. It has already been noted that representatives of the Kosovo Serbs and other minorities have to be included in the government. Article 3.1 of the Kosovo Constitution reads "[t]he Republic of Kosovo is a multi-ethnic society consisting of Albanian and other Communities, governed democratically with full respect for the rule of law through its legislative, executive and judicial institutions." Further, Article 61 specifies:

> Communities and their members shall be entitled to equitable representation in employment in public bodies and publicly owned enterprises at all levels, including in particular in the police service in areas inhabited by the respective Community, while respecting the rules concerning competence and integrity that govern public administration.

Therefore, as is the case in Macedonia, Kosovo legally ensures proportional representation of its different ethnic groups in the civil service. This, however, has proven to be a very difficult task. On the one side, a large number of Kosovo Serbs do not accept the independence of Kosovo and refuse to participate in its institutions and civil service. Serbia continues to pay salaries to those Kosovo Serbs that worked in the civil service in the province before UNMIK took over control in 1999. On the other side, key organizations such as the police and the army have been used by Kosovo's elite to ensure employment for former UCK fighters.

Veto Rights

Veto rights are very important in divided societies, because they ensure that no ethnic group can take major decisions against the will of others. As Lijphart (1977, p. 36) points out, mutual veto rights represent "negative minority rule." He focuses on the nature of veto rights as "mutual," an option that "all minority segments possess and can use" (Lijphart 1977, p. 37). As Bieber (2005) has pointed out, veto rights are present in the three cases in a number of institutions, including at the executive and legislative level. However, these are not always absolute and are often limited, and mediating institutions such as Constitutional Courts also play a key role in all three cases.

Bosnia applies the most complex system of veto rights. Veto rights are given to members of the House of Representative as representatives of the two entities.

This so-called "entity-veto" requires that all decisions taken by the House need to be approved by at least one-third of the representatives from each entity. However, there are also a number of ethnic veto rights installed in the Bosnian political system. Members of the constituent peoples can declare a decision to affect their "vital national interest" (which is nowhere defined or limited) and therefore block or delay the decision. Similarly, the upper House of Peoples can declare a veto based on vital national interests. Even stricter, a member of the Presidency can declare such a veto, in which case the decision is forwarded to the entity parliaments for consideration. Similar provisions about "national interest veto rights" were given to the House of Peoples of the FBiH and the upper chamber in the RS. Special majorities are furthermore required for changes to the constitution, namely a two-third majority in both Houses of the Bosnian Parliament. This amount of veto rights makes it easy for those that want to block the political system, in particular in the central institutions.

Macedonia and Kosovo have learned from the experience in Bosnia. Veto rights are much more limited in both countries; in fact Macedonia does not foresee any formal veto rights but rather uses special majorities for decisions concerning important elements of minority protection. Article 5.2 of the Ohrid Agreement reads:

> Laws that directly affect culture, use of language, education, personal documentation, and use of symbols, as well as laws on local finances, local elections, the city of Skopje, and boundaries of municipalities must receive a majority of votes, within which there must be a majority of the votes of the Representatives claiming to belong to the communities not in the majority in the population of Macedonia.

Kosovo applies the weakest form of veto rights. As Macedonia, Kosovo applies veto rights indirectly through special majorities. A special majority of two-thirds of the Assembly including two-thirds of the non-majority representatives is required in the case of constitutional changes. Furthermore, Article 81 of the constitution explains that in those areas that touch on the rights of the different Communities (such as language, religion and municipal boundaries), a special majority is required of those present in the Assembly and those representing different Communities.

What is notable in this comparison is the variety of veto rights applied in the three different cases. Bosnia uses veto rights in the form of a) territorial representation, b) ethnic veto rights and c) special majorities. Macedonia applies only special majorities, and so does Kosovo. What this demonstrates is a move away from fixed veto rights for clearly defined ethnic groups towards more flexible approaches that require cooperation through special majorities in parliament and avoid giving veto rights to specified groups. Further, conflict-resolution mechanisms differ between the cases. In Bosnia, as outlined in Article IV.3(f), an ad-hoc Committee of one Bosniak, one Serb and one Croat attempts to find a solution in case of a veto. Their decision has to be consensual; otherwise the issue will be referred to the Constitutional Court. In Macedonia in contrast the Committee for Relations between the Communities would have to decide by simple majority in the case of political conflict. The Committee consists of seven Macedonians, seven Albanians and one representative of each of the other communities in Macedonia, which means that theoretically minority communities have the majority in this political institution. However, in the past there have hardly been any issues forwarded to the Committee, because the informal power-sharing in the executive ensures that the majority of the non-majority population (namely the largest Albanian party) is part of the coalition government.

Autonomy

The provision of autonomy aims to ensure minority rule: "rule by the minority over itself in the area of the minority's exclusive concern" (Lijphart 1997, p. 41). If the different ethnic groups in a divided society are territorially concentrated, federalism will ensure the provision of autonomy and their inclusion in central decision-making. If however, the different ethnic groups are inter-mixed and have no connected territorial homeland, cultural autonomy will ensure that all members of the different ethnic groups are protected and can protect their culture and identity.

Autonomy has been implemented in different ways in BiH, Kosovo and Macedonia. BiH is the only successor state of the former Yugoslavia that has implemented a federal system (Keil, 2013a). It consists of two entities, the RS and the FBiH, whereby the FBiH is further divided in 10 cantons, five with a Bosniak majority, three with a Croat majority and two mixed cantons. In addition, Brčko District has been formed in 1999 as a third territorial unit as a result of international arbitration. Decision-making is highly decentralized and while some centralization has taken place since 1995, Bosnia remains a highly decentralized, asymmetric federation (Bose 2002, Woelk 2004, Bieber 2006). What is striking when looking at the federal system in BiH is its mixture of ethnic and territorial federalism and its reforms over the last decades that have to some extent strengthened the central state but have not fundamentally altered the nature of the Bosnian state. The *de facto* connection of territory and ethnicity, which despite the constitutional changes of 2002 remains intact on a symbolic level (such as in the name: Republika Srpska) and on a practical level, as refugee return has only had a limited impact, remains highly problematic to minorities. The focus on territorial autonomy has further led to continuous demands for further autonomy, such as the Croats' demand for a third entity, or RS calls for secession as demanded a number of times by the current President of the RS, Milorad Dodik (Toal 2013). There remains a fundamental lack of agreement on the nature of the state amongst the main political elites in BiH.[19]

Macedonia and Kosovo have abstained from implementing a federal system. In fact, Article 1.2 of the Ohrid Agreement enforces this apathy against territorial autonomy, as it argues that "Macedonia's sovereignty and territorial integrity, and the unitary character of the State are inviolable and must be preserved. There are no territorial solutions to ethnic issues." However, both Macedonia and Kosovo have focused on decentralization and the re-organization of municipalities to ensure that minority nations (in particular Macedonian Albanians and Kosovo Serbs) can practice autonomy in local government. In the case of Kosovo this also involves the devolution of power in the areas of culture and language to municipalities. Limited powers of self-government have also been devolved to the municipalities in Macedonia. However, both the Constitution of Kosovo and the Ohrid Agreement put their emphasis on the territorial integrity and unity of these two countries. Both countries provide extensive forms of cultural autonomy for members of minority nations, including in the areas of language, religion and education.

Successes and Failures of Power-Sharing in the Western Balkans

What is remarkable when comparing the power-sharing arrangements in BiH, Kosovo and Macedonia is not only their similarities and differences, but also the fact that forms of institutional learning seemed to have taken place among the different countries. This learning probably applies as much to the elites in the countries as to representatives of the international community and it focused on avoiding another stalemate solution like the one in BiH (Keil and Bieber 2009). Indeed, Bieber (2009) has demonstrated how different international peace treaties for the Western Balkans contained a number of solutions to the conflicts, all of them focusing in one way or another on power-sharing instruments. It is however important to discuss whether this variety of institutional mechanisms and indeed this form of institutional learning has had any positive effects, and, if so, to what extent one can talk about successes and failures of power-sharing institutions.

The notions of success and failure are not one-dimensional but multifaceted. What can look to one observer as a success (Bosnia's progress in state-building and consolidation from 2001–2006) might be a failure from a different perspective (when looking at the limited progress since 2006). Furthermore, while all power-sharing arrangements have been in place for more than 10 years, this can hardly be seen as sufficient time to overcome the results of war and build effective states. One only needs to consider Belgium and Spain to see how hard it is to adjust power-sharing instruments in a multinational society.

---

19   On the role of elites in Bosnia and Kosovo, see also Tina Mavrikos-Adamou's contribution in this volume.

Successes and Failures in Peacebuilding

Overall it is easy to conclude that the power-sharing arrangements in BiH, Macedonia and Kosovo have been successful in terms of ensuring the peace. BiH and Macedonia have seen no large-scale violence since the introduction of power-sharing institutions, and even the violent riots in Kosovo in 2004 and the latest eruption of violence in Northern Kosovo in 2011 are not comparable to the levels of human suffering in 1998 and 1999. Consequently, if we define peace by the sheer absence of violence, we can conclude that the power-sharing arrangements in the three countries have been very successful (Wallensteen 2007). Even if power-sharing institutions and the international community that has supported these arrangements would not have achieved anything else but to end the violent conflicts and create a *negative peace* (that is, the absence of violence) in the area, this already could be seen as a success. At the same time it is important that peacebuilding has also contributed to the transformation of conflicts into more constructive patterns of conflict-resolution (Ramsbotham, Woodhouse and Miall 2007). The fact that different party leaders have abstained from returning to violence is even more important if we recognize that the political elites in the new power-sharing institutions were often former commanders or political leaders of the military groups. Clearly, this success cannot be attributed to power-sharing alone since the peace plans for Bosnia and Kosovo included external peace-makers to ensure an end to the violence. Nevertheless, it is still very important to recognize that power-sharing agreements have generally contributed to the development of a political culture that sees violence as an illegitimate or at least potentially ineffective way of conflict-resolution.

While the relations between the former combatants in BiH, Kosovo and Macedonia are still conflictual and confrontational, there has nevertheless been a remarkable transformation. Institutions have become the main forum of inter-ethnic tensions and while boycotts, threats and open confrontation are still displayed in these institutions from time to time and all major political forces in the region have recognized the importance of peaceful conflict-management.

Successes and Failures in State-Building

While the record of power-sharing arrangements in their contribution to peacebuilding is very positive, its impact on state-building is less positive (Chandler 2000, Bose 2003, Ignatieff 2003, Woelk 2004, Marko 2005, Pejanović 2007, Krasniqi 2011). BiH, Kosovo and Macedonia remain contested states, fundamentally questioned internally and externally. In the case of BiH this challenge comes particularly from the Bosnian Serbs, but the Bosnian Croats have also voiced their disagreement with the current organization of the state. The power-sharing system that Dayton created has not been accepted by any of the main parties in BiH, and therefore it has been open to re-interpretation and political manipulation. Serbs continue to question the existence of a Bosnian state as such and resist all attempts of centralization. Bosnian Croats on the other side claim that they are disadvantaged by the Dayton system, because Serbs got their "own" entity and Bosniaks dominate the FBiH, while Croats remain discriminated. They, however, abstain from challenging the existence of the Bosnian state in contrast to the Bosnian Serbs and argue instead for a re-organization and re-structuring of BiH. The three main national groups in Bosnia fundamentally disagree about the nature of the state and its future constitutional organization.

A similar situation can be found in Kosovo, where the Kosovo Albanians see Kosovo as an independent state of all its citizens (who are mainly Albanian), but particularly as a result of the long struggle for Albanian self-determination, while most Kosovo Serbs (particularly in Northern Kosovo) do not recognize Kosovo's independence and demand a re-integration into Serbia. They receive support from all major Serbian parties. Serbs that live in the enclaves in Southern Kosovo have made their own arrangements to adapt to the new political reality and have started to cooperate with Albanians and the international community. A similar change of policy cannot be foreseen for the North, since Serbs there live independently from the government in Pristina and receive massive support from Belgrade (ICG 2009, 2012). The 2013 April Agreement between Kosovo and Serbia on the re-integration of the North has yet to be fully implemented (Bassuener and Weber 2013).

In Macedonia, the state as such is not directly challenged by the Albanian community. However, the relations between the Macedonian majority and Albanian minority must still be described as conflictual, and international actors, particularly the EU, remain important mediators between the two sides. The relations have suffered under the continued name dispute with Greece. Albanians have repeatedly declared that Macedonian politicians are not flexible enough in the negotiations with Greece and that they halt the further integration of Macedonia into the EU (and NATO) and contribute to Macedonia's slow transition (Koleka 2009).

While new institutions have been created in all three cases and have started to work more and more efficiently over the last decades, there remain a number of key challenges to the state-building projects. In BiH, it is of utmost importance that the state level receives the competences and financial resources to ensure effective governance and sufficient BiH statehood. This can only be achieved through constitutional reform in which all three parties agree on a joint definition of and vision for the state (see Perry, this volume). In Kosovo, the challenge is to strengthen the state by solving the status conflict with Serbia. If no final status agreement is found the state of Kosovo will remain weak and challenged from the inside and the outside. In Macedonia, it is the name dispute with Greece and the relations between Albanians and Macedonians that undermine Macedonian statehood.

Power-sharing arrangements have done little to strengthen these states and help to build more efficient polities. In highly decentralized states, weak state structures allow corruption and organized crime to flourish and local politicians often become part of these problems. In all three cases, boycotting, vetoing and questioning the legitimacy of power-sharing institutions have in fact become symbols of the contested nature of the overall states.

Successes and Failures in Democratization

Formally, all three countries are democracies. Their elections are regularly monitored by international observers and, with the exception of Kosovo, they are also generally proclaimed free and fair. The governments in all three countries are formed by party coalitions of the main (ethnic) parties and formally the judiciary is independent. Also, there exists a nascent civil society in all three countries, which has received considerable external funding. However, in reality, democratic decision-making is challenged internally and externally in all three cases. There is an internal challenge because the different ethnic parties often block decisions, boycott parliament or threaten unilateral actions. Cooperation as a classic element of democracy does not exist because politics is still seen as a zero-sum game. The judiciary is often weak and dependent on major political actors. Finally, civil society organizations find it difficult to take part in consultation and form a cooperative relationship with government bodies (Fagan 2010).[20]

These internal problems are overshadowed by the external threat to democracy, namely heavy international intervention. In BiH and Kosovo international representatives have the right to intervene directly and influence legislation as well as remove obstructive politicians (OHR 1999; Krasniqi 2011). In BiH these privileges have been used extensively to remove officials, impose legislation and stop unwanted laws (Chandler, 2000). The EU itself recognizes that its presence in Kosovo will need to continue in order to support state-building and democratization (EC 2010, EULEX 2011). However, it is not directly clear how the EU contributes to democratization in the country. When allegations of electoral fraud were voiced after the elections in 2010, the EU did relatively little to investigate those thoroughly and very quickly resumed its cooperation with the Kosovo government. In Macedonia there are fewer direct intervention possibilities but the EU remains a key negotiator between Macedonians and Albanians and also oversees the implementation of the Ohrid Agreement (Council of the European Union 2001, 2010).

While it is understandable that such a high degree of international presence (including civilian and military personal) was required shortly after the end of violence in the three countries, it is hard to see how these forms of intervention can contribute to democracy building. Whenever the High Representative vetoes a decision that has been passed in parliament, he undermines the fundamentals of Bosnian power-sharing.[21] At the same time it is hard to see how the relations

---

20   On this issue, see also Valery Perry's contribution in this volume.

21   However, since 2006 there have been only a few interventions of the HRs. With the international community trying to identify an exit strategy, direct intervention has become less of an issue. On this issue, see also Mateja Peter's contribution in this volume.

between Macedonians and Albanians can improve if they continuously fall back on European diplomats to help them find a decision. It is also difficult to imagine how the EU's involvement in Kosovo will contribute to democratization and not alienate the political elite. Having said this, this answer is of course not that the EU and the international community more generally should retreat from the area, but that their interventions should be limited to provisions that ensure peace and provide the environment for cooperative problem-solving. Rather than undermining power-sharing arrangements in the region, the EU and other international representatives should insist and promote their proper application based on cooperation and compromise.

Conclusion: Assessing Successes and Failures in Power-Sharing in the Western Balkans

In many respects it can be argued that the introduction of power-sharing mechanisms in the Western Balkans has been a success story. They have contributed to peacebuilding and a transformation of the political culture away from violence as a conflict-resolution mechanism. They have also contributed to better inter-ethnic relations in all three countries, although it needs to be said that the relations remain generally conflictual. However, we could not expect anything else taking into account that the wounds of the past are still relatively fresh and will take a long time to heal.

Furthermore, power-sharing arrangements have introduced democratic decision-making procedures and ensure the inclusion of minority nations. Different forms of autonomy have ensured that representatives of minority nations can focus on defending their rights politically rather than by the use of force, and power-sharing has generally contributed to the opening of the state to those that have been discriminated or neglected before. The number of Albanians in Macedonia's civil service has continuously risen since the Ohrid Agreement and also the inclusion of Serbs in Kosovo's institutions has been a success. In BiH, the political and civil service system remain divided between Bosniaks, Serbs and Croats, often making it difficult for members of other groups to enter leading positions. What the above discussion of power-sharing arrangements clearly demonstrates is that their success and their failure heavily depend on the status question. Because Bosnia, Kosovo and Macedonia remain contested countries it is relatively difficult to attribute a lack of reforms, cooperation and consensus to the failure of power-sharing. Instead, external and internal contestation of the states helps to explain some of the failures. What remains true is that some elements in the power-sharing arrangements in the region are flawed. The strict rules applied in BiH paralyze the political process. The rejection of Serbs in Northern Kosovo to take part in Kosovo's institutions makes all power-sharing attempts futile. Strained relations between Macedonia and Greece over Macedonia's name will also affect the relations between Macedonians and Albanians. Furthermore, we can witness that other minorities such as Roma and Sinti, Jews, Ashkali and Balkan Egyptians have been left out of the power-sharing arrangements and often remain in a disadvantaged political and social situation.

But despite these flaws in the arrangements one argument remains in favor of power-sharing. This is the argument that there is no viable alternative. Plural societies cannot simply be governed by the "One Person-One Vote" principle, because it will turn minority nations into permanent political minorities, and often leads to cultural assimilation and exclusion, or to violence and secession attempts. However, there must also be sufficient incentives to ensure that political leaders want to make the system work.

Bibliography

Bassuener, K. and Weber, B. (2013) *Not Yet a Done Deal: Kosovo and The Prishtina-Belgrade Agreement*. DPC Policy Paper, Sarajevo and Berlin, November.

Bieber, F. (2004a) *Institutionalizing Ethnicity in the Western Balkans. Managing Change in Deeply Divided Societies*. Working Paper No. 2. Flensburg: ECMI.

———. (2004b) Towards Better Governance with More Complexity? In: Solioz, C. and Vogel, T. (eds), *Dayton and Beyond: Perspectives on the Future of Bosnia and Herzegovina*. Baden-Baden: Nomos.

———. (2005) Power Sharing after Yugoslavia: Functionality and Dysfunctionality of Power-Sharing Institutions in Post-war Bosnia, Macedonia and Kosovo. In: Noel, S. (ed.), *From Power Sharing to Democracy (Post-Conflict Institutions in Ethnically divided Societies)*. Montreal: McGill-Queen's University Press.

———. (2006) *Post-War Bosnia (Ethnicity, Inequality and Public Sector Governance)*. Basingstoke: Palgrave McMillian.

———. (2008) Power-Sharing and the Implementation of the Ohrid Framework Agreement. In: Friedrich Ebert Stiftung (ed.), *Power-Sharing and the Implementation of the Ohrid Framework Agreement*. Skopje: Friedrich-Ebert-Stiftung.

———. (2009), Ethnicity and Territory in International Peace Proposals in the Former Yugoslavia. In: Woelk, J. (ed.), *Constitutional Dimensions of Cultural and Territorial Pluralism in the Balkans*. The Hague: Martinus Nijhoff/Brill.

Bieber, F. and Daskalovski, Ž. (2003) (eds) *Understanding the War in Kosovo*. London and Portland, OR: Frank Cass.

Bieber, F. and Keil. S. (2009) Power-Sharing Revisited: Lessons learnt in the Balkans? *Review of Central and Eastern European* Law, 34(4), pp. 337–360.

Bose, S. (2002) *Bosnia after Dayton (Nationalist Partition and International Intervention)*. London: Hurst & Company.

Brusis, M. (2003) The European Union and Interethnic Power-Sharing Arrangements in Accession Countries. *Journal of Ethno-politics and Minority Issues in* Europe, 4(1), pp. 1–21.

Burg, S. and Shoup, P. (1999) *The War in Bosnia-Herzegovina (Ethnic Conflict and International Intervention)*. Armonk, NY, and London: M.E. Sharpe.

Calic, M.-J. (1996) *Krieg und Frieden in Bosnien-Herzegowina*. 2nd edition. Frankfurt am Main: Suhrkamp.

Caplan, R. (2008) Who Guards the Guardians? International Accountability in Bosnia. In: Chandler, D. (ed.), *Peace Without Politics? Ten Years of International State-Building in Bosnia*. London and New York: Routledge.

Chandler, D. (2000) *Bosnia: Faking Democracy after Dayton*. 2nd edition. London and Sterling: Pluto Press.

———. (2008) From Dayton to Europe In: Chandler, D. (ed.), *Peace Without Politics? Ten Years of International State-Building in Bosnia*. London and New York: Routledge.

Chesterman, S. (2005) *You, The People, The United Nations, Transnational Administration, and State-Building*. Oxford and New York: Oxford University Press.

Comprehensive Proposal for Kosovo Status Settlement (2007) Available at: http://www.unosek.org/unosek/en/statusproposal.html [Accessed April 12, 2015].

Constitution of Bosnia and Herzegovina (1995) Available at: www.ohr.int.

Constitution of the Republic of Kosovo (2008) Available at: http://www.kushtetutakosoves.info/repository/docs/Constitution.of.the.Republic.of.Kosovo.pdf.

Constitutional Court of Bosnia and Herzegovina (2000) Judgment U 5/98 ("Constituent Peoples Decision"). Available at: http://www.ccbh.ba/eng/odluke/.

Council of the EU (2001) *Council Joint Action Concerning the Appointment of the Special Representative of the European Union in the Former Yugoslav Republic of Macedonia*. Council Document 12645/01, Brussels, October 26.

———. (2010) *Council Decision Extending the Mandate of the European Union—Special Representative in the Former Yugoslav Republic of Macedonia*. Council Document 6901/10, Brussels, March 8.

Daftay, F. (2001), Conflict Resolution in FYR Macedonia: Power-Sharing or the "Civic Approach". *Helsinki* Monitor, 12(4), pp. 291–312.

Daskalovski, Ž. (2006) *Walking on the Edge: Consolidating Multiethnic Macedonia 1989–2004*. Chapel Hill: Globic Press.

EULEX (European Union Rule of Law Mission in Kosovo) (2011) *EULEX Kosovo*. Council of the EU Fact Sheet.

European Commission (EC) (2010) *Kosovo 2010 Progress Report*. Commission Document COM(2010)660. Available at: http://ec.europa.eu/enlargement/pdf/key_documents/2010/package/ks_rapport_2010_en.pdf [Accessed April 12, 2015].

———. (2011) *Bosnia and Herzegovina 2011 Progress Report*. Commission Document SEC (2011) 1206 Final. Available at: http://ec.europa.eu/enlargement/pdf/key_documents/2011/package/ba_rapport_2011_en.pdf [Accessed April 12, 2015].

Fagan, A. (2010) *Europe's Balkan Dilemma: Paths to Civil Society or State-Building?* London: I.B. Tauris.

Gromes, T. (2011) Demokratisierung trotz fehlender Voraussetzungen? Bosnien und Hezegowina, Kosovo und Makedonien im Vergleich. *Zeitschrift für Vergleichende Politikwissenschaft*, 5(2), pp. 253–276.

Hartzell, C. and Hoddie, M. (2003) Institutionalizing Peace: Power Sharing and Post-Civil War Conflict Management. *American Journal of Political Science*, 47(2), pp. 318–322.

Holbrooke, R. (1999) *To End a War*. New York: The Modern Library.

Horowitz, D. (1993) Democracy in Divided Societies. *Journal of Democracy*, 4(4), pp. 18–38.

——. (2000) *Ethnic Groups in Conflict*. 2nd edition. Oakland, CA: University of California Press.

ICG (International Crisis Group) (2009) *Kosovo: Štrpce- A Model Serb Enclave?* Europe Briefing Nr. 56, October 15.

——. (2012) *Kosovo and Serbia: A Little Goodwill Could Go a Long Way*. Europe Report Nr. 215, February 2.

Ignatieff, M. (2003) *Empire Lite: Nation-Building in Bosnia, Kosovo and Afghanistan*. London: Vintage.

Keil, S. (2013a) *Multinational Federalism in Bosnia and Herzegovina*. Farnham and Burlington: Ashgate Publishing.

——. (2013b) Legal Misunderstandings, False normative Hopes and the Ignorance of Political Reality. *DPC Policy Note New Series #4*, November 2013.

Koleka, B. (2009) Albanians See Macedonian Will to Solve Name Row. *Reuters*, April 4.

Krasniqi, G. (2011) The International Community in Bosnia and Herzegovina and in Kosovo. *Südosteuropa*, 58(4), pp. 520–541.

Lijphart, A. (1969) Consociational Democracy. *World Politics*, 22(2), pp. 207–225.

——. (1977) *Democracy in Plural Societies*. New Haven and London: Yale University Press.

——. (1985) Non- Majoritarian Democracy: A Comparison of Federal and Consociational Theories. *Publius: The Journal of Federalism*, 15(2), pp. 3–15.

——. (2004) Constitutional Design for Divided Societies. *Journal of Democracy*, 15(2), pp. 96–109.

Marko, J. (2005) Post-Conflict Reconstruction Through State- and Nation-Building: The case of Bosnia and Herzegovina. *European Diversity and Autonomy Papers 4*. Bolzano: European Academy (EURAC).

McGarry, J. and O'Leary, B. (2005) Iraq's Constitution of 2005: Liberal Consociation as Political Prescription. *International Journal of Constitutional Law,* Vol. 5, No. 4, pp. 660–698.

Ohrid Framework Agreement (2001) Available at: http://faq.macedonia.org/politics/framework_agreement.pdf.

O'Leary B. (2005) Power-Sharing, Pluralist Federation and Federacy. In: O'Leary B., McGarry J. and Salih, K. (eds), *The Future of Kurdistan in Iraq*. Philadelphia: University of Pennsylvania Press.

Partos, G. (2001) Analysis: Casualties in the Macedonian conflict. *BBC News*, March 19. Available at: http://news.bbc.co.uk/1/hi/world/europe/1229991.stm.

Peace Implementation Council (PIC) (1997) PIC Bonn Conclusions. Available at: http://www.ohr.int/pic/default.asp?content_id=5182#11

Pejanović, M. (2007) *The Political Development of Bosnia and Herzegovina in the Post-Dayton Period*. Sarajevo: Šahinpašić.

Ramsbotham, O., Woodhouse, T. and Miall, H. (2007) *Contemporary Conflict Resolution*. 2nd edition. Cambridge and Malden: Polity.

Roeder, P. (2005) Power Dividing as an Alternative to Ethnic Power Sharing. In: Roeder, P. and Rothchild, D. (eds), *Sustainable Peace. Power and Democracy after Civil War*. Ithaca, NY, and London: Cornell University Press.

Rothchild, D. and Roeder, P. (2005) Dilemmas of State-Building in Divided Societies. In: Roeder, P. and Rothchild, D. (eds), *Sustainable Peace. Power and Democracy after Civil War*. Ithaca, NY, and London: Cornell University Press.

Sisk, T. (1996) *Power Sharing and International Mediation in Ethnic Conflicts*. Washington, DC: United States Institute of Peace.

Toal, G. (2013) Republika Srpska Will Have a Referendum. The Rhetorical Politics of Milorad Dodik. *Nationalities Papers*, 41(1), pp. 166–204.

UNMIK (2001) Constitutional Framework for Provisional Self-Government in Kosovo. Available at: http://www.unmikonline.org/pub/misc/FrameworkPocket_ENG_Dec2002.pdf.

UNSC (UN Security Council) (1999): United Nations Security Council Resolution 1244. Available at: http://www.nato.int/kosovo/docu/u990610a.htm.

Wallensteen, P. (2007) *Understanding Conflict Resolution: War, Peace and the International System*. 2nd edition. New Delhi and Thousand Oaks: Sage Publications.

Woelk, J. (2004) Federalism and Consociationalism as Tools for State Reconstruction? The Case of Bosnia and Herzegovina. In: Tarr, A. et al. (eds), *Federalism, Subnational Constitutions and Minority Return*. Westport and London: Prager.

Wolff, S. (2009) Complex Power-sharing and the Centrality of Territorial Self-governance in Contemporary Conflict Settlements. *Ethnopolitics*, 8(1), pp 27–45.

Conclusion

Bosnia and Herzegovina: A Failed Success

Florian Bieber

Bosnia and Herzegovina has been a failed success of international state-building. International intervention has been badly timed from the start of the Bosnian crisis. International officials, in particular the European Community, insisted that the republic hold a referendum on independence as a prerequisite for recognition, ignoring the complex multinational structure and the fact that the Serb boycott of the referendum undermined its legitimacy. There were hopes that international recognition would end the war, as it appeared to have done in Croatia, but instead the war escalated. As Bosnian Serb forces took control of a majority of territory and expelled and murdered Bosniaks and Croats living on it, international mediators proposed peace plans and stationed peacekeepers when there was neither a peace to keep nor a willingness to end the wars among the warring parties. International military intervention came only after 3.5 years of war, and Dayton offered a highly decentralized segregated state when it might have been possible to achieve a more coherent state structure. International state-building after the war was meant to be brief and to quickly transfer power and responsibility to elected officials—thus the haste in holding general elections in autumn 1996 in spite of many observers' concerns of the lack of conditions to ensure the ballot would be free and fair (ICG 1996). When, unsurprisingly, the same parties that fought the war won the elections just nine months later, intervention became more heavy-handed, and the EU and the United States began to understand the need to stay for the long haul. However, they never planned for it. Intervention by the High Representative peaked more than five years after the end of the war, and wound down only a decade afterwards. Since then, the international presence was consistently trimmed down, but nearly two decades after the war, there are still some 600 peacekeepers and a substantial presence of civilian international state-builders in Bosnia.

When the Bosnian war began, the UN sent peacekeepers, but later it was the warmongers who were pressed to make peace, with this wartime elite being legitimized by international efforts and then pressured once democratically elected to office. International pressure came late, between 1997 and 2005, and waned at a time when resistance to international pressured reforms among the political elites began to grow; possibly this domestic opposition grew because the international intervention was itself on the decline. Despite such a continuous track record of bad timing, Bosnia could be considered a success story in some respects. At the level of security and the risk for a return to war, as some chapters argue, international intervention has been a resounding success. Not only have the armies fighting the war in Bosnia been dismantled, the current army has a fraction of soldiers under arms in comparison to the wartime forces. Also, neighboring countries and parties to the Dayton Peace Agreement have seen major disarmament, with Croatia even joining NATO in 2009. Interethnic incidents have been rare—in UNDP surveys, in 2008 around 95 percent indicated that they had not experienced ethnic discrimination within the past year (UNDP 2008, p. 63)—and tens of thousands of refugees returned to their pre-war homes, even if they found themselves in a minority. Of course, this has happened against a backdrop where most Bosnian citizens live in relatively ethnically homogenous places where discrimination therefore is not—cannot be—an issue. Although Bosniaks and Croats in the RS and Serbs in the Federation often remain excluded and marginalized by the institutions, interethnic relations appear stable, and in 2005 a majority of all three nations indicated having friends among other nations/peoples, and would be glad to have more (O'Loughlin 2010), as ethnic distance shrank (UNDP 2008, pp. 64–65). This is in spite of diametrically opposed views of the war and divided educational systems. Surveys from 2005 and 2010 indicate high and steady level of Bosniaks, Serbs and Croats who see "their army" as being defensive and a large majority of Bosniaks and Croats consider that their nations only fought a defensive war, while among Serbs, a significant share only "somewhat agree" with this assessment in 2010 (Kostić 2012, pp. 655–656).

Despite these encouraging trends, the politics of Bosnia are characterized by constant emphasis on national identity, blockages of all state level legislation, strong secessionist rhetoric in the RS and stalemate.

Bosnia has been a key example of international intervention. The peace agreement was not just itself internationally mediated, but the implementation of the peace agreement was overseen by a plethora of international originations, from military peacekeeping by the NATO-led IFOR and SFOR, and later, EU-led EUFOR Althea, to the election and democratization support of the OSCE, and the ad hoc civilian implementation agency, the Office of the High Representative (OHR). Such implementation and the role of these agencies was built into the Dayton Agreement, in theory with as much weight as other elements of the Agreement, such as the constitution. While the immediate post-war period was characterized by international efforts to kick-start the Bosnian peace and leave, after a few years, more sustained and heavy-handed international intervention ensued. The Bonn powers of the OHR—the right to impose laws and dismiss officials in particular—led to key reforms and ensured that officials involved in war crimes and obstructing the peace agreement lost their jobs. The peak of international intervention was between the late 1990s and 2006, with new state agencies established, hundreds of officials dismissed and key laws imposed. Yet the transition from internationally imposed peacebuilding to a self-sustained process proved to be most difficult. However, once international assertion receded rapidly, Bosnian parties filled the gap and sought to protect narrow ethnonational interests, and are in the process of undoing many of the reforms.

This volume reflects the sober state of affairs. Whether in the sphere of politics, judicial reform or economic development, Bosnia has been stagnating for nearly a decade. The assessment of the state of the Bosnian peace project is not only relevant for the country itself, but also sheds a light on the broader question of international state-building. If peace in Bosnia cannot succeed, despite not just substantial international powers and financial investment, but also the possibility to join the EU, can it work elsewhere?

Few disagree with the diagnosis that the authors offer in this book: Bosnia is stuck in a steady, yet not stable, degrading deadlock. It is this paralysis that prevents it from moving closer to EU membership and establishing a functioning and more prosperous economy, and it is this paralysis that undermines the success of international intervention in terms of security and co-existence. While the symptoms are viewed by all, the diagnosis is contested. Some would argue that the institutions and electoral system, rigid national quotas and veto rights established at Dayton gave Bosnia a straightjacket, a popular metaphor (DPC 2008, OHR 2005, Perry 2014). Dayton thus appears as a type of Bosnian entrapment: An institutional trap imposed or at least facilitated by outsiders that make Bosnians choose ethnonationalism against their best interest.

At the other end stand the acceptance of ethnonationalist identity as given and inevitable. While such a view need not understand nationalism as primordial, it takes its salience as given, intractable and constant, irrespective of institutional arrangements (Hayden 2007). These are of course not mutually exclusive prepositions. Identity mattered, and while its relevance resulted from the choice of citizens at the first elections in 1990, and the politicization and polarization of these ethnonational identities through the war, there was a pre-history of political salience that pre-dates the 1990s. Yet, the institutions of Bosnia reward political actors for catering to only one and discourage them from appealing to multiple groups—or to those who reject affiliation with any ethnonational group. Despite this particular dilemma, it is important to note that the problems of Bosnia are by no means unique. The complexity of its government is shared with Belgium and it has paler replicas in Macedonia, and regional governments such as Northern Ireland or South Tyrol. Its corruption and unresponsive elite is not fundamentally different from that of its neighbors in Serbia and Montenegro. It is the combination of the two that has been particularly detrimental, as well as the horror of the Bosnian war that led to the death of over 100,000 Bosnians and the displacement of half the population.

Tony Judt in his masterful history of post-war Europe quotes British Labour Prime Minister Clement Attlee who warns of the fallacy that "it is possible by the elaboration of machinery to escape the necessity of trusting one's fellow human beings" (Judt 2005, p. 730). For much of the post-war period much emphasis has been on the machinery of government and little on building trust. In fact, the structure of Bosnia is based on the lack of trust in the other's intentions for the future of the country. Bosnia is a low-trust society, with low levels of trust irrespective of national belonging, low trust in political elites and institutions and low trust among the political elite (Bougarel 2002, UNDP 2009). While this reflects a larger post-Yugoslav trend, it is particularly pronounced in Bosnia.

For most of the post-war period, the low levels of horizontal and vertical trust have been demobilizing citizens and effectively empowering ethnonational elites. However, recent protests indicate that the country might be moving away from the post-war status quo. Two waves of protests have questioned the stability of the Bosnian system in 2013 and 2014. The protests were not large-scale affairs, involving a fairly small number of people for a relatively short duration, especially when compared to other protest movements in the region over the past decade. Nevertheless, they highlighted the structural weaknesses and strengths of the political system. The so-called JMBG protests in June 2013 were directed against the Bosnian parliament. It had failed to pass a new law to regulate the issuing of identity numbers, a pre-requisite for personal ID documents, including passports. As a number of cantons thus stopped issuing passports, newborns were unable to travel. The impact was most harshly felt on small children with serious health issues that could only be addressed abroad. A determined crowd of protestors encircled the Bosnian parliament in June 2013 and refused to let anybody leave the building. While a few follow up protests took place during the same month, they failed to gather mass support as parliament quickly took steps to overcome the impasse, even if the law adopted devolved ID issuing to the entity level, contrary to the stated interests of the protestors at the time.

The second wave of protests took place in February 2014 and began in the city of Tuzla over unemployment and privatization of several factories that had effectively stopped working a decade ago and are part of the larger deindustrialization of Bosnia (and the larger region) (ESI 2004). The protests turned violent and led to the burning of the cantonal government building in Tuzla. Subsequent protests and riots began in Sarajevo, Bihać, Mostar and other cities and towns, predominantly in the Federation. After the violence of the first days, the protests found a new form. Citizens' assemblies (called *plena*) were established and began to articulate the demands of the protestors' goals. Neither the protests nor plena had clear leaders, with all the advantages and problems this entails.[1] The plena have been unable to push authorities to more than a few concessions at the outset and continued to deliberate in some limited ways in some limited locations, but without re-shaping Bosnian politics.

The violence of the first days probably scared off potential participants as the levels of support were initially very high in opinion polls. The violence, including images of the burning state presidency could not fail to evoke the war. However, it is not just the emotional parallels to the war that rightfully made citizens weary of the violence. Once violence is used in a divided and contested polity like Bosnia, the risks of a "normalization of the use of force" is a considerable risk with potentially negative repercussions for those wanting change. The violence is

---

1   The protestors' demands and subsequent citizens plena are well documented here: http://bhprotestfiles.wordpress.com/ [Accessed April 12, 2015].

also indicative of the degree of frustration and the perceived inability to achieve change in the country through other, non-violent means. This hardly bodes well and also suggests that the post-Dayton status quo stopped being easily sustainable.

Amidst the protests that deliberately sidestepped constitutional issues and topics dear to ethnonationalist parties, it might be tempting to consider ethnonationalism a temporary phenomenon and to understand it as a type of "false consciousness," that is, a misguided and passing form of identity that will be eventually shaken off. The term "false consciousness"—popular among Marxist thinkers of the 1960s and 1970s—sought to explain why workers failed to act in line with Marxist expectation and follow their class interests and were instead bought off by other capitalist promises of upward mobility and consumption (Çelik 2007). Studies and debates in Bosnia often implicitly transfer this concept to ethnicity. The rise to power of ethnonationalist parties in 1990s and their consecutive successes are easily attributed to the war, international intervention and the Dayton system (Kurtović 2011). As a result, the parties in power are not genuine representatives of citizens, but some form of parasitical class. This perception is easily confirmed in the common every day reference in Bosnia and Herzegovina to "those politicians." As Kurtović explains, nationalism and national identity can be a pragmatic choice in terms of attaining a job or favors, and individuals make their choices often in contradiction or at least with a certain degree of eclecticism to the ideology of nationalism: "nationalist projects, like all other world-making ambitions, never fully subsume the forms of life which they produce through their own contradictions" (Kurtović 2011, p. 249). Nationalism is thus not false or real, but it is a lens through which to negotiate society. Thus, the persistence of nationalism—even through its deliberate absence in the protests in February 2014—is not a challenge to the constructivists' argument that ethnicity needs to be made and remade to remain salient (Brubaker 2006). Yet at the same time, this makes the process neither false nor inauthentic, but rather one of multiple venues in which elites can secure legitimacy and through which individuals navigate reality. The normative dimension in dismissing ethnicity is easily understandable, but is also detrimental to the understanding of post-war Bosnia.

As this volume highlights, Bosnia is plagued with uncertainty. The nature of the state, reflected in the constitution, remains contested and constitutes a source of legitimacy for ethnonationalist parties. While the RS claims greater self-government and rejects any decision, institution or law that would strengthen the state, Croat parties reject the status quo for what they consider to be discrimination against their community. Finally, parties representing the Bosniak electorate are dissatisfied with the high level of decentralization along ethnonational lines. Parties that seek to distance themselves from these dichotomies, such as Naša Stranka, and to a lesser degree Democratic Front and the Socialdemocratic Party have been either ineffective or captured by the larger ethnonationalist logic of political competition. Those who reject ethnonational markers or hail from smaller communities have been overshadowed and marginalized. One issue all parties can agree on is that no one is satisfied with the status quo, and there is little space for compromise or recognition of the demands of others. Consequently, EU integration has been delayed and Bosnia is a laggard in the region as questions over competence at the state, entity or cantonal level overshadow even the most banal legislation. Bosnia is thus far from a success story, and is rather a state where key questions over statehood and state structure remain elusive and thus continue to undermine all other policy areas, from economic to social reforms. Consequently, Bosnia remains a country both at peace and in limbo, uncertain whether it can survive the ambiguous peace that has shaped it for the past 20 years.

Bibliography

Bougarel, X. (2002) *Bosnia and Herzegovina. Local Level Institutions and Social Capital Study*. World Bank, ECSSD.

Brubaker, R. (2006) *Ethnicity without Groups*. Cambridge, MA: Harvard University Press.

Çelik, S.K. (2007). False Consciousness. In: Anderson, G. and Herr, K. (eds), *Encyclopedia of Activism and Social Justice*. Thousand Oaks, CA: SAGE, pp. 546–548. Available at: http://dx.doi.org/10.4135/9781412956215.n310 [Accessed August 17, 2014].

Democratization Policy Council (DPC) (2008) Understanding and Breaking Bosnia and Herzegovina's Constitutional Deadlock: A New Approach for the European Union and United States. *DPC Policy Brief 5*. Available at: http://democratizationpolicy.org/pdf/briefs/policybrief5.pdf [Accessed August 17, 2014].

European Stability Initiative (ESI) (2004) *Post-Industrial Society and the Authoritarian Temptation*. Available at: http://www.esiweb.org/index.php?lang=en&id=156&document_ID=63 [Accessed August 17, 2014].

Hayden, R. (2007) Moral Vision and Impaired Insight: The Imagining of Other Peoples' Communities in Bosnia. *Current Anthropology*, 48, pp. 105–131.

International Crisis Group (ICG) (1996) *Elections in Bosnia & Herzegovina*. September 22. ICG Report No. 16. Available at: http://www.crisisgroup.org/~/media/Files/europe/balkans/bosnia-herzegovina/Bosnia%202.pdf [Accessed October 2, 2014]

Judt, T. (2005) *Postwar. A History of Europe since 1945*. London and New York. Penguin Press.

Kostić, R. (2012) Transitional Justice and Reconciliation in Bosnia-Herzegovina: Whose Memories, whose Justice? *Sociologija*, 54, pp. 649–666.

Kurtović, L. (2011) What is a Nationalist? Some Thoughts on the Question from Bosnia-Herzegovina. *Anthropology of East Europe Review,* 29, pp. 242–253.

Office of the High Representative (OHR) (2005). Interview with Wolfgang Petritsch. *BiH Media Round-up*, January 29.

O'Loughlin, J. (2010) Inter-Ethnic Friendships in Post-War Bosnia-Herzegovina. Sociodemographic and Place Influences. *Ethnicities*, 10, pp. 26–53.

Perry, V. (2014) Is Substantial Political Reform in Bosnia and Herzegovina Possible through the Ballot Box in October 2014? DPC Policy Note, No. 7. Available at: http://democratizationpolicy.org/is-substantial-political-reform-in-bosnia-and-herzegovina-possible-through-the-ballot-box-in-october [Accessed October 20, 2014].

United Nations Development Programme (UNDP) (2008) *Early Warning System, Annual Report 2008*. Sarajevo: United Nations Development Programme.

——. (2009) *The Ties that Bind: Social Capital in Bosnia and Herzegovina*. National Human Development Report. Sarajevo: United Nations Development Programme.

Index

ACIPS 26–27
AFBiH 87, 101–103
  and politics 91–95
Ahtisaari Comprehensive Proposal for
  the Kosovo Status Settlement, see
  Kosovo Ahtisaari proposal
Alumni Association of the Centre for
  Interdisciplinary Postgraduate
  Studies, see ACIPS
Armed Forces of BiH, see AFBiH
Ashton, Catherine 73–74, 144

Banja Luka 26, 73–74, 85–86, 103

civil society of BiH 16, 21–24, 162, 207
  and constitutional reform 24–28, 30–35
  criticisms of 22–23
  and justice sector reform 68, 72, 75, 77
consociational democracy 181, 194; see
  also consociationalism
consociationalism 11, 41–42, 173, 181,
  186, 195, 197–198; see also power-
  sharing
  elements of 195–197
    autonomy 174, 194–197, 199,
      203–204, 208
    grand coalition 174, 194, 196,
      198–199
    proportionality 174, 194, 196,
      199–201
    veto rights 43, 195–197, 201–203
constitution of BiH 16–18, 35, 65, 144, 217
  constitutional reform 15–35
    April Package 15, 18, 24, 90
    bottom-up 24–28
    the Butmir Process 18–19, 144
    the Prud Process 18
    top-down 16–21
the Copenhagen Criteria 62, 126
Croatia 3, 89, 111, 122, 160, 214

Dayton Peace Accords, see Dayton Peace
  Agreement
Dayton Peace Agreement 4–5, 7, 11,
  41–42, 84, 132–133, 137–139, 197,
  213–215
  constitutional structure 43–44
democratization 1–3, 7–9, 193, 207–208
Dodik, Milorad 19–20, 30, 55–56, 70–4,
  90, 183, 203
DPA, see Dayton Peace Agreement

economy of BiH 109–127
  Central Bank 109, 120–121, 124
    Currency Board 109, 112–113, 116,
      120–121, 123–124
  and the EU 125–126
  foreign investment 124–125
  gray economy 115–116, 119
  macroeconomic performance 117–119,
    127
  and political fragmentation 116–117
  remittances 118, 123–124
  unemployment 111, 113, 117, 119–120
ethnonationalism 215, 217
the EU 10, 15–18, 33–35, 154
  EUPM 88–89, 98, 100
  EUSR 10, 32, 135–136, 139–140, 145
  and justice sector 74–75
  Police Mission, see EUPM
  Special Representative, see EUSR
European Commission for Democracy
  through Law, see Venice
  Commission
European Union, see EU

General Framework Agreement for Peace,
  see GFAP and Dayton Peace
  Agreement
GFAP 5, 83, 146, 196; see also Dayton
  Peace Agreement

the High Representative 6, 64–66,
        133–144, 213; *see also* OHR
        and the Office of the High
        Representative
    Ashdown, Paddy 6, 86, 87, 88, 140
    Inzko, Valentin 73, 132, 144, 187
    Lajčak, Miroslav 132, 141–143
    Petritsch, Wolfgang 6, 86, 87
    Schwarz-Schilling, Christian 90,
        140–141
Horowitz, Donald 194–195

ICTY 10, 84, 151–164
IMF 111–112, 116, 121, 127
    SBA 112–114
Implementation Force *see* NATO IFOR
international administration 131–146
International Criminal Tribunal for the
        former Yugoslavia, *see* ICTY
International Monetary Fund, see IMF
International Police Task Force 63, 84
intervention 1, 144–145, 207, 213–215
    civilian 6
    of the High Representative 6, 134, 213
    in Kosovo 207
    in Macedonia 1, 207
    military 5–6

justice sector 9, 61–77, 88, 152
    the Court of BiH 63–65, 70, 72
    High Judicial and Prosecutorial
        Council *see* HJPC
    HJPC 66–67, 71–72, 75–77, 88
    judicial reform 61–77, 215
        the Justice Sector Reform Strategy
            68–69, 71–72, 75–76
        the National War Crimes
            Processing Strategy 68–70
        the Structured Dialogue 31,
            74–76
    the Law on the Court of BiH 63–65
    Ministry of Justice 65, 68–69, 71,
        162
    the Prosecutor's Office 63–65, 70–73,
        77, 88
    reform, *see* judicial reform

Karadžić, Radovan 153, 157, 183

Kosovo 31, 85–86, 173–175, 178–180,
        196–197
    Ahtisaari proposal 178–180, 199
    constitution 178, 204
    political parties 184–187
        Kosovo Liberation Army 182, 184,
            196
    UNMIK 178–179, 196–197, 199

Lijphart, Arend 173–174, 181, 194, 198,
        201; *see also* consociational
        democracy; consociationalism;
        power-sharing

Macedonia 193–208
Milošević, Slobodan 86, 153, 159

National Endowment for Democracy, *see*
        NED
NATO 4–5, 84–86, 89, 95, 99, 101, 175,
        179–180, 196
    IFOR 84–86, 133
    SFOR 85–87, 89
NED 27
NGOs, *see* civil society

Office of the High Representative 1, 5, 64,
        132; *see also* OHR
OHR 10, 64, 87, 138–146; *see also* the
        Office of the High Representative
    Bonn powers 73, 133, 135, 144, 214
    closure 68, 90, 132–137, 140–146
        5+2 conditions 68, 92, 136–137,
            139
Ohrid Agreement 197, 200–202, 204, 207,
        208
O'Leary, Brendan 42, 195
Organization for Security and Co-operation
        in Europe, see OSCE
OSCE 8, 177, 181, 214
    Mission 9, 22, 69–70, 75

Parliament of BiH 18, 43–47, 51–52, 57,
        63–64, 67
    Bosnian 45, 143, 196, 199, 202, 216
party system of BiH 9, 11, 41–58; *see also*
        political system
    horizontal linkage 46–47

political parties 180–183
  DNZ 48–52
  HDZ 48–56, 85–86, 183, 187
  HDZ 1990 18, 26, 48–54, 56
  nationalist 54–56, 134, 177, 182
  SDS 47–50, 54–56, 183
  SNSD 26, 47–50, 55–55, 183
  vertical linkage 47, 52
Peace Implementation Council, *see* PIC
PIC 6, 64, 66, 84–5, 133, 135–136
  Steering Board 68, 95–96, 132, 134,
    136–138, 141, 143
political system of BiH 43, 117, 198,
    202
  fragmentation 42, 44–47, 52–53, 55,
    57–58, 116–117
  power-sharing 5, 11, 173–178, 193–209;
    see also consociationalism
presidency of BiH 18–20, 27–28, 94, 176,
    198

Republika Srpska 5, 61, 138, 196, 200,
    203, 217
  Law on Courts 75–76
  Law on Referendum and Citizen
    Initiatives 73
  National Assembly 43, 65, 72–75, 144
  party system 55–56
  referendum 73–74, 90–91, 144
RS, *see* Republika Srpska
RSNA, *see* Republika Srpska National
    Assembly

SAA 90, 98, 126, 136–137, 141–142
SAP 125–126, 141
security 9, 55, 83–102, 138, 144, 146, 213
  security sector reform 87–89
Sejdić-Finci 15, 19, 21, 27, 32, 35, 187
Silajdžić, Haris 19, 30, 56, 90
Srebrenica report 89, 161
the Stability Pact for Southeastern Europe
    85, 125–126
Stabilization and Association Agreement,
    see SAA
the Stabilization and Association Process,
    see SAP
Stabilization Force, *see* NATO SFOR
Stand-by arrangement, *see* IMF SBA
state-building 1–2, 6–8, 57, 131, 134–135,
    138–140, 145–146, 193, 205–207
  in Kosovo 179, 184
  international 8, 142, 144–146, 213, 215

transitional justice 151–164
Tuzla 2, 70, 92, 216

UN Security Council 64, 89, 100, 153
United Nations Interim Administration
    Mission in Kosovo, *see* Kosovo
    UNMIK
Venice Commission 17, 35, 65, 90

war 3–6, 54, 84, 111, 151, 213–214
  damages 111
World Bank 111–112, 114